*Go for Broke*

MY PHILOSOPHY
OF WINNING GOLF

by *Arnold Palmer*

WITH WILLIAM BARRY FURLONG

Simon and Schuster   *New York*

Contents

Contents   6

Part Four

ITS STRATEGY

 *Part One*

THE PHILOSOPHY

Everything is sweetened by risk.
—ALEXANDER SMITH (1830–67), *Scottish poet*

I

The Maddening First Hole

THERE was a sharp bite and sparkle in the mountain air. The Rockies loomed clearly in the distance—immense, clean, barren. I remember on the first hole at Denver, the sun was so bright that it hurt your eyes to look down the fairway. Standing on the tee, it was difficult to see the green without a pair of dark glasses. It took me four rounds to find it—but when I did, the whole thrust of my life was altered.

The time was 1960. The place was Cherry Hills Country Club. The event was the U. S. Open.

On the fourth round of that tournament, I tried a shot that I'd missed three times in three rounds. I tried it again not because I'd failed—or because I like failure—but because I was convinced that it was the shot necessary to win the tournament.

A bold shot?

Yes.

But you must play boldly to win. My whole philosophy has been based on winning golf tournaments, not on finishing a careful fifth, or seventh, or tenth.

A reckless shot?

No.

In eighteen years of tournament golf I feel that I've never tried a shot that I couldn't make.

On that summer day in 1960, I was young in what the world calls fame, but I was ripe in golfing experience. I'd been a professional golfer for five years, and up to then I'd won twenty tournaments. In those years, I'd learned something about the strategy of the game and its psychology and rewards. If there was any reward I treasured most, it was the way that the game responded to my inner drives, to the feeling we all have that—in those moments that are so profoundly a challenge to man himself—he has done his best. That—win or lose—nothing more could have been done.

My own needs were deeply driven ones: I could not retreat from a challenge. If the chance was there and if—no matter how difficult it appeared—it meant winning, I was going to take it. It was the "sweetness" of risk that I remembered, and not its dangers.

In looking back, I feel that in these years I was learning something of the subtle dimensions of all this—I was learning the *meaning* of boldness as well as its feeling.

For boldness does not mean "recklessness" to me. Rather it involves a considered confidence: I *know* I'm going to make the shot that seems reckless to others. I also know the value of the risk involved: A bold shot has to have its own rewards—winning or losing the match, winning or losing the tournament.

But perhaps it was not until the U. S. Open at Cherry Hills that I put it all together, philosophically as well as physically. For not until that summer day in 1960 did it become apparent to me how boldness might influence not just a hole but an entire round, an entire tournament, and even an entire golfing career.

It began, really, on the first tee of the last round at Cherry Hills. On the face of it, there was nothing terribly subtle about

this hole: You could see every mistake you made. It was down-
hill to the green; the tee was elevated perhaps 150 feet above
the green. It was only 346 yards long, not a terribly long par
4—and a terribly tempting birdie 3 . . . to me. It was guarded
on the left by an irregular line of poplars and pines and on the
right by a ditch that the membership had practically paved
with golf balls. A nice direct hole for the strong driver, somebody who could—in that thin, mile-high air—get the ball out
there 300 yards or so.

But there *was* one nasty little afterthought that had been
provided for the U. S. Open: The grass was allowed to grow
very long and become a "rough" right in the fairway, about
50 or 60 yards in front of the green. Moreover, the hazard was
heightened by a treacherous bunker guarding the gateway to the
green. It had grass in it that looked like it was three feet deep.
If you got in there, you might never be found again. I mean
it was the kind of place where you hunted buffalo—not par.

The idea, of course, was to penalize the strong driver, to
threaten him with capture by the rough—and a difficult second
shot—if he played to his own best game (a powerful drive) on
his first shot.

The safe way to play that hole, for most golfers, was not
to invite trouble—not to challenge the rough or the bunker in
the first place. In that sense, the first hole was an authentic
mirror of the entire course. For Cherry Hills was long in
yardage (7004) but not in reality: The thin air gave most tee
shots a much longer carry than on a sea-level course. But its
greens were small and well guarded by bunkers and water
hazards; there was an added danger that under the hot, direct
sun and the afternoon winds they would become so dried out
that it would be all but impossible to get the ball to stop on
them. If you hit those greens with power, the ball would roll
right over and off them on the far side. So it was a course that
took accuracy, touch, and an unflagging concentration. It
looked to many like a course whose yardage beckoned to

power—Mike Souchak, a powerful golfer, led at the halfway mark of the 1960 Open with a remarkable 68–67 for a thirty-six-hole score of 135. But it was, in reality, a course that catered to placement more than to power—in that opening round of 68, Souchak had only twenty-six putts, nine or ten short of normal for an eighteen-hole round. So he wasn't up there scattering power shots; he was getting good placement with everything he did.

To focus on the first hole: It was the kind of hole that shaped your entire approach to the course in that it could reward you for power or for placement.

To the pretty good amateur golfer, it was an opportunity for a par 4. He might put the ball out in the fairway pretty much where he could—far short of the rough—and then hope to get close to, or onto, the green with his second shot.

To the venturesome pro, it was an opportunity for a birdie. He'd use an iron to hit his shot off the tee, expecting to get enough accuracy from it (which he would less likely get from a driver) to drop the ball precisely in the fairway, where he'd have the ideal second shot. In short, he intended to place his first shot so that he could hit his second shot precisely to the cup—not just any old place on the green but *specifically* to the cup. For this was the kind of shot where the pro prefers—where he *intends*—to get his second shot so close to the cup that he'll need only one putt to "get down." So if he emphasized placement over power, he hoped to wind up with a birdie 3, not a par 4.

From my angle of vision—somewhat singular, I'll admit—this was an eagle hole, not a birdie hole. I figured that, with boldness, I could get down in two strokes, not three or four.

That meant being on the green in one shot, not two.

That meant getting into the cup in one putt, not two.

That meant emphasizing power over placement.

That meant using my driver, not my iron.

My intention was simply to drive the ball hard enough and

far enough so that it would bound through the rough in front of the green and run up on the putting surface to a good position near the cup. To get a ball to stop precisely on a green, you must give it backspin, so that it bites into the grass when it hits and then stops short, or even hops backward. That's fairly easy to do when you're using an iron from the fairway that is fairly close to the green; you merely strike straight downward at the ball, taking a divot after making contact with the ball, and take a normal follow-through. But it is difficult to do while driving off the tee and ramming the ball through the rough. For one thing, on tee shots you may be hitting the ground a microsecond before you make contact with the ball. At least that's what I was doing with my driver back in 1960 (though since then I've changed my style somewhat). Then you normally give the ball a considerable overspin when you hit the ball dead center (or thereabouts) and make the big follow-through. Normally you want to give the ball some overspin when hitting off the tee with a driver. Overspin will cause the ball to roll a little farther after it hits the ground. So my tee shot would, I expected, be hitting those small greens without backspin. And if the greens were dry and hard, as I expected, the ball might never stop rolling this side of the Continental Divide.

So I was proposing to use a power club—the driver—rather than a placement club—the iron—on a hole that demanded placement as well as power. And I was accepting overspin, not backspin, on a green that threatened to be faster than the Indianapolis Speedway on Memorial Day.

"Boldness" is what my friends called it. "Insanity" is what they meant.

But I figured to have two things going for me when the ball hit the green:

If the ball went through the rough, not over it, the thick grass would cut down significantly on the ball's momentum, and very likely on how far it would roll, once it hit the green.

Also, I'd be playing this hole relatively early in the morning on the first three rounds. (On the fourth and last round—because of the way the U. S. Open was run in those days—I'd be playing it in the early afternoon.) I knew that every green was being heavily watered at night, simply because the tournament officials were afraid that otherwise the greens would be hard and dry by the afternoon. So in the morning, the first green—obviously the first to be played—would likely be heavily laden with the water from the all-night sprinkling, and the water residue would slow down any ball hit onto it. That's another reason why the roll of the ball would be reduced.

(You didn't *really* think that I just went out there and hit the ball hard, without giving any thought to what would happen to it once it came down—now did you?)

The way I looked at it, all I had to do was pound the ball bouncingly through the rough and onto the heavily watered green. Then I'd one-putt and have an eagle. I'd have that course by the throat, and—as my fellow pro, Jerry Barber, once said—"shake it to death."

Only it didn't happen. Not on the first three rounds. That green was tough to reach with a rifle, much less a driver. In my first round I sent my tee shot into the ditch on the right. I didn't get an eagle or a birdie or a par on the hole. I didn't even get a bogey, for that matter. I got a double-bogey 6—two over par, instead of the two under par that I'd aimed for. After that, things got better—but not much. I got a bogey 5 on the second round and a par 4 on the third round. So in the first three rounds, I'd taken fifteen strokes on that hole, instead of the twelve strokes that playing it safe might have given me. And instead of the six strokes that—in wild flights of genius—my boldness might have given me.

More than that, starting off every round with a deep disappointment damaged my whole pattern of play. After three rounds, I had a total of thirteen birdies in the tournament, but they were so scattered that I'd never gotten any momentum out of them—no "charge," so to speak. The result was that I was in fifteenth place with a 215 after three rounds.

Just before lunch, and the start of my last round, I paused outside the vast white scoreboard outside the rambling, neo-Tudor clubhouse at Cherry Hills. There in the elaborate black and red numerals of golf, written in a manner as highly stylized as medieval script, I saw how the field lay. I was seven strokes behind the leader, Mike Souchak. But Mike wasn't the only hurdle. Between me and the leadership lay such great golfers as Ben Hogan and Sam Snead, Julius Boros and Dow Finsterwald, Dave Marr and Bob Goalby, and a twenty-one-year-old amateur named Jack Nicklaus.

By the time I sat down to a sandwich in the clubhouse, my mood was about as black as a witch's heart. Ken Venturi and Bob Rosburg, who also seemed to be out of contention, joined me, and a couple of newsmen stopped by our table to offer solace to the newly bereaved.

One of them was an old friend, Bob Drum, then of the Pittsburgh *Press*. He knew of my tribulations with that first hole and of my conviction that it was an eagle hole that would unlock the entire course to the player bold enough to attack it. He also knew that my failure in a daring power approach had—in an era of golf when meticulous precision was most admired—given a certain satisfaction to a few older hands around professional golf. "There are some guys out there who think you're just an upstart, a flash-in-the-pan," he'd told me. So when he began to console me, and hint that maybe it was time to play it safe and try to pick up some good also-ran money in the U. S. Open—since it was obvious I couldn't go from fifteenth place to first place in one round—the chemistry began working in me. Explosively.

"What would happen if I shot a 65 on this last round?" I

asked, perhaps more aggressively than in the thirst for pure knowledge.

"Nothing," said Bob. "You're out of it." He was an old friend but a realistic one. Only one man had *ever* shot a 65 in the final round of the U. S. Open: Walter Burkema in 1957.

But that got to me. And to my pride. Realism—and pessimism —I did not need.

"Well," I said, my voice lowering into my don't-tread-on-me tone, "the way I read it is that a 65 would give me 280 for the tournament. And 280 is the kind of score that usually wins the U. S. Open."

Bob gave me a startled look, as if he just noticed I had two heads.

"Sure," he said, "but you won't do it by taking another double-bogey on the first hole."

So there it was: I still looked at the first hole as a chance for triumph; Bob—and a great many others—looked at it as a place for patent disaster. I suppose they were right. If I'd played it safe on the first hole and teed off with my iron, instead of the driver, and gone for placement and par, I'd be three shots closer to the leaders after the first three rounds. If I'd picked up a birdie or two along with it, I might even be right on their necks. So the thing to do now was admit that the first hole had me beaten and go back to playing it like the other pros did—with an iron off the tee—and figure that by placing the ball and playing it safe, I might pick up enough strokes in the standing to avoid further shame.

But that's not the way I saw it. I wasn't playing golf to avoid shame. I was playing it to win championships. And the last round of a National Open is no place to start changing your whole style and philosophy of golf.

The way I looked at it, being fifteenth made it more *imperative* that I play boldly. It couldn't cost me much: The difference between being fifteenth or twenty-fifth or fifty-fifth is not terribly meaningful—at least to me. It's the difference between first and second that has meaning. And a considered boldness might—I was sure—still win me the tournament.

So when I got to the first tee, I reached for my driver. Even though it was now one-forty-five in the afternoon and the green figured to be dried out and it would take incredible accuracy to hit the green and hold it. One of my luncheon companions (not Bob Drum) had come along, and he looked as if there were nothing wrong with me that brain surgery couldn't cure. I addressed the ball as if it were my enemy—or my slave—and hit it with everything I could get into it. The ball went up and hung in the sharp, clear air as if it had been painted there. When it came down—with overspin—it leaped forward and ran through the rough and right onto the middle of the green.

Twenty feet from the hole.

Three hundred and forty-six yards and I'd not only driven the green but drilled it right in the heart!

Just like I'd been planning it all along.

Right? Right!

Okay—two putts. A birdie, not an eagle. But that didn't much depress me. For I'd shown that my idea *did* work—that boldness could conquer this hole. And that if it made the first hole yield, then the whole course could be conquered with boldness.

Suddenly my whole spirit, my entire attitude changed.

I charged onto the second hole—a 410-yard par 4 with an elevated green and trees right in the fairway. In two shots I was not quite on the green. But I chipped the ball from off the green right into the cup for another birdie 3. I charged onto the 348-yard third hole and birdied it. I charged onto the fourth hole and birdied it with a twisting 40-foot putt. Four holes: four birdie 3s. A par on the fifth, a birdie on the sixth, a birdie on the seventh: six birdies on seven holes. I finished the first nine holes in 30 strokes, just one short of a record.

"Damn!" I said to Bob Drum when he finally caught up to

us. "I really wanted that 29." Bob exhibited deplorable self-control: "Well," he murmured consolingly, "maybe next time."

By the tenth hole, I was tied with Mike Souchak. By the twelfth, I was ahead of him. But it was not all over: There had been fourteen men between me and the lead, and before the afternoon was over, a half dozen or more held or challenged for the title. "This was, to put it mildly, the wildest Open ever," said *Sports Illustrated.* For me, the birdies disappeared, but the pars survived. The final five holes at Cherry Hills are a punishing finishing stretch: Ben Hogan, then forty-seven, felt it, and he faded here; Nicklaus was twenty-one, and so did he. I managed to play each of those last five holes in par and to come in with a 65 for the eighteen-hole round. Boldness had paid off: That surge at the start was, in the words of golf writer Herbert Warren Wind, "the most explosive stretch of sub-par golf any golfer has ever produced in the championship. . . ." I finished the tournament with a seventy-two-hole score of 280. That was enough to give me the U. S. Open championship and, as it developed, a certain hold on history.

For the "charge" didn't stop there. It was not, in the long perspective, to be confined solely to one round or one tournament. It became a sort of phenomenon that marked my career: In the period 1960–63, I was to win thirty-two tournaments —and go on to become the first million-dollar winner in golf history.

II

The Watershed Year

JUST inside the front door, on a wall of the foyer leading to the living room, is a small painting with a calm beauty and serene dignity. There is nothing strained or sophisticated in its composition but, as a farmyard scene—a barn, a corral, a horse, the deepened colors of nature—it has a certain grand integrity. It's an original but it's initialed, not signed, and I don't know that it would have a value to anyone but me. The painter was a man named Eisenhower.

In a bookcase just inside the door of the master bedroom is a book about a critical moment in the life and career of Thomas Jefferson. It has a message, insight, and significance that has no special value to anyone but me. It was the gift of a man named Nixon.

The point of all this is not to brag. It's really to do the opposite. These are highly personal items, not a part of a public display of accomplishment. In fact, I don't think there are many people outside of the family who know they're there. The fact is, there isn't much of the flashy public bric-a-brac around the house to reflect the run through history that I've enjoyed. Most of the golf trophies are at the Latrobe Country Club, where my father, Deacon Palmer, was and is the head pro and course superintendent. He put a lot of his life and sweat into that country club, and if there are any symbols of my success in life, I feel that they should be in a public place where they'll be a reflection of his labor and his love.

The one thing that we cherish—and that has a small "public" flavor—is in the den. It's a cracked old walnut table—round and low, like a cocktail table—that we have sitting at shin-barking height just in front of the sofa. The only noticeable thing about it, I guess, is that it doesn't fit into the décor of the den. It's old and broken and faded, whereas the den is done in what you might call the Palmer method: It has a rug the color of a holly-berry, sober paneled wood walls, and a bookcase that has a thick volume in rich leather sitting on top of it—it's called *The World's Greatest Book* and it opens up into a tiny bar with bottles of liquor secreted in it.

The reason that we like that battered old walnut table is because it tells more about these last few years than all of the other mementos we have around the house put together.

For it's inlaid with some of the medals that I've won in golf. There are four gold medals from the Masters tourney there. There are two gold medals from the British Open. There's one gold medal from the U. S. Open and four silver ones.

Altogether, there are thirty medals in this old table.

And one empty space.

We could fill it, of course. But we're holding off. We'd like to fill it some day with another Masters medal, or a U. S. Open gold medal, or my first PGA gold medal.

But as soon as we did, we'd bore another hole into the table. And leave it empty—for the *next* medal.

For the way I feel, there should always be a little room for the future.

That's why in turning backward—in focusing on the 1960 U. S. Open—I feel I may have done you a disfavor.

For I am one of those people who feel that it is today's game, not yesterday's, that is important. It is the present challenge, not the past, that commands devotion.

The other day, a newsman asked me which year I felt was my most successful year—1960, or 1961, or 1964, when I played as close to a "perfect" Masters as some people thought possible. Or was it 1971, when I won $209,603—almost exactly five times what I won in the year we began to build our house?

Or was it some year yet to come?

I don't know, of course. I hope it's still in the future. The single advantage of going back to 1960 is that it gives us a perspective on the years that followed. For we know now that something else was happening to all of us in 1960. And that golf—while assuredly not the substance—became a symbol of that "happening."

We had, you may remember, come through a period when our whole national being—in life, much more than in golf—was bound up in the meticulous avoidance of mistakes. And thus in the avoidance of defeat.

There was something in this—something quite subtle—that frustrated the American spirit. If only because we, as a people, have been bred boldly to victory rather than to the avoidance of defeat. It was a moment that cried out for somebody—anybody—who could not merely challenge defeat but charge boldly after victory. What I did in golf in 1960 was, mysteriously, to touch the temper of the times. For we all know now that the basic drama of the 1960s—the whole insistent pulse of life, from the civil rights marches to the reach for the moon —was a reflection of the feeling that man must not only define his life but control it. No matter how enormous were the odds. If 1960 was anything, it was the beginning of one of those historic moments when it seemed important—personally, and as part of the nation—to go for broke. And it was a time when a symbol, any symbol—even this compelling, obsessive, utterly maddening game called golf—might come to reflect, however vicariously, the emerging style of our times.

It was my fate, and extraordinary good fortune, to become part of that symbol. At the time I didn't know it. None of us were sitting around intellectualizing about the future then. I was absorbed by an entirely different, and masochistic, preoccupation: hitting a small round ball into a hole in a large round ball. And if anything will give you perspective, *that* will.

As I look back on it, it was not important, in 1960, that I won. It was important that I won against the odds. That I clearly enjoyed bucking the odds. And that I did it time and time again.

For my success in the 1960 National Open had an important prologue as well as many happy epilogues. The prologue took place in the 1960 Masters tournament, and it had for me—and perhaps millions watching on television—an enomous emotional punch. That was the tournament in which I had to beat off the charge of other golfers and go birdie-birdie on the last two holes to overtake Ken Venturi. And I had to do it after what could only be called spectacularly mixed play.

In the opening round, I got three birdies and an eagle on the four par-5 holes at Augusta. That helped me come in with a 67. After that, everything seemed to fall apart. Particularly my putting. In the second and third rounds, I shot a 73 and a 72. At the time, I was breaking in a new putter, and with it I felt I had all the subtle touch of a punch press. It got so bad that I wasn't sure I could drop it in from three feet up, much less putt it in from three feet out. At the end of the third round, I was tempted to throw the putter away—and I might have done it if I'd known then that the championship would depend on my making two crucial putts successfully.

As I was coming down the stretch on the last round, Ken Venturi was in the clubhouse with a 283, enough—it seemed—

to win. At the seventeenth green, I faced a 39-foot putt, uphill and to the cup, and a hard decision: whether to play it safe or go for broke.

There was still a chance I might win, albeit a very small one. I'd have to sink this putt for a birdie on the seventeenth hole. Then I'd have to birdie the eighteenth hole, too. And—considering the way I'd been putting—that was a formidable problem. The first putt would be the toughest one. It was not only a long one—and thus susceptible to the subtle vagaries of the grain and grass—but it had the potential for total failure. For I knew I'd have to hit it hard; if the ball missed the cup, it would likely go a long way past it. That could mean that I might have to take two putts coming back—three putts altogether—and that would mean no chance for the title.

On the other hand, I could play it safe and lag the ball up close on my first putt. That would give me a good chance of sinking the second putt. I'd only have a par for the hole, but if I followed up with a birdie I could salvage a tie for the title and get a chance for a playoff against Venturi the next day.

So here was the classic situation that defined the times—a chance to avoid defeat. A chance to *tie*. Not win. By playing it safe, I *couldn't* win; but then I might not lose, either.

There was only one trouble: Avoiding defeat on this hole wouldn't guarantee that I'd avoid defeat on the next hole. It might get worse there, not better.

So I decided to go boldly for the cup.

Never up, never in—that's the way I looked at it. If it was going to be a bad putt, it was going to be a spectacularly bad putt. For I wasn't going to fall short of the hole: I was going to hit the ball so hard that if it missed the cup it might not stop until it hit the far collar around the green.

It *was* a spectacular putt. The ball homed crisply on the hole, almost went right over it, rammed the far side of the cup —and dropped in.

For the birdie.

Now I faced another challenge: to keep my emotions under control. A putt like that is going to send anybody's spirit soaring. It would have been easy to relax and say that if I could sink a putt like that, there's nothing I could do wrong. But I knew better; you play this game with brains as well as boldness.

I still had to get a birdie on the eighteenth hole in order to win. That meant building the birdie right from the tee to cup, not just going out there and swinging from the heels.

Take my first two shots: The eighteenth at Augusta is an up-hill 420-yard par-4 with a gentle dogleg to the right. The shortest route to the green is down the right side, and the opening to the green is toward the right. Those attractions are there for a purpose: to lure the golfer into trouble. For along the right side of the fairway where it bends to the right, some 230 yards from the tee, there's a dense stand of tall, thick-trunked Georgia pines. The golfer who goes down the right side of the fairway toward the opening to the green is likely going to wind up in those trees, where there are birds but no birdies.

I knew that a well-placed drive to the middle of the fairway would leave anything from the five- to a seven-iron to the green. The left side of the fairway was then a hazard-free target that offered a certain security: The rough on that side had been well trampled by spectators in the four days of the tournament (remember, this was the last hole on the last day), and so it might be just a little flattened out. You might find a reasonable lie in that kind of rough and—to be candid about it—you'd find a lot of spectators whose sheer presence would stop the roll of the ball. So if your ball happened to go that way, you'd still likely wind up in a spot much better than in the woods on the right.

(There's now a large two-tiered sand trap down there, in the left fairway, just about where you'd go around the outside corner on the dogleg right. It was built in 1967, and its purpose—I'm convinced—was to keep the pros from booming their tee shots to the left, risking the rough or the crowd. Now they'll boom it into the sand trap—or be forced right by the threat toward the trees.)

So my goal was to go for the middle of the fairway, favoring a miss to the left that would keep me away from the trees. On the tee I set up in a very slight "hook" stance (my right foot drawn back slightly from the line of flight) so that if anything went wrong, it would go "wrong" toward the open spaces on the left instead of toward the trees on the right. I teed the ball up low, to keep it from getting up into the wind, and I remembered some advice of my father's that was particularly useful in a high-pressure situation: Don't rush the shot or swing fast in order to get more distance. "Start deliberate," he often told me, "and come back slow on the backswing, and then give it everything you've got on the downswing."

That's exactly what I did. And I got the ball out there 260 yards or so—right in the middle of the fairway, where I had a good, clear view of the green and the flag.

It would be a solid six-iron. And I would go for the cup —not for the green, but precisely for the cup. For to get the birdie, I *had* to one-putt. And to get into a position to one-putt, I had to hit this approach shot exactly right.

It was not going to be easy: The 18th green at Augusta is fairly narrow and rises to the back in three distinct plateaus. It is trapped on the right and on the front and falls off sharply into some TV towers on the left. It is a green that cries out for small errors—then it magnifies them. As I saw it—in seeking the birdie—it would not be enough to hit the green. It would have to be hit precisely, in a spot so close to the cup that a one-putt was more than merely possible; that it might even be said to be probable.

In short, all I had to do was hit a great six-iron approach shot.

The trick was in the sense of self-discipline. For the temptation in a crucial spot like that is to look up so that you'll know instantly what you've done—for better or for worse. Yet on a six-iron shot like this, or on any comparable approach shot using a middle-to-short iron, the most important single thing is not to yield to temptation—never to look up at the ball. Because looking up causes the golfer to quit on his shot at impact. It prevents him from hitting *through* the ball on the downswing so that he literally makes his ultimate impact with the ground—after hitting the ball—and digs a divot with the club beyond the ball.

It took a good deal of self-control, but when I hit this six-iron —again coming back slowly and deliberately—I made sure that I never saw the ball in the air. But when I heard the crowd around the eighteenth green yell, and saw the spectators swarm all over the fairway, it was more satisfying than the shot itself. For the ball hit to the right of the cup, bounced in a twisting motion back toward it, and stopped five feet from the hole.

As I walked up to the green, I thought about how boldness had turned this game around. It had kept me in a position to win the tournament, and it had given me the "charge" to make two excellent shots. Now I had to go for the win—and sink the putt. My resolution must have been contagious. "The ball's scared of him," said Bob Rosburg as he and other pros watched the action on closed-circuit television in the clubhouse. "He'll get it in the hole if he has to stare it in."

In looking back, we can see the pattern-in-common now. At both Augusta and Cherry Hills in 1960, I won because I wasn't stopped by the fear of failure. It wasn't that I was playing all my shots brilliantly but that I ready to overcome the challenge of my own bad shots. At Augusta, I won by overcoming my own worst fault of that tournament—putting. At Cherry Hills, I won by overcoming my own worst fault there —flawed tee shots on the first hole. I won because I refused to accept the avoidance of small mistakes. I would win boldly or lose the same way. But I wasn't going to lead a life of dear-and-near-misses.

That my philosophy worked was important to me: In two seasons or so I was to win fourteen tournaments and establish a certain security in golf.

That it worked with a certain style was one of the accidents of history. For the way I did things appealed to the unspoken inner instincts of the nation. I didn't know it. I didn't even *think* about it. But we all know in looking back that there was rising then a yearning for the bold play, the bravura gesture, the indomitable defiance of odds. It was a time when the American people were beginning to feel once again that anything might be accomplished if only we were bold enough to try.

In this new spirit of busting loose, there was—to many people—something meaningful in the way I attacked a golf course. Until then, golf was a game that demanded subtlety and control rather than a brazen expenditure of energy. It responded to a superbly meticulous touch that focused on the avoidance of mistakes—and thus an avoidance of defeat—and it not only fit the earlier times but had an accomplished symbol: Ben Hogan. That's why I tend to look to 1960 as a sort of watershed in golf. For it not only involved a change in the temper of the times, and golfing style, but it involved the matched drama of two careers: mine and Ben Hogan's. They happened to come together at Cherry Hills—and then again later in the decade.

By way of explanation, let me stress that golf is not only a game of touch and feel; it's also a game of heightened sensitivity. It must respond to the inner needs and character of the golfer. Every man must measure his skills against his goals and his purpose. The integrity with which he puts them together is his own best measure of success. A man must respond to what is within him. I did not fit my style to the times; I fit my style to my own needs. I *have* to go for broke. I could not be comfortable with myself otherwise. To be sure, mine is a measured boldness rather than a reckless one: I'm bold when the rewards are right, not just because risk or recklessness is attractive in itself. The meticulous player, as I see it, does not challenge risk at all; he avoids it. He may also achieve an enormous success—and insist that it is a genuine measure of his inner drives and fears. I'd like to think—as an advocate of boldness—that the bold player takes greater risks in pursuit of greater goals. But the more meticulous player might claim that his goals are just as genuine and that his style is just as satisfying to his own special drives.

That, I think, is the measure of the man and the game: that his golf has the integrity of himself in it.

What would happen, for example, if I didn't go for broke?

What happens to any player when he denies what is within him?

Ben Hogan can tell you. And so can I.

And the evidence was in the 1960s.

Take the U. S. Open at Cherry Hills in 1960. It was on a course that catered to placement more than to power. It was on a course that appealed to the style of Ben Hogan—precise, meticulous, fading the ball in here, punching it in there, always being in just the right spot in the fairway so as never to risk missing the green. He didn't play the course with the power that Mike Souchak did: Hogan was three strokes off the lead as he started the final round. But he did play it with somewhat the same touch: By the seventeenth hole of the final round, he'd hit the green in regulation strokes on thirty-four consecutive holes. [*"Regulation strokes" is a short way of saying "par for the hole minus two." Every hole is designed with an expectation of two putts on the green (a short pause for hysterical laughter). To reach the green in "regulation"—i.e., to move from tee to green—you have to figure the score without those two putts: one stroke on a par 3, two on a par 4, three on a par 5.*]

You couldn't imagine a much finer expression of a style of golf than Ben Hogan's. Or a more successful one. On the seventeenth hole at Cherry Hills, he was tied or thereabouts at four under par with me and with Jack Fleck. He may have been a little surprised by what I'd done, what with my coming from so far behind. It was no secret: My 30 on the first nine—and how I'd gotten it—was the hottest gossip on the golf course.

Fleck posed an even more interesting challenge. He was the man who'd tied Ben Hogan in the 1955 U. S. Open at Olympic Club in San Francisco. At the time, Ben was as close as a split hair to becoming the first and only man to win the U. S. Open five times. He'd walked off the seventy-second green in that tournament—an apparent victor with a "lead that nobody could overtake"—to one of the greatest and most honestly earned acclamations in the game. He was, himself, so sure that he'd won his fifth U. S. Open that, as he walked off the eighteenth green that day, he handed the ball he'd used to Joe Dey, then the executive director of the United States Golf Association. "Here's one for Golf House," he said, referring to the USGA museum and headquarters then in New York.

Then suddenly along came Jack Fleck, then a pro with just a hint of a reputation, who operated a couple of municipal golf courses in Davenport, Iowa. In 1955, he'd never won a professional golf tournament. In fact, he'd never finished as high as fifth. Nor could it be said that he was the one pro who could conquer Olympic: He had, after all, taken an 87 in a practice round. There was one last irony in all this: He was trying to shatter Ben Hogan's world by using Ben Hogan-endorsed golf clubs.

As it happened, Fleck represented not only an unhappy reality—to Ben—but also a haunting memory to Ben's fans. For back in 1955, Fleck came into the last hole needing a birdie to tie Hogan. The eighteenth green at Olympic tilts severely from back to front, and it was—at that time—quite slippery. (I remember because that was my first U. S. Open as a pro. I finished twenty-first with a 303 for 72 holes, and I walked away with $180 in prize money.) Most of the pros had been ver-r-y careful on that green. They'd been babying their putts and hoping to catch a corner of the cup. Jack Fleck came up needing a birdie to tie Ben Hogan for the U. S. Open championship and—in a defiance of tradition—he rammed the ball hard into the center of the cup, just as if he didn't have a care about the grain or the tilt or the scourge of the golf tournament. It was not—in terms of the very meticulous temper of the times—playing the game.

In the resulting playoff of the 1955 U. S. Open, Fleck sank putts as if he were in a trance. By the last hole, Ben needed to pick up a stroke to catch Fleck on the last hole, but he didn't get it; he drove into the rough, took three strokes to play carefully back into the fairway, and lost to Fleck by three strokes.

Ben was forty-two at the time. Now here he was, five years later, in a good position finally to win his fifth U. S. Open. He looked up on the seventeenth hole at Cherry Hills—and Jack Fleck, of *all* people, is coming at him. I can't say that it bothered Ben a great deal; he is too unflappable a character. But there were people who admire him who were struck by the irony of this little drama.

Ben was playing with Jack Nicklaus at the time, two pairs in front of me, four in front of Jack Fleck. Nicklaus and I have discussed from time to time what took place at the seventeenth hole. Indeed, it was debated through the long hours of that night by everybody involved in the Open. For there was an instant on that seventeenth hole when Ben Hogan was challenged—as I had been a few hours earlier, on the first tee—to switch to a game other than what was within himself.

To understand the decision facing him, you must understand the hole and the situation.

As he stood on the seventeenth tee, Ben knew he had only two holes on which to improve his score: this hole and the eighteenth.

He knew also that the two men who were tied with him had more room for maneuver. I was at about the fifteenth tee, and

I had four holes in which to improve my score. Jack Fleck was at about the thirteenth tee, with six holes in which to lower his score. Ben knew that neither of us was likely to sit back and play for a tie: We both had the boldness to go for the throat—*his* throat.

Of course, you could look at it another way: that I had four holes and Fleck had six holes in which to blow the tournament. But I was playing a hot streak of golf, and Fleck had shown a certain resistance to pressure when he went head on head against Hogan in the past.

Beyond all this, Ben Hogan is, superbly, a realist. He couldn't rely on us to fail. He had to rely on himself to succeed.

And so he had to make his score-lowering move now.

These were his choices: The seventeenth was a 548-yard par-5 hole. The green was set on a small island in a lake and, on this day, the pin was toward the right-front edge of the green. It was not what you would call an easy birdie hole. None of the leaders birdied it on that last day, and some of them bogeyed it.

The eighteenth was no better. It was a strenuous 468-yard par-4 hole, uphill and climbing to a high and plateaued green. Mike Souchak, then the tournament leader, had double-bogeyed the hole at the end of his third round, only a few hours earlier. Of the eleven top finishers in the tournament, eight of them—including Nicklaus, Julius Boros, Souchak, Fleck, Jerry Barber, Ted Kroll, Dutch Harrison, and Hogan— would bogey, double-bogey, or triple-bogey the eighteenth on the last round. It was clearly not the kind of hole that even the best of golfers could be sure would provide him with a stroke-saving opportunity.

So for Ben Hogan, starting the seventeenth hole, it was now or never: He had to make his bid to pick up strokes on the seventeenth. The first two shots had to be executed to get position for the decisive third shot. Most golfers liked to lay their second shot up in front of the lake so they'd have an easier and safer shot on the green. The safe way to play the third shot was to go for the fat part of the putting surface—the big broad sweep of the green, however far from the pin that it was. For if you got daring about playing to the cup—at least when the pin was so close to the front—you took the risk of plopping into the water.

The safe way meant accepting the two-putt approach, at the very least. The daring way gave you a chance to go for one putt—and a birdie.

Jack Nicklaus played it safe. He laid the ball up there close to the water with a four-iron on his second shot. Then he used a wedge to lob the ball over the water onto the fat part of the green. Then he two-putted for his par 5.

Hogan, playing with Nicklaus, put his second shot right in the center of the fairway—where else?—about 25 or 30 yards short of the water. The moat wasn't terribly wide, perhaps 8 or 10 yards from the edge of the fairway to the front of the green. So Ben had only 35 or 40 yards to go to clear the water.

But it wasn't the distance from pin to green that concerned him. It was the distance from the pin to the potential putt—his first putt. For on that last round, the pin was set only about 9 feet—perhaps only 3 yards—beyond the edge of the water. Thus there was precious little landing area on the front of the green, up in the one-putt territory. Even if you could place the ball in there with enough backspin to keep it from rolling far beyond the cup, you'd take a chance that it would bounce back and off the green, down into the moat in front of the green. If you didn't place it with backspin, the ball would hit and run on toward the back of the green, where it would take two putts—or perhaps more—to get back to the cup. So it took a very delicate, almost incredible touch to hit the front of the green exactly and get the ball to hold there.

So the decisions facing Ben were these:

Did he want to go for the two-putt and a par? It was the

safe play. Or did he want to go for the one-putt position, with all the risks involved in it? In short, should he take the big risk for the birdie and a chance to take the lead in the tournament? Or should he ignore the risk and play it safe for a tie?

Nobody knows what was in Ben Hogan's mind at that moment. Certainly I don't know, and I'm sure Jack Nicklaus doesn't. But Ben was forty-seven years old by then, a man who'd recovered from a near-fatal auto accident to come back to win three of his four U. S. Opens. He'd have to play thirty-six holes on that Saturday to wind up the U. S. Open, an exhausting experience in high-pressure golf for any man whose legs had been all but crippled. Now he faced the likelihood that —if he played it safe—he'd have to go around the next day in a grueling, high-pressure playoff. And it was possible, just possible, that he'd be meeting Jack Fleck again in that playoff. Nothing could present a more final or tormented irony than that his fifth U. S. Open title should be taken away from him —in a playoff—by the same man who'd done it before.

But if he played it boldly—against the natural grain of his career—he might end it all there. A successful gamble could take it all away from Fleck and the rest of us.

He chose to gamble. This extraordinary golfer with an almost celestial sense of where and how to play the safe shot to avoid defeat took a risky shot in a bold bid for victory.

He took out his wedge and laid the blade back almost flat with the ground. Then he hit the ball with a short decisive chop, pitching it up low and to the very front of the green with a dominant backspin. It did almost exactly what he wanted— but not quite. It hit the bank on the far side of the water— and popped backward. The ball settled down right at the edge of the water.

It was all over. Right then and there, Ben Hogan knew that he'd lost the gamble. Now all it would take would be a miracle —hitting from a bad lie into the hole.

At least he could try to salvage something less than disaster.

And he tried. He took off his right shoe and sock and climbed down into the moat; he lofted the ball out of that atrocious lie and dropped it just 18 feet from the pin. It was a remarkable recovery, considering his position. But he two-putted from there and took a bogey 6 instead of the birdie four he'd been seeking. The risk didn't work for him. He dropped out of a tie for the lead at that point, and he never regained it.

Moreover, going against his own internal grain seemed to drain him of his purpose, his drive, his energy. On the eighteenth tee, he hooked his first shot and dropped it in the water on his left. It took him a total of four shots to get to the green, and he three-putted from there. He took a 7. That gave him 13 strokes for the final two holes, four over par. In a matter of minutes, he dropped from a tie for the lead to a tie for ninth place.

He wound up with a 284. Fleck beat him with a 283. So did I with a 280. If he'd played it safe and gone for par on both holes, he would have tied me—and beaten Fleck.

That one moment of boldness—that single departure from a lifelong style of meticulous and superbly calculated play—cost him his chance for his fifth U. S. Open title.

And, perhaps as much as my own victory, it symbolized the changing temper and evolving style of the golf that was soon to be.

I would be less than candid if I did not relate the long-delayed aftermath. For I tried Ben Hogan's way, just as he tried mine. For a longer period of time. And with no more success.

The time was in the middle 1960s—I can't remember exactly what date or what place. All I know is that I was becoming increasingly disturbed about my game. Three years were to pass in which I'd win only one major tournament. In fact, one whole year passed, 1965, in which I won only one tournament of any kind. I began thinking that maybe I'd had it too good, that the hard, remorseless resolution needed to win week after week on the pro golf tour had somehow slipped away from me with my rising affluence. Ultimately, I began to wonder if I *could* win—if I was afraid to win.

So I decided to change all my tactics. I was getting "old"— thirty-six at the time—and I feared the days of boldness were over. Maybe, I thought, *maybe* I should play it cozy: Go for the "percentage" shot, keep the ball away from the trees by controlling it with a three-wood instead of a driver, hitting the fairways in just the right place, hitting the greens even better, using the divots of one round to mark the shots for the next.

There was only one trouble: It wasn't in me. I *have* to play with a sense of abandon, with "full release," without the cunning and coziness that goes with the kind of game that I was trying now. In this change of style I was denying my own nature; I could only ruin myself by trying to play in somebody else's skin.

The result was that by the autumn of 1965, I was totally unsure of my game. Between seasons, I came home to Latrobe, Pennsylvania, and worked on my physique and my psychology. I built up my strength by exercising. I built up my determination that I could win—and that I would win.

In the Los Angeles Open, at the start of the 1966 season, I felt I *had* to win, to prove myself to myself. And things went beautifully—at least until the last round. I went into it with a seven-stroke lead—and a sudden sense of fear. I worried about that lead: I began protecting it, not extending it. Again I began playing the game like Ben Hogan played it, more cautiously than I know how. The result was that I'd lost six strokes off that lead with four holes left to play. Here I had the tournament won, and I was so afraid of losing it that I didn't know what to do. At that moment, I turned within myself and said, "I've *got* to get hold of myself and play my own game." It was just in time: I reverted to my old bold style of play. The result: I hung onto the lead in the L. A. Open and went on to win five more tournaments and tie for the title in three others before losing in playoffs.

It wasn't easy. I had to place all kinds of little disciplines on myself to keep from falling prey to Man's Natural Fear. At the Champions Tournament in Houston that year, I tried a few fancy shots early on the back nine and lost a last-round lead to Gardner Dickinson. But I made sure that I didn't quite know the true dimensions of disaster. I stopped to read the scoreboard—I've always been a big scoreboard watcher. But this time I was afraid of knowing too much. So I cocked my head and slitted my eyes a little so I could focus on the score, not the names. I could see my big red "9" at the top, indicating I was nine under par. So I started down the line, glancing hurriedly for fear I'd get the bad news, and I didn't see anything close to it. Until I got to the bottom line, where I saw another red "9." Deliberately I turned away without even looking to see who'd caught me. I didn't want to know. "Never mind who it is," I told myself. "Never mind being smart and setting the strategy for him. Just go out and hit the ball and beat him." That I did. I went out to the eighteenth hole, hit a bad tee shot —and then got hold of myself. My mind and spirit began working my way again. I found I was blocked from the green by a fairway bunker and the pin was tucked behind a yawning bunker that guarded the green. It seemed an impossible shot to go for the flag; the safe way to play it was to go for the "fat" of the green and away from the flag, and then putt gradually back to the cup. But I just "bust loose": I resisted the temptation to play it safe, and I went boldly for the flag. The ball dropped just 12 feet from the cup. I sank the putt for a birdie and won the championship.

With that approach shot, I found myself again. I *have* to be an aggressive player. I have to do it my way. I can't be happy playing somebody else's game, even if that game has been a proven success. A golfer—a *man*—must feel right within himself about himself. His greatest wealth is his integrity. In nothing else is he rich. In nothing else is he poor.

III

Three Plaques

IN THE MORNING, the sun shines in through the picture window and warms my back between the shoulder blades. Down below the window to my office, beyond the slopes filled with pine and oak and birch, is the Latrobe Country Club, where my father has worked for half a century. I grew up on that course: From my chair I can still see the copse of trees where—as an eight- or ten-year-old—I'd go to practice shooting out of the rough by the hour.

It's just after sunup when I get to the office in the morning. It's quiet then—the staff doesn't come in for an hour or two. And I'm a "morning" person: I like to get up early and enjoy the solitude of working alone. That's a dramatic change from my "work" on the professional golf tour, where solitude isn't just a distant virtue—it's an absent one.

That may be one of the reasons why I always come back to the hill country of western Pennsylvania. It has feeling and substance and solitude. I'm a provincial. I always have been. I'm not ashamed to say that I love coming back to this small town—in a time when cosmopolitan "urban living" is supposed to be the high style—and that coming home has a profound sense of renewal for me.

["*I think that attitude helps explain why Palmer has succeeded so well," says Dr. David C. Morley, a psychiatrist and psychological consultant to* Golf Digest, *who's played golf on occasion with Palmer at Latrobe. "He knows who he is, likes what he's got, and doesn't desire anything beyond that. His ability to feel genuinely happy within the confines of his home town, and to see himself realistically, is what holds him together."*]

My roots run deep here. The old values appear and reappear. I'm not much of a one for keeping all the bric-a-brac of success around me: The only trophy in the office is a battered little cup—that's still not engraved—that I got for my first professional win, at the Canadian Open in 1955. But there are three plaques that have a special significance for me—one of them on the wall of my office and the other two on golf courses around the world. Together they suggest the tone and style of my attitude toward golf.

The framed plaque on the wall of my office is part of the process of renewal and reminder. It is a simple expression simply put, but it reveals nevertheless the energizing thrust of my career. Here is the first part:

> "If you think you are beaten, you are,
> If you think you dare not, you don't,
> If you'd like to win but think you can't
> It's almost certain you won't."

The second part is the positive side:

> "Life's battles don't always go
> To the stronger or faster man,
> But sooner or later, the man who wins
> Is the man who thinks he can."

In these words, you can see much of the philosophy that guides me in golf. Just as every individual's philosophical approach to golf, and to life, must possess an inner integrity, so also must his actions. He must carry out what he thinks, in the expectation of success but never in the fear of failure. But the individual must not merely try; he must try to the *utmost*. My goals have always been the impossible ones: "This guy," Sam Snead said after I'd teamed with him in the 1960 Canada Cup matches, "wants to hole out everything from the tee."

Of course. No other way to go. For golf has always represented self-fulfillment to me. Perhaps, as some have said, it is an elaborate and addictive rite. And perhaps it is in a class by itself for the anguish it imposes. But it also lightens and ventilates the days. and—for millions of people—makes them more bearable. For to every golfer, whether he's a duffer or a top pro, golf offers a magnificent combination of hope, joy, exasperation, and rue. It is singular in that its goals never disappear —it has something that always beckons compellingly to every golfer, no matter how much he's succeeded. A few years ago, Jack Nicklaus walked into a press tent after shooting a 64 in the Tournament of Champions.

"Dog-*gone!*" he said. "Try as I might, I haven't ever been able to break a 64."

"That's a terrible thing," said Jim Murray of the Los Angeles *Times*, "to have to go through life with."

The point here is that life is a combination of success and of failure—that in your greatest success you may yet be suffering a certain failure. But only if you set your goals high enough. That's why the other two plaques I mentioned are a reflection of my basic attitude toward golf: They commemorate my particular goals as well as particular golf shots. One is a memorial to success and the other a memorial to failure. But both are suggestions of what aggressiveness and confidence can do. For you. And to you.

The plaque for success is at Royal Birkdale in England. I

went there in 1961 to play in the British Open, in a year when the challenge was not only from the golf course and the golfers but from the hardy weather. A steady rain fell, and a stiff, remorseless wind blew constantly after the first round. The third round had, in fact, to be postponed because of the weather. (When the British won't play their Open, you'd better *believe* that the weather is bad.) Fortunately my game was well geared for a bad blow. My shots were teed up low then, so that I hit low line drives that bored through the wind, not lofty fly balls that might surrender to the caprice of every gust and gale. On approach shots near the green, I'd choke down on the shaft so much that many people thought I was half-topping the ball on many occasions. Actually I was choking down on a one-iron, which has no loft, and thus I could ram the ball low and straight, under the wind. In that way, I got the shorter distance that I'd usually be seeking from a four- or five- or even a six-iron, but I'd be keeping the ball on a low line drive, instead of popping it up into the air—and the wind—as would happen if I'd used the higher-number irons with the more sharply lofted heads.

Halfway through the tournament, I was one stroke out of the lead. On the morning when the third round was played—in a stiff gale—I shot a 32 on the front nine. The next best score was a 38. That figured to end it all there, but it didn't. For I couldn't quite shake the pursuit of Dai Rees, a remarkable golfer from Wales. He was as intent on winning—and as unwavering in the wind—as I was, and by the time I reached the fifteenth hole of the last round we were still pretty much neck and neck.

It was a par-4 hole, and I hit a poor tee shot. It got up a little high, was caught by the wind, and landed very, very deep in the rough to the right. It was so far in there—perhaps five feet from being out of bounds—that you wouldn't need a caddy to find it; you'd need an archaeologist. The rain was still falling, and the rough and underbrush were wet and tangled. Most of the experts took one look and wished me well; it was their view that the only way I'd get to the green from there was with a safari and a native guide. There was, of course, the safe way: Dig the ball out of there with a wedge and pop it back onto the fairway—coming out in the direction from which I'd come. Going backward that way would cost me a minimum of a stroke: Even if I played the hole as well as could be expected, I'd very likely wind up with a 5—three strokes to get to the green and two putts. So I'd bogey the hole —and going that one-over-par might hand the tournament to Dai Rees.

I looked for another way out. My basic attitude is that when you're in the rough, go for the green. I'd urge anybody to look to the green when you're in the rough. Most of the time, you'll save yourself a stroke—*if* you're sure you can execute the shot.

The way I saw it, it would take a six-iron to get me out of there and land me on the green. Middling loft to dig the ball up out of the rough. Plus extra musclepower needed to get out of the tangle and carry all the way to the green. I saw the opening, and I was sure I could make it. Nobody else did. To most people, it seemed like a shot that was not merely impossible but utterly insane. For even the slightest flaw in execution would keep me in the rough or send the ball careening in an utterly unpredictable way. The way they looked at it, sacrificing one stroke—by playing safe to the fairway—was the best deal I could make; anything else would cost two or three or four strokes. Actually, it never entered my mind that I'd hit into the rough again or come up short. You go for the cup or you crawl to it—that's my attitude.

The only comment I could make was with the golf club: I took the six-iron and rammed the ball out of there—just right on the loft, just right in the direction, just right on the musclepower—leaving a foot-long scar in the rough. [". . . *Few will see it,*" *wrote one British golf writer, "for it is an unfrequented spot ringed by perdition.*"] The ball shot toward the green, bounced once on the soggy turf, and came to a quick stop on the wet green. Two putts and I had my par—and my plaque. For that shot helped me win my first British Open: I wound up edging Dai Rees by just one stroke.

The other plaque that holds some significance is for a shot —actually, four of them—that I made in the Los Angeles Open back in 1961. It's a tournament I like to do well in: I've won it three times and finished second or third two other times. It's played at Rancho Park Golf Course, a public course where 150,000 or so rounds are played every year. The significance of this particular plaque is that the public could play the hole better than I did.

It was on the ninth hole of the golf course—the eighteenth hole of the second round for me. (Because there were so many players in the tournament, the field had to be split in half, and I happened to be in the half that finished that day on holes one through nine.) I came up to the hole some two strokes under par. To wind up with a 69, I needed only get a par 5 on this hole. But I wanted to do better—I was thinking of getting a birdie or, if possible, an eagle. [*"He doesn't play a golf course, he tries to obliterate it," wrote Jim Murray in the Los Angeles Times.*] The hole is something of a funnel, narrowing in the distance until the green—flanked closely by two out-of-bounds fences—seems locked in the neck of the funnel. The opening to the green is quite narrow, but you can reach the putting surface in two strokes—and bid for a birdie—by going over the hazards with a wood instead of laying up to the green with an iron. Or so I figured.

My tee shot carried me well into the fairway, and I decided to go for the green on the second shot by hitting with a three-wood.

I hit a good shot—but it went wrong.

You've heard that one before? Well, let me tell you—this ball looked like it was going to settle just where I'd hoped, when a little wind came up and gave it a fair nudge to the right. It faded off fast, hit the top rail of the fence, and bounded out of bounds.

The only thing I could do was take a penalty stroke and go back to my original lie in the fairway.

I did—and I went for the green again. I didn't quit now and decide to play it safe by hitting with an iron. I took out my three-wood because I was still sure I could make the shot. And—even though I'd missed my birdie—I was still playing the numbers: That second fairway stroke with the three-wood was only my fourth stroke (including the penalty stroke) of the hole. If I got it close to the pin, I might one-putt and—since the putt would be stroke No. 5—get par for the hole. With an iron, it would certainly take two strokes to the green, and the best I could get would be a bogey.

So I played for par—and missed.

I corrected for the fade ever so subtly. This time the ball hooked and went out of bounds over the fence on the left.

At least I had the green bracketed, and the next shot should drill it in the heart. Right?

Wrong!

I took the penalty shot and played again from the fairway and, correcting ever so subtly for the hook, hit a ball that . . . faded again and went out of bounds, over the fence to the right.

The important thing was confidence. Or stubbornness. No —I like to think of it as confidence. My decision was right: I could hit that three-wood onto the green—I *knew* that. [*"He doesn't play a course," wrote Murray. He collides with it."*] So I played the three-wood again, with a little more hook into the shot, and the results were pretty much what you'd expect: over the fence and out of bounds to the left. Four shots and four penalty shots and I was right where I was when I started. [*Murray: "It's nice to see Arnold Palmer find out what it's like. You feel like leaning over to the television set and leering, 'Aggravating, ain't it, Arnie? How do you like it, boy?' "*]

Now I figured it was time to quit all this foolin' around, that there was just one thing left to do: play the three-wood direct to the green. So I did it: The ball took off, clean as a clergyman's conscience—no hook, no fade—and it dropped pin-high onto the green, about 15 feet from the cup.

Simple—just what I'd intended all along. It just took a little more practice than I expected.

Two putts later and I'd finished the hole with a 12, seven over par for the round.

When I got to the clubhouse, somebody asked me what had happened.

"I missed a putt for an 11," I told them cheerfully.

(The dénouement: the next year the Los Angeles Junior Chamber of Commerce, which sponsors the Los Angeles Open, came to me and asked how I'd feel about them putting up a plaque to memorialize the feat. "Like 'Arnold Palmer wept here'?" I inquired. Actually, they had a neat and bizarre idea: to memorialize a colossal failure. The kind of failure that might comfort—if not enlighten—the regular clientele. But they didn't want to hurt my feelings while they did it. "Okay, go ahead," I told them. "But what makes you think you won't need another plaque next year?")

Over the years, there were to be a great many more frustrations in golf. And just as many satisfactions: By the middle of 1972, I'd won sixty tournaments in the United States and sixteen more overseas. Each had its own character and its own touching memory. But in the establishment, and reflection, of a philosophy of golf—with its ups and downs—nothing has been more pointed, or pungent, than the insights of these three plaques.

 *Part Two*

ITS ROOTS AND REWARDS

Everything is the cause of itself.
—RALPH WALDO EMERSON (1803–82)
American essayist

IV

The Road Up the Ridge...

THE OLD frame house is gray and weathered now. And empty. It sits like a distant memory beside the fifth hole at the Latrobe Country Club. I can see the old house from my bedroom window, looking through the birch trees and the oaks and pines. I grew up in that old house, and much of what I learned of life, and golf, was learned within its now-slanting walls.

Today, our home is a cozy one. White with black shutters, set into a ridge overlooking the Latrobe Country Club and out onto the lovely wooded foothills of the Allegheny Mountains. It's not a pretentious house. It started out as a three-bedroom home. I didn't like mortgages. I didn't like debt. I'd grown up in a time and place—in a Pennsylvania steel town during the Depression—when people were literally broken under the burden of impossible debt. It's a steep climb and a difficult one up that ridge from the old house to the new: When Winnie and I first climbed it, we had to have a hatchet to cut our way through the tangled underbrush. When I look out from it now, down toward the old house, I can't help but think how short a

47

distance life's trip is. And how stern it is.

When I was a boy, the frame house was green, and golf was even then at the very center of my life. My father was on the construction crew that built Latrobe Country Club, and when it opened in 1921, he was hired on the groundskeeping crew. In 1926, he was named greenskeeper, and in 1933, when the club couldn't afford both a pro and a course superintendent because of the Depression, he was asked to take over both jobs "until things got better." They never seemed to get enough better. He's still the pro and he's still the course superintendent: You can see him now—after a half century of pouring his sweat into this club—hunched over the controls of a gangmower, working the golf course today as he always did.

[*In the summer of 1971, Arnold Palmer bought the Latrobe Country Club. Palmer was asked then if Milfred "Deacon" Palmer would be retained in his role as pro and greenskeeper: "If he behaves himself," said Palmer with a puckish grin.*]

My father didn't just teach me to play golf. He taught me a discipline. It wasn't the kind of discipline that just says what you can't do—"don't do this" or "don't do that." It was the kind that said what you *had* to do—always do everything as hard and well as you can. Pap *had* to do it. As a boy, he'd suffered an attack of polio that left him bedridden, though not permanently paralyzed, for a long time. This was back before World War I, and when he finally got up out of his sickbed, he had to learn how to walk all over again. It was a struggle: he'd grown up in one of the little towns that surround Latrobe —it's called Youngstown—and there weren't many doctors around who could work with a pre-teen-age boy, helping guide him through a rehabilitation program. So Pap did it all himself, and it toughened him as a person as well as physically.

When I was growing up, he was a tough, taciturn disciplinarian. He taught me the value—and the need—for hard work. And he started at an early age. Some of the earliest memories

I have—as a kid three or four years old—are of riding around the club grounds on a tractor, between my father's knees. It wasn't too long before he had me doing it alone. Some people think I developed my strong arms by working in the steel mills around Latrobe. Not so. I got them when I was a little kid, seven or eight years old, working on the tractor for Pap. As I went chugging up and down those hills, it took everything I had—standing up and heaving the wheel with both arms—to "horse" that machine around.

Pap always had a job for me. For a while, he had me working in the pro shop, but he came to the conclusion that I wasn't a great success at the job: On nice days, I'd lock up the pro shop and take off over the hill to practice my drives. [*"I finally had to get rid of him," said Deacon Palmer dryly—just like he'd let any teen-ager go who didn't work out on the job.*] Of course, I was a caddy, too—but I fear I was less than a submissive success at that. For I figured I knew as much about the course as any member did, and I couldn't help but let them know about it. Not by anything I said: One thing I learned from Pap—never be bold or brassy. It was through my face, which—as you may have noticed—is a little expressive. In fact, you can read everything about how I feel by watching my expression. [*Years later, Harry Saxman, a top executive of Latrobe Steel—which owned most of the stock in the Latrobe Country Club—was to say of caddy Arnold Palmer: "I might ask for a four-iron and Arnie'd look up at me like I didn't know what I was doing. He wasn't being fresh; he'd just shake his head as if he felt sorry for me—a golfer like me not knowing I was using too much club." At that time, Saxman was the club champion, but his eleven-year-old caddy figured he could "club" anybody. " 'All right, Arnie,' I'd say, 'give me the five.' Then if I hit it just where I'd want, he'd just grin up at me and never say a word. We'd all laugh about it. But Arnie was usually right—he knew all there was to know about the course."*]

I learned it by working on it—as an old-time pro worked a course. And I learned it by playing on it. Because when I was about three years old, Pap fashioned a special set of golf clubs for me. It wasn't hard, for him. He simply cut down a set of battered old wood-shafted clubs to accommodate my height and then rewrapped the grips so I could wind my fingers around them. I'm sure if he had to, he could build a set of golf clubs from scratch today. It's something he passed on to me: One of the greatest joys I have is working endlessly over my clubs—new and old—in a workshop behind my office.

The big thing about getting the clubs early was not that I became an instant champion (I was seven years old before I ever broke a hundred). My dad taught me the overlapping grip before I'd ever been corrupted by handling a baseball bat. Because I learned to hold the club at age three, I never felt that the golf grip was awkward; it is as reflexive as blinking to me. Never in my life did I want to pick up a golf club—as do most boys who learn baseball first—and grip or swing it like a bat.

My dad taught me some basic and profoundly important things about golf. He taught me the compact swing—people now consider the "square-to-square" swing an act of genius— and he told me to remember just one thing: "Always hit it hard." It was never a matter of him spending hours and hours with me on the golf course; he never had time for that. It was more a matter of him looking me over for ten to fifteen minutes, teaching me this, steering me away from that—and then leaving me alone to work it out. I'd practice as long as I wanted, and then—I was a very little kid at this point—I'd yell: "Hey, Pap! Watch me, Pap! Look at how I do it! [*Years later his father was to say: "You'd get so sick of him yelling, you'd want to give him a swat." But another member of his family remembers affectionately: "Arnold had a little of the show-off in him. He'd always do better at something when somebody was watching him. So he always wanted an audience."*]

Pap gave me the time to practice. But not always the place. For Pap was a strict man. Scotch-Irish with a hard set of rules. For himself. For me. And for the members.

For himself, he'd never set a foot in the locker room or the dining room or the bar unless he was specifically invited by a member. He'd eat his meals in the club kitchen or at home, before he'd ever venture uninvited into the dining room. He'd never let me swim in the club pool. He'd never let me play with the members' kids. He'd never let me take the trophy home when I won the caddy tournaments—that was for some other father's son. He never let me play the course except on Monday—when the course was closed to members—and sometimes very early or very late in the day. But one thing he did let me do: learn respect for him and his contemporaries.

So there was this great big playground out there but not much chance to play it—at least for a full round. Nor were there many people to play it with. Latrobe was a steel town, and the kids in steel towns dream of growing up to play baseball or football, not golf. Moreover, the country club was four or five miles out of town, and it wasn't often that many of the kids could get out to play with me: These were the Depression years, and if you had a car, you sure didn't use it to chauffeur the kids around for playtime between the country club and home. And you can bet the kids weren't going to come of their own accord. They could go out in the street and play football and baseball; they didn't have to hike eight or ten miles round-trip to play golf with me.

So I had to make my own opportunities. For a long while, when I was small, I'd nag my mother into letting me go around with her and her friends when they played golf. That was not quite a mother's dream, and so I tried to make myself useful. I'd carry the bags for her and her friends. And I'd volunteer to "help" them out on the tough holes. That got to ge a prosperous little business for me: Whenever ladies would come around to the fifth tee—right beside our house—and saw a creek running along down there near the tee, I'd turn up and volunteer: "Show you how to hit it over the creek. For a nickel." When they saw that a little kid could do it, they felt a little more confident about doing it themselves. One thing about that kind of work: you sure could get motivated for a nickel—and a grateful smile.

There was another thing I had going for me: my imagination.

Any kid who doesn't have a lot of friends to play with is going to make up games. That's what I'd do. I'd go out in the rough—in among the elms and oaks—and practice chipping out to a specific spot on the fairway. Some spot where nobody was playing. The reason: I couldn't practice chipping up to the green. My father wouldn't let me. He wouldn't let *anybody* practice around the greens. I remember one time, a member came into the pro shop, bought around five hundred dollars' worth of equipment, and then took some of it out, along with a half dozen balls, to practice chipping up to a nearby green. Pap went out—after having just made a big sale to this guy—and shagged him out of there: Not even the members could use the playing greens for practice.

So since I couldn't use the greens for practice, or use the tees and fairways—except at restricted times—I used the rough. That's probably made me so confident a pro in the rough: As a kid I practiced hitting off one foot and then the other, hitting with the club turned around, hitting from pine needles and leaf-covered lies and branches and twigs. That became my natural environment: I don't know if that's the reason I get in the rough so much these days, but I do know that—as a pro—I was never fazed by landing there. Or much mystified by how to get out.

But when I'd practice I didn't just hit the ball. I love competition—but there was nobody to compete with. And so I'd make up some competition for myself. I'd be out there among the trees and I'd say, like a sports announcer, "Now

---

here's Arnold Palmer in the trees at the right on the eighteenth hole at Augusta. . . . He needs a birdie to win the Masters. . . . He swings and—there it goes! Right up to the cup and in!" Or maybe I'd play the role of some of the great golfers of the day: "Here's Byron Nelson . . . chipping out for his birdie three. . . ." Or, "Here's Lloyd Mangrum taking out a five-iron . . . the ball must be buried deep in there." Old Lloyd was always a shark with the irons. The wonderful thing is that I didn't *need* playmates as long as I had my dreams. And in my dreams, I never lost.

In those days, I didn't read instructional books on golf. Pap didn't think much of them. I learned the game by working at it. The Latrobe Country Club became my laboratory, and the game that I learned had much of its personality in it—and much of my father's. It was tough, stubborn, and it didn't yield easily, either to logic or to a particular gift. When I was a little boy, there wasn't a pine tree on this golf course—not a single one. It was a barren course, and yet it resisted the skills of some pretty fine players. Tough: just like Pap.

In a sense, the Latrobe Country Club is an enduring work of art. It's never been finished: Pap changes it from year to year, month to month, even day to day. You can see his touch in it everywhere: It has an intimacy that he feels more deeply than anybody else. I can remember when he began to plant pine trees on the course. He'd go out and haul in a load of pine trees brought in by the Vanadium Alloy Steel Company on the northwest side of Latrobe, heaving along in an old Model T truck, and I used to sit on top of the trees, all edgy and wriggly—trying to avoid the needles—as we jolted along the road to the club. My dad plotted and planted every pine tree on this course; there are thousands of them now, and because of the way he's used them, the fairways have become narrower, the par-4s have become more demanding, and it requires a considerable facility with the irons to make your way around it.

In the old days, it was a nine-hole course. Par 34. It had no par-5 holes, two par-3s, and seven par-4s. But to a kid growing up, it was an exciting course—somehow tailored to the outer limits of my skills, with no truly easy holes, no place where you'd be sure of picking up a birdie. The best that was ever shot on it in those days was a 30, four under par for the nine holes.

Then the club acquired a little more land and—though keeping it a nine-hole course—lengthened two of the par-4s, making them into par-5s. That increased over-all par to 36, and gave a little chance for the long hitters—or for a boy growing up—to stretch out a little bit and eat up the yardage with a display of muscle. I shot a 29 on it once, which was more a display of ego than the difficulty of the course. Then when the club got still more land and expanded to 18 holes, I went back to work on it and finally shot a 60. That may not be a true test of the course, for I had a chance to study it as no other player ever did. The best anybody else ever shot on the course may be a more faithful reflection of its nature: It was a 66.

It was the very design of the course that led to my strengths and weaknesses. I've already mentioned my long self-instruction in getting out of the rough. But there were other elements:

The course had rather small but moist (or "heavy") greens —slow ones. So they played better to low, hard shots that would arrow on a line underneath the wind and, if they hit hard, the momentum for a long roll would be cut to nothing by the softness of the greens. So I grew up with a low-liner power drive instead of the lofty, high-fly tee shot that would settle softly to the ground, bounce once or twice, and stop without a roll. (I've changed since then, as we'll see a little later on.)

The course had a good many holes that demanded precise iron shots to the small greens. So I became quite facile in using the No. 1 iron for distances of 210 to 230 yards. Not many pros ever use the No. 1 iron; in fact, few of them bother to carry it in their bag (and very few manufacturers include it

in the "matched sets" they sell, presumably because most amateur golfers don't have the extremely strong wrists and forearms needed to put the club to its optimum use). But I found
the No. 1 iron extremely useful as a result of my "training" at
Latrobe Country Club: It has very little loft, and it offers somewhat greater accuracy (which was needed for the small greens)
than a wood would. Even today, I carry the No. 1 iron as
often as its logical alternative, the four-wood. The four-wood
will give me a higher trajectory than the No. 1 iron, as well
as just about the same distance. So it is considerably more useful on steep and hilly courses, where you have to get your
long fairways shots high in the air. But on no-slope or low-
trajectory courses, the one-iron is still my favored weapon.
The course had almost no sand traps. The reason is simple:
They are extremely hard—and costly—to maintain. When I was
growing up, there wasn't enough money to maintain them, so
Pap was loath to put them in. That meant that I didn't get
much chance to practice out of sand traps. (I'm sure that if
there had been a lot of sand traps on the course, Pap wouldn't
have wanted his kid tramping around in them, practicing shots
to the green. In fact, he wouldn't have allowed members to
practice in them. He respects the golf course as a place to play
golf, not to play around.) The lack of sand traps, and the lack
of permission to practice endlessly around the greens, left my
chipping and work with the sand wedge the weakest parts of
my game for years.

Though I couldn't practice all the shots, or all the time, I
could make up for it by practice all through the year. I'd be
out on the course in the winter as well as the summer—I'd go
out and shovel off the back lawn in the winter and hit balls
that Pap painted red. Eventually he put in a putting green out
there, as a nursery to help grow grass for the playing greens.
I could practice on it—but I didn't like to. I wanted to practice
hitting the ball, not putting it. And when a practice tee was
built, I'd be out there by the hour. [*Says one friend—and fellow*

caddy—who worked with Arnold: "It was a pleasure to shag balls for Arnie. He'd tell you just where to stand and then he'd drive it off the tee to where you were on exactly one bounce. He was uncanny."] I'd won the local caddy tournament a few times by the time I got to high school, and that helped convince me: Everything I did was going to be geared toward golf. I lost only one match in high school. That was in my first year —and I lost to a senior. [*Bill Yates, who coached Palmer in high school, has recalled: "I was his coach but I didn't teach him anything. He knew more about golf as a freshman than anyone in school. He taught the team. I managed it." He recalled that Palmer was always serious about his practice. "If he hit a bad five-iron shot in practice, he'd let everybody go ahead. Then he'd get a bag of fifty balls and bang away at the five-iron shot." The practice—or the need for practice—never daunted him. "He exuded confidence," Yates said. "Most kids went out to play. Arnie went out to win."*]

There were other fascinations. In those days, we had a fifty-minute lunch period in high school, and there were many days when a few of us would grab our brown lunch bags, run down to the pool hall, and munch sandwiches while we got in a game of pool. [*"He was," recalled a friend from those days, "the best pool player in Latrobe."*] I liked to play cards, then, too. In those days it was poker—where I'd play with a great zest that somehow impressed but didn't altogether deceive my friends. [*"He was a wild man—he'd press anything to the hilt on a gamble," recalls one of them.*] More recently it's been bridge—that was one of the games that drew us together with the late President Eisenhower. [*One newsman who played bridge with Palmer says: "I got the impression that his skill and confidence alone can help him win, much as it does in golf. But he overbids miserably and gets impatient with bad hands." Another friend, a pro golfer who played bridge with Palmer, has observed: "He throws good money after bad. If he doesn't have the cards, he'll bid anyway."*]

Outside of golf, I played, or played at, baseball: I could really hit the ball—when I hit it at all. And I played a little football: I was strong enough—but mostly in my arms. But I wasn't big enough—at 5-10 and maybe 150–60 pounds in high school—to play the position where strong arms and forearms would be most valuable: in the defensive line or at linebacker. The fact was that my strength was keyed to my sport: golf. And my dad warned me then—not so much about the danger of injury in football—about spreading my energies too thinly. "If you want to be good at something, Arnie, you can't play a dozen things," he said.

So I played golf—on the high school team, in tournaments at Latrobe Country Club, in amateur tournaments all over the state. [*One of his contemporaries remembers that as a result of his success in state and local tournaments, "Arnie had watches running up one arm and down the other and more luggage than you ever saw before."*] My father came along with me to most tournaments, and he tried to instill in me a discipline about winning and losing—about success and failure. I was always to go for the win, but I was never to express disappointment about losing. He really drilled it into me: There've been many times when I lost tournaments that I felt low as a turtle's toenail. But —because of my father's training—I never let it bust out of me. And so, thanks to that regimen, most people remember today the look of elation on my face in tournaments I'd won, but never the pervasive heart-aching disappointment I felt over losing.

There was another thing he taught me: Never make a display of my frustration—the kind of frustration everybody experiences in golf. I remember that Pap had taken the whole family over to see me play in one junior tournament in another city, and at one point I got so mad at myself that I threw a club far up into a tree. That afternoon, when I got back into the car for the ride home, Pap didn't speak to me. Neither did anybody else. Here I'd won a tournament, and everybody treated me like I'd done something *bad*. Well, to Deacon Palmer, I had. "If you ever throw a club again," he finally told me on the ride home, "you'll never play in another tournament. That will be the *last* time you play competitive golf."

He meant it—I knew it. I've been with some pretty good club-throwers since then. In my early days on the pro tour, my wife and I were very close to the Tommy Bolts. We traveled with them, played cards with them, and shared kitchens with them. Tommy was—I hasten to tell you—an extraordinarily thoughtful man and a thoroughgoing gentleman, off the course. But his temper got just a little bit the better of him on the course. In the 1960 National Open at Cherry Hills, I remember, he got a triple bogey on one hole, then put his tee shot on the eighteenth hole into the water. He hit his second tee shot into the water. Then he threw his driver into the water—he figured that it should be where the ball went. Herbert Warren Wind, the golf writer, said at the time that "considering the size, beauty, and beckoning nature of the water hazard, there was something classic about Bolt's performance, like Hilary scaling Everest or Stanley finding Livingstone." But much as I liked and admired Tommy Bolt, I never dared to imitate him: I was too much impressed by the threat of my father. I never threw a club again.

When I was a senior in high school, I traveled to the West Coast for the Hearst National Junior Golf Tournament. There I met Buddy Worsham, the brother of Lew Worsham, who is a pro up our way now, at Oakmont Country Club. Lew won the U. S. Open in 1947. Buddy was to become my closest friend. In fact, he got me into Wake Forest on an athletic scholarship: He'd already won a scholarship there, and he sent a wire urging them to pick up another prospect—which they did.

["*I remember the day Arnold came to Wake Forest,*" *said Johnny Johnston, his golf coach in college.* "*He and Buddy*

Worsham showed up in the morning, and they wanted a game right away. We got up a foursome with one of the other coaches and went over to the Carolina Country Club course in Raleigh. Arnold had a 67 that afternoon and Buddy had a 68, and neither of them had ever seen the course before.

"*Neither of us had ever seen that kind of college golf before.*"

Arnold and Buddy were the best of friends: they lived together and worked together for three years. In their sophomore year, they persuaded Wake Forest to change from sand "greens" to grass greens, and then he and Buddy and the rest of the Wake Forest golf team went out and did the labor on the job. "One time Buddy set a course record of 63 over at Raleigh and he couldn't wait to tell Arnie about it," Johnny Johnston has recalled. "Palmer just told him to hold on for a while. Then he went over to Raleigh and shot a 62 to break Buddy's record."

His teammates knew that chipping and wedging up and out of sand traps was the weakest part of Arnold's game. "But he was so strong it didn't matter," Dick Tiddy, the No. 3 man on the team, has said. "He was hitting 260 and 270 on the tee shots even then . . . I can remember him almost driving the green several times on the fourth hole at the Carolina Country Club, and that's a 335-yard hole," Johnny Johnston added: "He was as strong in the hands, arms, and shoulders as anybody I've ever seen. We used to do a little wrestling, and he was strong as a bull. He'd take on Buddy Worsham and myself at the same time, and he could handle us both." Dick Tiddy, now the head pro at Palmer's Bay Hill Club in Orlando, Florida, remarked that Arnold never lost a match in the two years that they played on the same team. And that he beat such famous-to-be players as Mike Souchak and Art Wall and Billy Maxwell. In fact, this was a time of great golfers-to-be. Dow Finsterwald, who was to become a close friend of Palmer's on the pro tour—and who was to win the 1958 PGA and rack up one of the longest in-the-money records in golf—was at Ohio University. Ken Venturi, who was to fight Palmer down to the wire in the 1960 Masters and then win the 1964 U. S. Open, was at San Jose State. Gene Littler, later to become the 1961 U. S. Open champion, was at San Diego State. Don January, who went on to win the 1967 PGA, was at North Texas State. And the in-state competition of North Carolina was pretty stiff. Souchak was at Duke, and Harvie Ward—who would twice win the men's U. S. Amateur championship after Arnold turned pro—was at the University of North Carolina. "Arnold thought he was as good as any of them," Tiddy has said. "He wasn't cocky; he just knew." One year he went over to the Azalea Open to find out how he'd do against the pros and he finished fifth. "You've got to have a lot of confidence to do something like that," Tiddy said.

In the end it seemed dry and pointless. On an autumn night in 1950, Buddy Worsham came to him and urged Arnold to drive over to Duke with him for a homecoming dance that night. It was only about 15 miles away from Wake Forest's campus then—the campus has since been moved—and it promised to be a wonderful bash. But Arnold was already deep into another commitment at Wake Forest that Saturday, and he decided not to go. That night, Buddy Worsham was killed in an auto accident on his way back from the dance in Durham. Palmer was stunned. Even now he finds it very difficut to talk about. He was quoted then—and later—as saying, "I felt it wouldn't have happened if I was along." Palmer went back to Buddy's home in Washington, D.C., with the body, and a short time later—in youth's ever-present shock at finding the world ordered in a way different than it dreamed—dropped out of school. He was just a semester short of getting his degree in business administration. "I didn't know what to do with myself," he was quoted as saying. "I stayed in school until I thought I'd go crazy—every time I turned around to tell him something, I'd realize he was gone forever."]

The Korean War was on then, and I decided to join the Navy. But I never got into the Navy; I went into the Coast Guard instead. My first assignment was to Cape May, New Jersey, at the southern tip of the state where the Atlantic joins Delaware Bay, where I worked with a civilian staff in air-sea rescue. I was always enthusiastic about flying, and this gave me a little taste of it. Later on I was transferred to the Great Lakes division at Cleveland. There, among other duties, I found myself building a driving range in a supply depot: The admiral liked golf and wanted some place to practice. I made a good many friends in Cleveland—friends who had a manic appetite for golf. There were a lot of times when we'd play the Lake Shore course in Cleveland on such cold winter days that the pins were frozen solid in the cup. Nevertheless, with all that had happened—and with a growing maturity—the life of a golf pro didn't seem quite as attractive as it had in the past. When I got out of the Coast Guard, one of my friends offered me a deal: If I'd go back to college to get my degree in business administration, he'd give me a job working for him, in sales. I'd call on customers in the morning and play golf in the afternoon, usually at his request and with customers he selected. Just like a lot of other guys who spent some time in the service, I figured it was time to settle down and get started on a job. I felt I could satisfy my passion for golf as an amateur who could play with customers most of the week and then take the weekend for some serious amateur competition. So I took his offer and went back to school as soon as I got out of the Coast Guard. By the summer of 1954, I was back in Cleveland, working for his painting supplies house.

[*Mark McCormack, Palmer's attorney and business representative, has observed: "Having been raised with the subconscious idea that the country club golf pro was a kind of servant —and many private clubs still foster this attitude—Arnold finally concluded, 'I was too proud to lead my life as some sort of sec-*

ond-class citizen.' He decided he would become a businessman and pictured himself as a top amateur golfer playing in all the big tournaments."]

I'd played in the U. S. Amateur championship since 1948: I lost in the first round that year and again in 1950; I lost in the third round in 1949. Because of my service commitments, I didn't play in 1951 or 1952—in fact, I didn't play golf much at all for a year after Buddy was killed. But in 1953, though still in the Coast Guard, I got a leave—the admiral *really* loved golf—and beat Congressman Jack Westland 1-up in the second round. (He'd won the U. S. Amateur championship in 1952; he was up in his forties or fifties then, and his celebrity as a late-blooming champion was so great that he got elected to Congress that year in the Eisenhower landslide.) Then in the third round I beat Ken Venturi, 2 and 1. That was the end; I lost my fourth-round match, and Gene Littler—then just out of college on the West Coast—went on to win the '53 U. S. Amateur.

By 1954 I was out of the Coast Guard and itching to play something more than salesman's golf. The U. S. Amateur was to be played at the Country Club of Detroit, and it was still being held as a match-play tournament in those days. That means you were matched head-on-head with one other golfer, and whoever won the most holes won the match. (You don't necessarily have to play eighteen holes to win. If you've got a two-hole lead and you've only got one left to play—the eighteenth—there's no sense in continuing with the match: Your opponent can't win. The score goes down as 2 and 1: a two-hole lead with one hole to play. Similar with, say, 6 and 4: You've got a six-hole lead with four holes to play. So in the latter case, you might as well quit after the fourteenth; your opponent has no chance to catch up.) Some very good players get knocked out in match play. In the 1954 U. S. Amateur

I beat Frank Stranahan, the long-time "strong man" among the amateurs, and Don Cherry, the singer who went on the golf tour (though an amateur, he finished in a tie with Ben Hogan in the 1960 U. S. Open). Harvie Ward, who was a very good amateur, lost in the early rounds and so did Billy Joe Patton—this was the first time he'd been outscored by any opponent in a 4½-month string in which he'd been paired against the likes of Ben Hogan and Byron Nelson and Lew Worsham and Lloyd Mangrum. In the semifinals, after I eliminated Don Cherry, my opponent was Ed Meister. (There were people of a certain wit who lamented that if I hadn't beaten singer Don Cherry, the semifinal might have been billed as a Meister-singer affair.)

I managed to beat Ed on the third hole of a sudden-death playoff—*after* a thirty-six-hole match. (He had me on the thirty-fifth, thirty-sixth, thirty-seventh, and thirty-eighth holes, but missed putts of 5 to 16 feet on the various greens to give me a new life. Then on the thirty-ninth hole—the third hole of the third round that day—I put my second shot on the green on the 510-yard par-5. Then I two-putted for the birdie and won.

The next day I was matched against Bob Sweeny, then in his early forties, a gray, sinewy, slim-as-a-one-iron investment banker who'd won the British Amateur in 1937, helped organize the Eagle Squadron in World War II—the group of American pilots who flew for the British Royal Air Force— and who now made his home in London, with rest stops in Palm Beach. I was still pretty much of a dark horse: I don't think there was anybody who expected a thin kid who was a pro's son from Latrobe, Pennsylvania, to conquer this kind of glamor.

Particularly after the fourth hole. Sweeny birdied the second, the third, and the fourth holes. Four holes played, and already he was 3-up. He was a considerate man and he didn't want me to get too discouraged, just because this thing was developing into one of the great all-time disasters for me. "Arnie," he said, as he threw an arm around me on our walk off the fourth green, "you *know* I can't keep this up."

That I was glad to hear. He went a little too bold on the fifth hole and wound up three-putting to break the birdie-birdie-birdie string. I picked up three holes—the eighth, ninth, and tenth—and he stopped me on the eleventh. But I was even. He was ahead 2-up on the eighteenth, 1-up on the twenty-ninth. I fought back to take the lead—for the first time—on the thirty-second; he fought back almost to tie the match on the thirty-third. He played beautifully—and boldly—to the green, then barely missed a putt that lipped the cup. I holed out to take the hole, and Sweeny never quite caught up. The United States Amateur championship was mine before I'd turned twenty-five. S*ports Illustrated* saw it as a "battle of the classes" where a kid from a steel town beat a "graying millionaire playboy who is a celebrity on two continents." All I can say is that I saw it as a darned hard golf game—I wouldn't want to take on those "graying millionaire playboys" too often.

But it was an important win. Because a sneaky little thought had entered my mind: Maybe I should play a little more golf. For money. On the pro tour.

That thought was paired with another sneaky thought: Maybe I should get married. If you ever want to pair two threats to peace of mind—and prosperity—try putting going pro and getting married back-to-back. Fortunately I was young and bold and . . .

I was playing in the Waite Memorial tournament at Shawnee-on-Delaware over the Labor Day holiday, a day or so after I'd won the National Amateur championship, and I figured, quite naturally, that I could do anything. I met this girl who was one of the hostesses for the tournament—freckled, crisp, somehow unadorned by all the sly deceits of adolescence. Her name was Winifred Walzer, and her father had a cottage at Shawnee. He was president of a canned-goods company, and

I can remember being impressed with how fresh and natural Winnie was, coming from such a "rich" family—she was Pembroke, interior decorating, soon-to-be New York University biz-administration. So I fell in love, and three days later asked her to marry me. It didn't dawn on me that she might say "No." Or that her family might have certain reservations about their teen-age daughter giving up everything to marry an itinerant salesman who spent most of his time on a golf course.

To impress them, I wanted to give Winnie a huge engagement ring. It was a problem: I was seven months out of the Coast Guard and not making much money as a salesman—particularly since I was playing golf most of the time, and wasn't making many sales—and so there was a conspicuous lack of money. My boss in Cleveland—a happy soul who didn't mind a little give and take in golf—said he'd make me a deal: He'd pick a par-70 course—one he'd never played before—and we'd go around on it. If I got a 72, we'd break even. Everything under a 72, he'd give me $200 a stroke. But I'd have to give him $100 a stroke for everything over 80. In between—nothing.

It was the kind of bet every friend likes to lay on you: It was a sucker bet. I'd have to play a great game to make a penny. I'd get nothing for playing a pretty good game—72 to 79. And I'd have to pay and pay and pay if I had a bad game. But I figured: What the hell; I was young and in love, and what is life like without friends like that?

Then he picked the course: Pine Valley in Clementon, New Jersey—only one of the toughest golf courses in the United States.

A par-70 it was. But you can't say par was abused on this course: It was open for twenty-five years before par 70 was bettered on it (by Craig Wood—the 1941 U. S. Open champion —on October 29, 1938). In the arcane math of golf, Pine Valley had a course rating of 73. That may have been a generous enough rating. The late John Brookes, a club member who was also once president of Burning Tree Country Club in Washington—the club where President Eisenhower played so much—once took 44 strokes on the fourteenth hole. And when Bryan Field, then vice president and general manager of Delaware Park, took a 12 on the par-4 eleventh, his caddy remarked: "Never mind, sir. The captain of the British Ryder Cup team once took a 17 here."

That was significant because Pine Valley—though only about 15 miles from Philadelphia—was as close to a Scottish links as anything ever developed in America. It was an unusual, not to say fantastic, concept. For a "link" under the original Scottish interpretation, is a sand hill among level or undulating land, as you sometimes find along the Scottish seashore. In most of the seaside courses of Scotland, the "link" was made up of sand and Scottish broom and an assortment of underbrush. That's exactly what Pine Valley—built into the lush green suburban landscape near Philadelphia—was made up of: sand, Scottish broom, some underbrush, and a few scrub pines. (The man who designed and started to carve Pine Valley out of a thick stand of heavy pines—George A. Crump, a multimillionaire who moved out to Pine Valley to live in a tent there—once said that he hauled out twenty-two thousand tree stumps before he stopped counting.) There are, to be sure, no hidden bunkers here, no out-of-bounds, and no unnatural hazards—the whole course is a natural hazard. For not only is so much of it made up of sand, not grass, but it is unraked sand: footprints and gashes slashed out with clubs are part of the natural play of the course. "Pine Valley is the shrine of American golf," Ed Sullivan of TV fame once said, "because so many golfers are buried there."

The fact is that Pine Valley is not a tournament site. The general feeling is that galleries cannot be handled well there—consider the number of footprints *they'd* leave in the sand. (In fact, the club has a rule limiting play to a hundred golfers a day.) To my knowledge, only one major tournament has ever been played there: the 1936 Walker Cup matches. This is a match between the finest amateurs in Britain and the United

States. Interestingly, the United States whomped the Britishers, 9–0, on the Scottish-style course. But everybody of both teams had such trouble on one hole—the 217-yard par-3 fifth hole—that one Scottish lad and an American amateur got together to memorialize it in verse:

> "This course was made for you and me
> But only God can make a three."

So this was the course on which I was to "earn" Winnie's engagement ring.

My start was not unusual: I bogeyed the first hole. It looked as if my friends and playing partners had picked the course specifically to frustrate me: I'd grown up on a course virtually without sand traps (so I didn't master the art of playing in sand). And here was a course that looked like one continuous sand trap. Actually, there are stretches of grassy fairway leading to many of the greens, and I quickly discovered a fundamental truth: If you could control a fairly strong tee shot, you could hit the greens—most of them were comfortably large—or you could hit the grassy part of the fairways fairly consistently. I had the strong tee shot, and I was confident that I could keep it under control. So I scrambled and hustled and played over, around, and above the sand. Quickly I began picking up momentum and confidence. The result: I went around in 68. And picked up $800 for Winnie's ring.

That wasn't enough to express my love for her. I went out and borrowed a lot more money in order to get her the ring that I wanted. It wasn't easy; I was more than broke. I'd started in business at $500 a month—$6000 a year—plus expenses. After I won the U. S. Amateur, I was raised to $750 a month plus expenses. That was good—but not enough to meet all my debts. Or my ambitions.

Because now I *really* wanted to get out on the golf tour. I began looking around for financial backing. The idea of a group of businessmen backing a golfer on the tour was rather new at the time, but there were several offers to help me: One of them was for $10,000. But I turned them down; here I'm dying for money, and I turned down ten grand! But my reasons were good ones: The offers involved the sponsors taking 50 percent of all my earnings. They didn't ask that I repay the loan and a reasonable interest along with it. They wanted half of everything I earned for a certain number of years. That meant that over the first three years—as it turned out—they would have gotten back $30,000 on their $10,000 investment. And over the first four years they would have gotten back almost $53,000 for that $10,000 investment. In the meantime, I'd be paying all expenses—perhaps $15,000 a year in those days—and it would have cost me $60,000 just to earn that same $53,000. That didn't seem like sound business to me: taking a loss so that some others could make back their initial investment five times over. I was looking for backing, not for bankruptcy. The way their offer looked, I would have been worse off after four or five years—even though I'd won more than a hundred thousand dollars—than when I started. So I told these various groups: "No, I'll give you a profit on what you lend me, when I'm able to, but I won't give you half of everything I earn."

That ended that.

But it didn't end my hopes. There was a sporting goods company that agreed to back me: They'd give me between $1500 and $2500 to get started in return for giving them my endorsement for three years. It seemed like a good deal to me, and some of the clauses whizzed right by me. (The company was generous in providing equipment—balls, bags, clubs—but the equipment always remained the property of the company. Contractually, the golfer was obligated to return all equipment to the company at the end of the contract period. Which might have been quite difficult—if you have to recover and return all the golf balls.) That gave me a start: I signed the contract and I formally turned pro on November 15, 1954.

Then I borrowed some money from my family and from

Winnie's family and from my friends in Cleveland. Altogether, I had about $5000 to get started on the tour. Then to cut expenses, Winnie and I decided to buy a second-hand trailer so we could park where we wanted and make our own meals, instead of paying hotel prices for room and board. Where did the money come from? From Winnie's folks.

It took me a year—but only a year—to pay them all back.

It was a tough year. I started out on the pro tour with a wife who was brand-new and a trailer that was not. The wife was petite; the trailer was not. It had three rooms and a bath and it was too big for our car to pull—you can really wreck a transmission hauling a big trailer like that up and down mountain roads. The jumps between tournaments were huge ones: 500, 600, 700 miles a day sometimes—hauling the trailer behind. I remember driving all night to get to a nontournament event in Palm Beach, getting in about five o'clock in the morning, getting out on the golf course about eight o'clock in the morning—and shooting an 85. I remember another night when we just couldn't get that huge old trailer up an icy mountain road. So Winnie got out and pushed while I tried to ease the car-and-trailer into motion. In those days, it wasn't just the tournament that was the test; it was getting *to* the tournament.

The rules of the Professional Golfers Association barred rookies on the tournament from taking any prize money out of PGA tournaments for the first six months. Technically, the rookie could win ten straight tournaments and not get a penny for it. Nobody did, of course. And the rules have been changed since then. Now the rookies have to go through a qualifying program to get on the tour, but they get paid for everything they achieve. My achievements were spotty: I finished sixth a couple of times, tenth a couple of times, seventeenth a couple of times, and fortieth or more a couple of times. I was paid nothing for these efforts. But I can remember trying so hard to win—to be first, even without money—that I almost wrecked my health practicing. The first winter down in Arizona and

Texas, I got a sharp and recurring pain in my right shoulder. It became quite intense, and I feared that I'd have to go off the tour only a couple of weeks after I'd gone on it. Finally I found a doctor who diagnosed the cause of the pain: I was practicing so much on those hard, sun-baked tees and fairways in the Southwest that my shoulder was damaged by the constant impact of the club on the hard ground. (In those days, I used a driving style that caused the clubhead of my driver to make impact on the ground an instant before it hit the ball.) He gave me some cortisone shots that cleared up the pain and—almost elated that nothing pathological had developed—I continued hectically on the tour.

Actually, there was a way to pick up some income, even though you couldn't take any prize money from PGA tournaments. That was simply to compete in the non-PGA events whenever possible. The pro-ams, which usually preceded the tournament in any city, were an example: I won something like $700 in the first pro-am I entered, in January 1955. I won another at Greenbrier later in the spring. I went down to the Panamanian Open—another non-PGA event—in January and finished second and took home $900. I was invited to the Masters tournament—as the winner of the U. S. Amateur the previous year—and finished tenth and won $696. (The Masters is not a PGA-run tournament; it is run and supervised entirely by its own tournament committee.) It wasn't until June that I was able to take some money out of a PGA tournament: I finished twenty-fifth in the Fort Wayne Open and was paid $145. After that, things picked up. I placed third in St. Paul and won $1300. I won the Canadian Open and won $2400. (In six or seven months I'd gone from second in Panama to first in Canada —a big piece of geography and a big range of achievement.) By the end of the tour, I'd won $8226 and paid off all my debts. I was way down the money-winning list; Mike Souchak and Gene Littler—both college contemporaries of mine—had each won around $29,000 that year.

But in another three years I'd passed them all. By 1958, I'd won five times as much money—$45,608—and led the whole money-winning list. I began taking flying lessons that year. And we built our house that year.

The climb up the ridge was begun. And ended.

Now I had to look to new heights.

V

The Gifts That Golf Gave

[*For a cookout at the Palmers', Winnie had made a noodle casserole. It was delicious. Arnold, who had been raised on more slimming diets and earned his way to gourmet banquets, turned to his mother.*

"This is good—wonderful. But not as good as yours used to be, Mother," he said. "How come yours tasted so much better?"

"You were a lot hungrier then," said Doris Palmer.]

*

When I was young and "hungry," I never coveted money much—not for its own sake. Oh sure, I wanted to win and I measured the prize money carefully, not because it was money but because it would help me get onto the next tournament and do what I wanted most to do: play golf better than anybody else in the world.

Perhaps I was lucky in my attitude. Because the money wasn't all that much when I started playing professional golf. In

1954, the year I announced I was turning pro, the total prize money available on the golf circuit came to $600,819. By 1972, it was $7.2 million—twelve times that earlier figure.

Just three of us earned more money on the pro tour in 1971 than all the golfers combined in 1954—110 percent of their purse, in fact: Jack Nicklaus, with $244,490; Lee Trevino, with $231,202; and myself, with $209,603.

The reason that I say that I was lucky is that the winner's checks in the day when I got my start were $1500 and $2000. That's a long way from $50,000—but it wasn't bad. I think that working my way into the big money the way I did—winning $3000 at a time, then maybe $5000 or $6000, then $10,000 and $20,000 and $30,000—was good for me. Because it happened gradually, I learned to handle the money—I grew up with the purses. It was my added good fortune to be able to turn success at golf into extra money on the side so that I was doing as well or better there than I was through purse money. But money for its own sake never had much attraction for me. It offered security—that I liked. But I did not see it in terms of wealth, power, and prestige.

The one thing that it could give me was the one thing it *did* give me: a chance to arrange life so that I could concentrate on doing well what I like doing best—play golf.

We bought five or six acres on that wooded slope above my boyhood home. We have our own home there and a small office building and workshop. And we were able to provide land for two or three of our closest friends to come in and build their own homes next door to us. So "home" for me isn't just a single structure where I eat and sleep. It's a total environment. It doesn't have much in the way of luxury, but it does have what I want most: convenience.

For instance, from the front door of our house, it is:

Just 100 steps to the front door of the office.

Just seconds to the front door of two of our fondest friends.

Just one minute down the road from Pap's house—he also moved up the ridge and down the road from the old frame house.

Just two minutes to the first tee of the Latrobe Country Club.

Just four minutes from the airport where our Lear Jet is hangared.

Literally everything I need to fill my life—golf, family, friends and flying—is only a matter of seconds from my front door.

As the money kept coming in, the structure of our house changed a little over the years. We added a game room downstairs and built another bedoom just off it. We put in a new dining room, we redid the kitchen, we walled in the carport to make an in-the-house office, and—when we built another office up the hill—we turned it into a den. There's a swimming pool out back now; in the winter it's housed with a blue polyethylene covering to turn it into an indoor pool—I take about 50 laps a morning to keep in shape during the winter. Like most people, we don't use the living room much, except for Peggy, our oldest daughter: She loves to sit there and play the piano by the hour. (There was a music book of Bach on the piano stand the last time I looked.) And of course there's a basketball backboard out by the garage. When the people ask why it's there—I have only two daughters, no sons—I tell them the truth: "The girls wanted it there." Perhaps because they knew that the boys would like it there.

Until late in the 1960s, I tried to concentrate everything in this house—work as well as pleasure. I had a workshop in the basement for eight years and the office was in the old walled-in carport. But it got pretty crowded, what with Patty Aikens, my secretary, at one end of a 12-foot room and me at the other; we didn't quite know where to put Doc Giffin, my administrative assistant. Finally we put him in a tiny A-frame outside the house—up on the hill a little farther. But that was a trifle inconvenient; in fact, Doc was in better condition than I was, what with running up and down that hill all day long. So finally we built a special office building just up the hill. It's white and colonial in style, and it looks as much like a home as an office.

There's a big difference in attitude, though: The office reeks with golf, whereas our home doesn't.

The doorstops are made of golf balls. The wallpaper in the "executive" washroom is a series of my golf lessons from a magazine. On a wall in the reception room is a battered and lumpy old golf ball that my friends—and mentors—from childhood will swear was hit by "little" Arnold Palmer in the misty depths of yesteryear. In short, there's much in the building that communicates "Golf!"

My wife says it's the smell of lacquer from the workshop in the back.

(That's how she can tell if I'm in the workshop—as soon as you open the door to the building, you catch the pungent smell of lacquer. It's like that of the airplane cement I used when I was building model airplanes as a child. I'm beginning to think that's why my wife consented to—or lobbied for—building the office and workshop farther up the slope from our home. Until then, the office, the workshop, and the smell of lacquer were all in the house.)

The office building is large enough to give me some "roaming" room—I'd go crazy if I had to sit behind a desk all day, so I'm usually up and around, working from every room in the building. It's got an office for me and another for Patty as well as an office for Doc and another for Darrell Brown, my pilot. Both Doc and Darrell have certain executive duties that range far beyond their obvious work. Doc now oversees the operation of the Latrobe Country Club. Darrell, who got his master's degree in business administration and who was a senior accountant for Kerr-McGee Oil Company before returning full-time to flying, runs a farm for me up the road—I raise a few quarter-horses and some cattle—as well as a nearby game preserve, where we have about six hundred birds.

When I'm home, I can get up to my office in a matter of seconds. I like it best—as I've already suggested—in the early morning. The solitude helps me concentrate, and in the first hour or so—before the phones start ringing—I can get a great deal of the desk work done. Thus it becomes something of a refuge in itself—a place where I can retreat from the commotion of the tour and its remorseless pressures.

[*The muted elegance of the office reflects the many tastes and various incarnations of Arnold Palmer. It's paneled with a knotty pine stained a faint green. It has a beamed ceiling and a rug the color of Augusta's greens in the spring and a chandelier over the desk that is right out of the Federal period. Around the light switch is a frame representing the "Tom Morris Green" at the Royal and Ancient Club at St. Andrews, Scotland. The style, tone, and amplitude of the elegance are often astonishing: In the "executive" washroom, the finger towels were designed by Yves St.-Laurent.*

Off to the side of the main office—to the right as Arnold sits at his desk—is a "sweat room." It has a shower and steam bath, an exercycle, and some block-and-tackle exercising equipment anchored to the wall. Palmer doesn't use it now for sweat produced by exercise. Instead he's got a drafting table under a window in there, and on it he's laid out maps and charts of every detail of the Latrobe Country Club so he can sweat over what needs to be done and what he wants to get done on the golf course.

The main office has a personal touch, of course: It has everything from old golf clubs stacked in a corner to model airplanes crowded onto a table—a dozen models, from a helicopter and lunar module to a B-47 and a 747. In a corner is a short-wave aircraft radio receiver to pick up transmissions to and from the control tower at the Latrobe airport. Says Doc Giffin, "Sometimes—when Arnold is flying in from the tour— we'll listen for the tower talking with 'N1-AP.' That's Arnold's number, and if we don't have a car up there, somebody drives to the airport to pick him up." The range of Palmer's life— and its grand as well as homely dimensions—are suggested by just two other mementos. One is on his desk: a pair of his baby shoes, saved and silvered by his father and mother and given to Arnold as a gift on his forty-second birthday. The other is on the wall: a letter framed and glassed and written on the stationery of the White House. It was sent by President Nixon after Palmer won two tournaments toward the end of 1969: "Only the truly great champions," it says, "ever come back."]

We've got a pretty close-knit group in the office building. And a carefree one. (I just noticed my secretary hanging up a new example of poster graffiti: "Our boss runs this place with an iron head.") In fact, I can't even say there's a solemn attitude toward golf. I'd guess that one member of our staff has never played golf in her life. It's Patty Aikens, who's been my secretary for ten years. She's sweet, young, terribly competent, and *very* formidable: One day President Nixon called up about something or other and she wouldn't give him the number to my house down below—she wasn't about to give out that number to just any old caller who announced, "The President of the United States is on the phone." But Patty is not in love with golf. She can take it or leave it—that's my guess—and it wouldn't break her heart to leave it. But she loves the people in golf. The joy she gets out of being with them just glows in her very being. The way she reaches out to people is reflected in the slogan she keeps on her desk: "Have a *Happy* Day!"

Doc Giffin is a pretty good golfer, for a guy who's spent his life in newspapering and public relations and other hedonistic activities. He won't agree. The other day he pointed to the wallboard down in the locker room of the Latrobe Country

Club, and it showed that he'd been posting poorer scores than Darrell Brown. This is probably the truest possible reflection on Doc: Most men want to brag on their golf game a bit, but Doc is such a stickler for accuracy that he'll put his own game down. [*Doc says that he is a fifteen-handicap player and that no matter what his boss—or I—say, he is not as good a golfer as Darrell Brown.*] That was Doc's value when he worked for the pro golfers on the tour for five years before joining me— he was so accurate that he wouldn't even brag about his golf game. [*Says Doc: In that environment, who would?*] He'd done a lot for me over the years. He may very well be the best man for his job in the entire profession. But I can't say I've done much for his golf game. He won't let me: He even turns me down when I want to get out on the golf course in the afternoon. Says he's got too much work to do.

Now Darrell Brown—there's something special. He's a great pilot and a well-disciplined one. He even got me to stop buzzing the house when I flew home so that Winnie would know when to come down to the airport to pick us up. He's a fine administrator—he majored in business administration at the University of Oklahoma—and a most efficient planner: If we have an early-morning flight, he'll file a flight plan, check all the weather, and have the plane fueled and ready to go before he even comes up to the office. But a great golfer he is not. I've tried to help him; Lord *knows* I've tried to help him. But that boy just does not take well to teaching.

[*Darrell—in defense: "I played golf maybe six or eight times a year before I met Arnold. I found it a pretty frustrating experience, and I'm a little like the boss—I like to do well at everything I try. But I stayed with it and finally I got down into the 80s, pretty much with a style like a kid falling out of a tree. I mean, I found a way of getting things done in golf even if they aren't the right way. So the first time I played with Arnold, he looked at me very sympathetically and said, 'I do believe you've got the worst swing I've ever seen.' He likes to be helpful, and he wanted me to play golf the right way. He helped me change my swing, my grip, my stance, my alignment. So now I'm back in the 100s."*

Doc Giffin wants to get in a word: "If you meet Darrell on the first tee somewhere, don't give him any strokes. You'll find that here's a guy who talks in the 100s and shoots in the 80s. He's an eleven-handicap and I'm a fifteen-handicap and—let me tell you—that's something I learned the hard way.]

Probably the best thing about the whole office layout is that it's 15 steps from my office to the door leading downstairs to the storeroom. And 17 steps to the workshop. That means I can get to working with my hands any time I want to—a few strides and I'm liberated from desk work and deep into the kind of work, and clutter, I love best.

[*There are eighteen shelves of old golf shoes in the basement storeroom. Palmer hates to throw old shoes away—he keeps thinking of hard times and the possibility he may need them again. So he just builds more and more racks for his old shoes —and for his old clubs. There are a couple of thousand old clubs down there: I counted 522 woods one day not long ago; add to them the hundreds upon hundreds of irons and the hundreds of putters, and you see why he needs a big storeroom. The clubs are divided neatly in slanting horizontal bins—for drivers and woods up to the four-woods, for each iron or wedge or putter. It seems that each club has a personal memory attached to it. For it's part of Palmer's phenomenal memory that if you asked him what clubs he used to win the 1954 U. S. Amateur, he'd be able to pick them right out of the bins.*]

Upstairs, the workshop has some impedimenta, too. The other day I counted up and found I had almost a hundred irons lined up on my workbench, waiting for a little work to be done on them. There are a half dozen golf bags scattered around—from the Ryder Cup teams of '61, '63, '65, '67, '71—and some skis belonging to my wife and daughters are stacked in a corner. There's a telephone with an extra-long cord. I get about ten calls an hour while I'm in the office, and—with that extra-long cord—I can take them in the workshop and wander about, doing my work with the clubs, bending over the workbench while I talk with the caller.

The workshop is a big one. In one corner you'll see a wall display outlining the sixteen steps in making a wood, the twenty steps in making an iron. I've made many a golf club, right from scratch. In fact, I still like to finish and refinish my clubs myself. I'll likely put on my own grip and shaft and reweight them. There's plenty of equipment to work with: machine tools such as jigsaws, bandsaws, sanders, buffers; hand tools such as reamers, countersinkers, oyster openers, screwdrivers, chisels; special tools such as loft and lie ball-setting gauges, and a golf club swing-weighting system. There are even a few little tools that I've been able to put together myself.

[One afternoon last spring, Arnold bent over a naked wood and peered at it intently. It was old and bruised. The clubhead had been stripped of its shiny gloss, and the screw—the Phillips screw that holds the wooden insert to the sole plate and the front of the clubhead together—had been stripped of its head. There was just a metal stud about an eighth of an inch wide imbedded in the wood. But it still held the clubhead together.

"How would you get that screw out," said Palmer, "without defacing the clubhead?" He meant without gouging into the wooden insert around the stud and trying to pry it out with a chisel or gripping it with a pliers and lifting and twisting it out. The top of the stud was flush, of course, with the face that Palmer did not want defaced.

One try, then another was made at it. Any tool available would have left deep nicks in the clubface. No pliers known could get that stud out without making a large halo around the stud. The phone rang, and Palmer picked it up. "No, can't do it—that's our day at Hilton Head," he said. He walked over to another bench—with the phone tucked between shoulder and ear—and picked up a small homemade hand tool. "Yeah— I have to be there in Dallas before breakfast," he said into the phone. He walked back to the vise where the clubhead was locked. With tiny, purposeful strokes—as small and furious as the drive rods on an HO-gauge model railroad—he worked at the stud. "No, I'm not sure. We may go to Florida tonight. Maybe tomorrow morning," he said into the phone. He picked up a very thin, very narrow screwdriver and—with his powerful hands and wrists—gave a twist. The stud began moving: he'd carved a small slot into the top of the stud and now was using a screwdriver to loosen it. "The TV people won't be ready to start taping before eight o'clock," he said. "We can leave here at five-thirty and be there a little after seven." It is one hour and fifty minutes of flying time in his Lear Jet from his home in Latrobe to the Bay Hill Club that he owns in Orlando, Florida. The next day, he'd be using the club to film a television spot. "Uh-huh," he said—not into the phone. The stud's head was clear of the clubface now. He disposed of the phone call, handed the phone to a bystander to put back on the wall hook, and twisted the stud out of the hole with the pliers. He looked up at it and examined it in the light, like a dentist who's just removed a tooth. "Now all you have to know," *he said, immensely and boyishly pleased, "is about something like this." He held up a tool he'd fashioned around the shop. It was a portion of a hacksaw blade that he fitted into a handle for a tool used to carve grooves in a clubhead. "With this, I can cut a slot into the top of a stud and turn it into a screw. Then I can move the screw far enough to work out with a pliers," he said.*

He seemed as proud of what he had accomplished with his hands in his workshop as anything he'd ever done in a golf tournament.]

My wife kids from time to time that I couldn't fix the kitchen sink if I had to. And she's right: That's one machine that I know nothing about. But she goes one step further: "It isn't that he doesn't know how to be a plumber," says Winnie. "It's that he doesn't even know how to call one."

That hurts—now, *that* hurts.

Unfortunately, she's right.

For you see, I have very satisfying skills with my hands—but very selective ones. And if you study those skills carefully, you'll find that they are all connected with golf and not at all connected with the home. A handyman I am not. For I happen to have one of the most thorough, reliable, and endearing deputies in the home-support field—a wife named Winnie—that any man could desire. I feel that I'll take care of the important things—like the shape of the clubheads—as long as she takes care of the details, like the house sliding down the hillside into the road below.

That's one thing money couldn't buy—the help and solace that a family offers in trying to maintain the edge for competitive golf.

One thing money could buy was the Lear Jet. It is a convenience that has given a vast new dimension to my life. It's an enormous business asset: I can handle business opportunities of a size and nature that would be impossible without the plane. Instead of spending two or three days traveling in a trailer from one tournament to another—as I did with Winnie in the early days—I can leave one tournament before sundown on a Sunday, tackle other business for three days, and still make an early tee-off time for the next tournament on the next Thursday. In fact, there are a few tournaments that I can commute to via my jet: I fly home regularly every night during any of the tournaments at the Firestone Country Club in Akron—it's only about a twenty-minute flight by jet from Akron to my home in Latrobe. At a few of the other tournaments in the East and near-Midwest, the jet allows me to get home almost every night to be with my own family and to sleep, soundly, in my own bed. That way I avoid the commotion and the cocktail party excitement of the tournament city, and I'm fresh for my next round the next day. And, because I'm a "morning" person —one who feels at his peak in the morning—it is no trouble for me to get up early in the morning to fly back to the tournament site. In fact, I rather enjoy early-morning flying. When the U. S. Open was held at Oak Hill Country Club in Rochester, New York, in 1968, for example, I flew home after the third round—it was only a half hour by Lear Jet—to stay overnight and to pick up my wife and children to take them back to Rochester for the final round the next day. (It was the first time our daughters had ever been at a U. S. Open final round.) Did lousy in that tournament, though.

The jet has also made it possible for me to commute to my other "business" home. I bought a twenty-seven-hole private golf course in Orlando, Florida, a few years ago. It's a place to go to sharpen up for the winter tour—I have a condominium there, and the family and I fly down during the Christmas holidays so I can play in the sun for a couple of weeks before flying out to the West Coast. I also use it for a great many business obligations—taping television commercials, for example. With the jet, I can leave the house in Latrobe at five-thirty in the morning and be on the golf course at Bay Hill by seven-forty-five to start my taping.

Of course, it's not the plane alone that's convenient. It's also the airport: It's just down at the end of the road—Darrell or I can phone down to the airport to roll out the jet and within ten minutes of leaving my home, we can be in the air. Compare that with taking regularly scheduled commercial flights, and you can see what it means in terms of time saved and tension avoided. The Greater Pittsburgh airport is 60 miles from my home, and a good part of it is going through traffic-clogged Pittsburgh. You've got to allow ninety minutes or two hours to get over there, plus another half hour to check in and get the ticket and put the bags on the plane. I figure that for every round trip I made out of the Pittsburgh area, I'd be spending four to five hours of ground time—getting to and from the airport and handling all the ticket details. It makes a lot of difference—mentally and temperamentally—to be able to cut that four to five hours down to ten to twenty minutes; to be able to choose when to go myself instead of having to meet somebody else's schedule.

In the old days, the Latrobe airport wasn't too much— a grass runway with a few biplanes hangared in old frame buildings there. I'm not sure that I ever saw anything as big as a DC-3 come in there. It was all by-gosh and by-God flying: there was no control tower or instrument landing or radio direction. Today, it's a wonderful little airport. It has a 5000-foot runway—more than enough for a business jet—and a control tower that's open sixteen hours a day (from 7 A.M. to 11 P.M.). It has an ILS (instrument landing system) and a glide path that's illuminated: You don't have to rely on making your approach any more by the lights of the Chevrolet agency down on Highway 981 near U. S. 30.

As you can see, I love to fly. I figure I've logged more than three thousand hours at the controls of my own plane. So flying isn't just a method of transportation for me. It's a method of satisfaction. And rejuvenation.

It started when I was a little boy. If there was anything that could compete with my interest in golf, it was flying. Those were the pioneering days when you didn't build preassembled or precast plastic model planes. You built them out of balsa wood stringers with water-shrunk and lacquer-hardened paper for a "skin." Building model planes was "workshop labor." It allowed me to do the same thing I loved to do in golf: work with my hands. But I was also getting into the verbal, the communal, atmosphere of flying. For when I wasn't building, and breaking, model planes, I was running down the country club road to the airport. There was a flight room where some of the pilots would gather around an old pot-bellied stove, and I'd sit there listening to all the glories of the sky.

From time to time, somebody would give me a ride in a plane off the Latrobe airport. But it wasn't until 1956 that I ever took a flying lesson. And then it was all very tentative: Most of my concentration was devoted to establishing myself on the pro tour. By 1958, I'd won the Masters and collected some $42,000 in prize money that year—and I was able to make time for flying lessons. I soloed then, and two years later I was able to buy my first airplane—a twin-engine Aero Commander.

Since then, I've traveled more than a million miles by air. It's not terribly unusual for me to fly across the country— sometimes twice each week. Nor is it unusual for me to fly from home to New York for a business breakfast and then to an exhibition in Georgia around lunchtime and finally to our golf course at Orlando, Florida, for dinner. If I'm at the controls of the plane, I feel almost "liberated" from the pressures of tournament golf. [*Winnie says: "This is one thing that Arnold is not bold about. He's a very careful pilot."*] Flying is still a learning experience for me. I'm as anxious to improve in my flying as I am in my golf; so far, I've qualified for an instrument rating and am licensed to fly multi-engined aircraft. The happy fact is that—through the good offices of my friends—I've been at the controls of everything from a jet fighter to a 747.

[*Says Darrell Brown: "He's a very quick study in these matters. To qualify for instrument rating, a pilot normally takes a ten-day course under an FAA-rated instructor. The way Arnold went about it was to fly up to LaGuardia one day and take about four hours of intense instruction. Then we went to a hotel near the airport and he sat down to study. After a while, he said, 'Okay, start firing questions at me.' We went at it and didn't stop for dinner—he just wanted to go on testing himself. The next morning, he went back to the instructor and stayed with him 'til about noon. Then we had to leave—he had an exhibition that day back home. But as soon as he could, he took the FAA instrument-rating written exam—it's a four- or five-hour job—and passed without the least bit of trouble. Then a week or so later, he took the flight exam—we had an exhibition in Philadelphia, and he decided he was ready. So we left and flew over to Allentown and went through the test-in-flight with an FAA supervisor. No sweat—he had it all down pat: What normally takes ten days, he'd picked up in about a day of intense study and instruction. And he was able to do it— under all the pressures of his life—because he brings to it the same concentration he brings to golf."]*

So far, I've had a few surprises while at the controls of a plane, but no real accidents. Back in 1966, I got a surprise on a trip into back-country Georgia for some quail shooting. The nearest airport didn't have a runway long enough to handle the jet, so we flew into Albany and then used a chartered pilot and Aero Commander for the trip in close to the hunting spot. I'd owned and flown that kind of plane, so I knew a little about its characteristics.

After the hunt, the hired pilot and I were ready to fly back to Albany. We had some passengers aboard, and they were going to ride with me in the jet back to New York City. We were rolling down the runway when I pushed in the pedals and discovered that the rudder wasn't working. (That's the vertical control surface on the tail of the plane that helps you turn the nose to the right or left.) I knew that sometimes you don't get any response from the rudder when you don't have quite enough speed to put pressure on the control surfaces. Since we had a lot of runway left, I waited for a moment or so to pick up more speed. Then I tried again. Nothing—no rudder response.

"We don't have a rudder," I snapped to the pilot. I was reaching for the controls to throttle back and stop the plane before we ran out of runway. But the licensed pilot beat me to the throttle. He jammed the throttle forward and grabbed the controls, figuring that I didn't know what I was talking about and that all we needed was more airspeed.

Now we'd gone past the point of no return. We could never stop the plane before we reached the end of the runway. But we couldn't get it more than a few feet off the ground either. At this point, the plane started to veer to the left; the torque of the propellers was pulling us in that direction, and we couldn't correct it by using the rudder. Suddenly we were skimming across a cornfield, with stalks licking at the bottom of the plane; I looked ahead and saw that all we had to do was clear a line of scrub pines at the far end of the field.

We could have packed it all in right there. For we were only going about eighty miles per hour, and the plane was at stall point—where it doesn't have enough airspeed and the nose just comes up, and you squash down to the ground. Hard. (If you're up high enough, the plane stalls and then goes into a spin.) The stall alarm in the plane was clanging away, and I knew we had barely enough speed to keep us in the air. Moreover, we *had* to lose airspeed the more we pulled up the nose to get over those trees—just like walking up a hill that gets steeper and steeper; you tend to walk more and more slowly. And yet somehow we did it. We just barely cleared the trees and picked up enough speed to stay in the air. We kept climbing—we didn't dare risk a turn—for a while. Then the pilot decided to swing around to our destination. He pressed the rudder pedals.

"My God!" he cried. "We don't have any rudder!"

"So what else is new?" I thought to myself.

Well, we managed to use the other controls and the throttles to turn the plane and fly 170 miles to our destination without a rudder control. We got into the proper flight pattern and landed the plane without further trouble.

Then we piled out of the plane and went back to take a look at the tail. No rudder cable—it had been broken.

And it had almost broken us—up into very small pieces.

[*Says Darrell Brown: "Arnold has very quick and sure reflexes at the controls of a plane. In 1970, after the Crosby, we got a little surprise that he reacted to beautifully. He had a speaking engagement in Modesto, California, and so we flew over there—Arnold and Winnie and myself. When he finished there, he decided that he didn't want to stay out on the Coast overnight—you know Arnold. He's got to keep things in motion all the time. So we leave there around eleven or eleven-thirty at night and hop over the mountains and make a refueling stop at Grand Island, Nebraska. And then Arnold takes over the controls and we get over the Latrobe airport shortly before seven in the morning, before the control tower opened. That's four and one-half hours elapsed time from California home, including the time spent refueling. So you can see the flexibility Arnold gets by using the jet.*

"Of course, it's winter in Latrobe—we could see mounds of snow a couple of feet high bordering the runway. What we couldn't see is that during the night, a layer of very clear ice had formed on the runway. And because it was so early, there was nobody in the control tower to tell us about it. To us, up in the air, the runway simply looked clean and clear. If we'd known about that ice, we would have brought that plane in like a feather—dropping it just right for the minimum roll. Like a good chip shot to the cup. But we didn't know about the ice and we came in like one of Arnold's punch shots—where he's going to make it low and hard and let the ball roll to the cup. The glide path was beautiful—for our purposes—and we're

rolling beautifully along the runway, using the rudder to steer the plane. When we got down to fifty knots, Arnold went over to nose-wheel steering. That's when we got two surprises: We found out about the ice and the nose-wheel circuit breaker popped, so we didn't have any control over the wheel.

"In a situation like that, the plane will go where the nose wheel points. And since it was on the loose, it began pointing sideways and suddenly that's how we're going down the runway: skidding sideways. Just a very little bit.

"Arnold didn't panic. He looked over the alternatives, like a computer working. He knew he had to act fast. He needed to steer the plane by the rudder before we dropped so far in speed that the rudder wouldn't respond. After that, steering the plane would rest on the landing gear brakes, and that can mean trouble without nose-wheel steering. So just before our speed died, he hit the left rudder pedal and eased the plane into a snowbank at the left of the runway, nose first, before a high snowbank could catch the wingtip and perhaps spin us around. Or at least damage the wingtip and the wing tank.

"That's when things really *got dangerous. For Arnold got out on the ground—and ice. We popped the circuit breaker back in to get the nose wheel under control again; it wasn't much more trouble than flicking the circuit breaker in your home. We cleared the snow away from the landing gear, and the idea was to rev up to about 95 percent power and back the plane out of there; since the ground crew wasn't around with its tractors, we didn't have a way to tow it out. I climbed back into the cockpit while Arnold volunteered to be the guidance man on the ground. He climbed out of the snow heap, moved out onto the ice to give me signals, and splat! He went down flat on his back and smacked his head on the ice.*

" 'My God!' I thought, 'he's fractured his skull!'

"He got up quickly and signaled he was okay. We got the plane in position on the taxiway and put chocks under the wheels and took a good look at it. The plane was okay. We took

a good look at Arnold. He insisted he was okay, too. So we climbed in the car and drove home and I phoned the airport a little later to have the mechanics double-check the plane. Arnold didn't bother to double-check his bump. By two o'clock that afternoon, Arnold was back in the plane, flying up to New York."]

Usually when we're airborne, and have the details of the flight under complete control, I can indulge one of the vast pleasures of flight: its magnificent perspective. If I've had a golfing problem, I can let it roam around in the back of my mind—knowing the perspective is different when I'm in the sky—and hope to come to some solution. The same way with business: Darrell will save up some notes, and when we're up there—with no phones and no interruptions—we can talk things out, even while tending to the absorptions of flight. I'm more of a aural person than anything else—I pick up things better by hearing about them than by reading about them. And Darrell is shrewd enough to know just how to handle that quality: He keeps me focused on the flight—yet he knows how to talk out some problems with me that might get completely overlooked in an earthbound perspective. Winnie figures he's a genius: She says the smartest thing he ever did was let me take the left-hand seat—the captain's seat—in the cockpit the first time we ever flew together. Now, I'll admit that was pretty impressive: I *wanted* to fly from that seat at that time, and he seemed to sense it. When you've got a man like that, you don't often want to let him get away.

[*Says Darrell: "When Arnold wants something, he won't quit until he gets it. I was the pilot who was asked to check him out the first time he switched from a propeller-driven plane to a jet. At the time, I was in sales and was working as a test pilot for the manufacturer—I'd already decided to give up accounting for the oil company and to go back to flying full-*

time. Well, I spent three days with Arnold, helping him check out his new equipment. Then the company assigned me to spend another thirty days with him as the pilot provided under the leasing contract. It was in that time that he began talking to me about coming to work for him full-time. I didn't want much to leave Oklahoma City—we just had a new home down there. But Arnold just wouldn't give up. He pointed out that with my business background I could do other work for him as well as be his pilot. And he said he'd take the risk of it: He said that if I bought a house here and then found out I didn't like it, he'd buy the house back from me and make sure I didn't suffer any losses. So I took him up on it and haven't ever given a thought to leaving."]

From all this, you might get the impression that I'm a pretty strong-minded person. I am. I get it from Pap. But I got something else from Pap: to do things well for their own sake. It didn't leave me with much lust for money—though I didn't fight it off when it came my way. But what I did seek was the chance to organize the world—my world—in a particular way. And if there's anything that golf has given me, it's the chance to do it.

 *Part Three*

ITS APPLICATIONS

. . . the most terrible reality brings us,
with our suffering,
the joy of a great discovery . . .
—MARCEL PROUST (1871–1922)

VI

Dealing with Reality

SOMETIMES at night, when we're flying home under a star-bright sky, I remember a fragment of a poem I heard many years ago. It was by "AE" (whose real name was George W. Russell), and it went something like "Our hearts were drunk with a beauty/That our eyes could never see."

That's how it is when you're alone at the controls of a jet and your whole spirit comes together and you have that soaring sense of oneness gazing out to a land—and universe—that you can't quite see.

If there's a difference between flying and golf—in my inner enthusiasms—I guess it's the difference between the romantic and the realist. Flying has always held a vast sense of romance for me, and golf has always been its realistic twin. In golf, I'm down to earth—literally and symbolically—and I never forget the hard discipline of realism that it imposes.

To be sure, there are a good many people who see a certain romance in my boldness and the bid always to go for broke. That's because boldness is—at least for most of us—rooted in a sunny optimism. It speaks of the hard shot, or the impossible one, that can and *will* be made. But it is not an escape mechanism. It is not a way to avoid reality and seek the beguiling miracle. It is only a way to view reality in a different light and use it to achieve your purpose. Take the growing sense of frustration that any golfer feels when he is not doing well. It is easy for him to give up and just do about as well as he can—to stop striving, so to speak. But this is not a reality; it is a surrender to a fiction—i.e., that because you're near defeat, you must suffer defeat. There's been many a time when boldness helped me to go on trying to win, even when common sense told me I had no chance. And it was boldness that developed within me a tradition of coming from behind—a momentum that people call a "charge."

In the Los Angeles Open of 1963 I was in sixth place, three strokes behind the leader going into the last day. Yet through aggressive play, I managed to win the tournament. In the 1962 Palm Springs Classic I won on the last day with five straight birdies in the final round. In the Texas Open that same year, I birdied three of the last four holes to win the tournament by one stroke.

But I know what it is to have the momentum going the other way, too. And how hard you have to fight to overcome it.

Take the 1971 Masters: I was playing poorly—well, even par—through the first six holes. I hooked my tee shot on the seventh hole into the trees and when I got to the ball, I found that I couldn't see the green. The tree blocked me out from it. There was an opening in the line of trees but it was not in line from my ball to the green. The safe shot, of course, was not to go for the green—to hit through the trees to the fairway so I could see the green, then to take another stroke from the fairway to the green. But I could "visualize" the shot that had to be made; I literally could "see" in my mind's eye how I'd hit the shot straight through the trees and yet give the ball a finishing hook that would put it on the green. I went for the bold shot. I took out my six-iron, dug the ball out of the pine needles, and arrowed it straight between the trees, then—though I couldn't see it—let it hook up to the green. It stopped seven feet from the hole. I dropped the putt for a birdie: I'd managed to convert a very bad lie in the woods into a birdie situation, and I could just feel the "charge" coming.

On the eighth, I hooked my second shot into the trees. This time I could see the green and—with my success in coming out of the woods a few moments earlier—I had no doubt I'd make a good recovery. But this time I stubbed the shot and left the ball short of the green. (The eighth is a 530-yard par-5, some 165 yards longer than the seventh hole.) So I wasn't on the green in three with a chance for a one-putt for a birdie. I was still off the green hoping to chip up close enough to get a one-putt for a par. But my chip shot ran past the hole, and it took me two putts to get the ball down. I wound up with a bogey—when I was sure my momentum would carry me to a birdie or par.

On the ninth I had a chance for a birdie. But I two-putted from 12 feet and took a par. On the tenth, I missed an 8-inch putt and three-putted for a bogey 5. Now I knew the momentum was all downhill. The whole experience became a fight to regain my charge—and to get the ball in the hole. I missed several more very short putts on the next few holes and sank deeper and deeper, and nothing seemed to work; my putting and driving faltered and I wound up eighteenth in the tournament.

That kind of performance inspires thoughts of defensive golf. Almost four months later, in the summer of 1971, I was leading the Westchester Classic by three strokes on the par-3, 154-yard fourteenth hole of the final round. My tee shot was bold enough—it went over the green and into tall grass down an embankment. As I scrambled down that embankment, I began thinking of protecting my lead, of trying to place the ball close to the cup, not in it. It was a reflexive thought, and it resulted in my hitting the wedge shot too weakly. The ball bounced short of the top of the embankment and dropped back. Now the anxieties were really rolling. I walked around for a while to settle down, and then I went back to aggressive play: I flicked the ball up and over and 12 feet past the cup. Then I went over and calmly sank the putt. That putt was the key: It gave me a bogey 4, but even the one-over-par managed to help me hold the two-stroke lead. And I went on from there to win the $50,000 first prize by five strokes.

If there's any change in my attitude toward golf over the years, it's reflected in the pairing of these incidents: Now I remember when the momentum failed me. And I have to fight it.

When I was young on the tournament trail, it never occurred to me that a shot couldn't be made. And that a tournament couldn't be won. There was no yesterday: Like all young people, I didn't remember the past—or much believe in it. It was all *now*. There was nothing else.

Today, when I take a shot that seems bold, it also never occurs to me that I might miss it. If I don't believe in the shot, I don't take it. If I miss it, I don't worry about it. Much . . .

But if I miss it, I know now it may sink into my subconscious and that it might influence me in the future. So I have to be more determined and more purposeful in my gearing up to golf. That's what an extra fifteen or twenty years will do to youth: Suddenly you know there were yesterdays as well as tomorrows. And that there is a link between them.

As I look back on it, I can see a link—and even a pattern—developing in a number of tournaments where I did not discipline myself to focus on the realities.

Take, for example, the match-up between the 1960 and the 1961 Masters tournaments and the 1966 and 1967 U. S. Open tournaments.

You remember how I'd come from behind to get in contention for the 1960 Masters title? And how I'd gotten birdies on the seventeenth and eighteenth holes to clinch the win?

Well, the very next year everything turned around.

There was, to be sure, a "charge" in 1961. But it took place a few holes earlier, away from the television cameras.

In the first two rounds, Gary Player and I had played virtually stroke-for-stroke. In the third round I shot a pallid 73, and Gary took a four-stroke lead on me. But I made it all up in the last round. And I even managed to grab a one-stroke lead —within one minute of play. That minute came when I birdied the thirteenth hole while Gary, playing two holes in front of me, bogeyed the fifteenth. That gave me a chance to pick up two strokes and—at that stage in the tournament—move from one stroke down to a one-stroke ahead.

I still held that lead as I came up to the eighteenth hole. Gary had shot a 74 that day and was in the clubhouse with a 72-hole total of 280. All I needed was to get a par 4 on the eighteenth hole, and I'd win the tournament. Nobody had ever won the Masters two years in a row but, in anticipation of the event, somebody came up to me on the eighteenth hole and said, "Congratulations, Arnie. You did it again." I thanked him and—in foolish anticipation of the event—was inclined to agree with him. It was a failure of my basic discipline. No longer was I focusing on the realities of the situation but out of a wish—and an assumption—that were rooted in the tournament of a year past.

My tee shot on the eighteenth was, if anything, better than the comparable shot a year earlier. I avoided the trees on the right, got the ball out to the left fairway, but put it perhaps ten yards closer to the green. So all I needed to try to hit the pin—located on the left front—was a seven-iron.

I blew it. My approach shot, with the seven-iron, went into a sand trap on the right front. I suspect, in looking back at it, that I lifted my head a little early and thus didn't hit all the way through on the shot.

I was annoyed—with myself, mostly—but not despairing. I figured I could blast out near the cup, get the ball down with one putt, get my par 4, and win.

But I was a little hasty. Instead of taking a moment to cool down to study the shot, I went up to it abruptly—hurrying to get my "win." This time, on my explosion shot out of the sand trap, the ball went all the way across the green and down a slick bank on the other side. Now I'd be using my fourth shot just to get up to the green. But I figured if I got it up close to the hole where I could get down in one putt, I'd still have a one-over-par and a tie with Gary and a chance to win a playoff. But I came up too hard off that slope, and the ball rolled 15 feet past the cup. The putt—for a tie—was going to be a tough one.

Too tough. I rolled the ball past the cup again, just slightly to the right.

I sank the second putt. But now I had a double-bogey—a six on this par-4 hole—and I'd given the championship right back to Gary.

On exactly the same hole where I'd won it the year before.

It's an experience like this that teaches you about the yester-days—and the tomorrows.

[*A year later, Gary Player was to comment on competition with—and against—Arnold Palmer. It was after the 1962 Masters. Palmer had come from two strokes behind Player on the final nine holes once again: On the par-3 sixteenth hole, he'd holed an electrifying wedge shot for a birdie 2; on the seventeenth he dropped a 12-foot putt for another birdie. He'd tied for the title, then won a playoff the next day against Player and Dow Finsterwald. Said Player: "I have a very uncomfortable feeling when Arnold is behind me, breathing down my neck. I'd rather be a stroke behind him than a stroke ahead of him. I think this is the feeling of just about everybody on the tour."*]

There was a repeat of the pattern in 1966, when I forgot the realities—and my sense of discipline—by assuming that a tournament was won . . . when it wasn't.

That was the year, 1966, that the U. S. Open was played at Olympic Club near San Francisco. The Olympic Club had its own special history, even before it spawned a country club: Gentleman Jim Corbett was a member in 1892, when he beat John L. Sullivan at Olympic for the world heavyweight championship. It was not until 1918 that the Olympic Club bought a set of bare sand dunes hard by the Pacific Ocean, planted some twenty thousand trees on them, and sat back to await the forest—and the glory. By 1966, it was a curious mixture of a course: It had no water hazards—though the ocean was only 500 yards away—and only one fairway bunker. What it *did* have was a lot of steep hills mounted by dense, towering evergreens that either slap down errant golf balls or swallow them up altogether. (Some years ago, when three limbs were pruned off a large tree on the eighth hole, 105 golf balls fell out.)

I'd played at Olympic in the U. S. Open of 1955, my first year on the pro tour, and I remembered it as a tight golf course with very narrow fairways and small greens. I'd also concluded that the "secret" to conquering the golf course lay in the way you played the first nine holes. I decided to focus on beating those holes, and I succeeded: In three rounds, I averaged 33 for those holes compared to 38-plus for the back nine.

In fact, I did so well in 1966 that I had a seven-stroke lead over the second-place pro, Billy Casper, as we started play on the last nine holes of the tournament. I felt so confident of victory that I let my attention wander from the realities—winning this tournament—to pursuing another goal: beating the U. S. Open record of 276 shot by Ben Hogan in 1948. I already had set the British Open record several years earlier, and I was beguiled by the thought of holding both the U. S. and British Open records.

I wasn't alone in my expectations of victory. As we stood on the tenth tee, Casper—my playing partner in this final round—turned to me and said: "I'm really going to have to go to get second, Arnie."

My reply sounded like a pompous gaffe. "Don't worry, Bill," I said, "you'll get second."

I was trying to reassure him, not put him down. For I knew he was thinking about the pursuit of Jack Nicklaus, who was just a stroke or two behind him.

This was the bizarre "discipline" of that final nine at Olympic: Bill Casper with his mind on the man behind him—not on a win; myself with my mind on a record—not on the win.

In that atmosphere, the first subtle shifts in momentum were not much noted. On the tenth hole, I lost a stroke to Bill. On the thirteenth, I lost another. But I still had a five-stroke lead and a good chance to come in with a 275. Now we came up to the fifteenth hole, a par-3, and I was trying to play the perfect shot—going for the record, not just the title. With a lead that big, who needs to play for the perfect shot?

Me.

The perfect shot would not have been just to the green but right to the cup. For a potential birdie and a leg up on Hogan's record.

Casper took out a seven-iron—for the 150-yard hole with an elevated green surrounded by bunkers. The pin was tucked tightly in on the right-hand side. Billy's tee shot hit safely on the green, and he one-putted for a birdie. That was the safe shot, and a superbly successful one. I chose the bold shot, to go for the cup. Unfortunately, the ball hit an inch wrong; an inch or so the other way to the left, and it would have licked in to the left and held near the cup, in good birdie distance. But it went an inch or so the wrong way and trickled down into the trap on the right side. I blasted up onto the green and two-putted. One over par for me, one under par for Billy—and now my lead was down to three strokes. With three holes to play.

For the first time, my attention was dragged back from breaking Hogan's record to playing the 1966 Open. For the first time, it dawned on me that Billy Casper had a chance to win this tournament. But, to me, it didn't look like a very good chance. The sixteenth was a long par-5—604 yards from the back tees used for the U. S. Open. It was not an easy birdie hole. Neither was the seventeenth. The eighteenth was a possible birdie. So I didn't see him making up three shots in those three holes—he'd have to play three-under to do it.

What I didn't expect was what I might do to help him.

As I stood on the sixteenth tee, I knew that I could play it safe and shut Billy off completely. I could take out a one-iron and bump and nudge the ball down the fairway, keeping it under control—while sacrificing distance—and accepting that it would take three shots to get to the green. If I played it safe all the way, I'd be in a good position to two-putt and get my par. Then I thought of how I'd look to myself: "There goes Arnold Palmer, playing it safe with a one-iron when he's got a three-stroke lead with three holes to play." It seemed silly. Billy Casper is a cautious and precise player, and I'd been struck by the irony of his strategy in this round of golf. "Here's a guy trying to catch me and *he's* playing it safe."

I couldn't do it. I have to be aggressive. I have to play the hole as I *feel* it, not as somebody else plays it. So I decided to go for broke: to use my driver.

But I used it poorly. I pulled the ball sharply left into a line of evergreens about 150 yards down from the tee and dropped into some heavy rough. Now I had another hard choice: Should I sacrifice a stroke by playing cautiously back to the fairway? That way I could make my way up to a bogey 6. Or should I go for broke and head for the green in search of par 5? I went toward the green. There was only one thing wrong: The grass was tougher and more wiry than I thought. I'd taken out a three-iron, more club than I'd customarily use in such a situation, because I wanted to get its accompanying power and distance to the hole. But the clubhead did not have the loft I needed for such a muscular, resistant rough. The result was that I could not get the ball up high enough to reach the fairway. It dribbled only about 75 yards, still in the rough. [*Later Casper, watching from the fairway and getting a glimmer of hope about finishing first, not second, was to say: "I was surprised when I saw Arnold take such a shallow club for his second shot, but nothing Arnold does really surprises me. When he is playing well, he feels he can do anything."*]

At this point, I had only one shot to play: a conservative little nine-iron that got me out onto the fairway. But my troubles weren't over: I hit my fourth shot—a long three-wood —into a bunker before the green. Now Bill was in a good spot to take over right then and there. For he'd come safely down the fairway and reached the green in three shots. Then he one-putted for a birdie four. I was still in a sand trap after my fourth shot, and the odds were that it would take me three more shots to get down. But I beat those odds: I hit a delicate little shot out of the sand to about four feet from the cup. Then I sank the first putt for a bogey 6 (instead of two-putting for a double-bogey 7).

But Bill had gained two more strokes on me—he picked up four strokes in two holes—and now he was only one behind me with two to play.

And he'd done it by playing safe while I was chasing the phantom record of Ben Hogan.

On the seventeenth, I was in trouble again. It's a 435-yard par-4 in which the fairway tilts from left to right and then breaks upward to a narrow-throated green. I was in the rough off to the left after my second shot, while Billy was on the fringe of the green. But I pulled myself together: Trouble, I figured, is my métier, and I've had to learn to live with it. So I pulled out my wedge and lofted the ball out of the rough, over a bunker, and onto the green, about 5½ feet from the hole. Joe Dey, then the executive director of the USGA, was to say later that it was as fine a recovery shot—given the circum-stance—as he ever witnessed.

The putt would be ever-so-slightly uphill, and I hit it ex-actly as I wanted to. I thought I had it made—the ball was right on line and seemed to have the roll to carry to the cup. But it stopped an inch short of the cup. A lousy little inch. It was perhaps the first time I'd ever come up short on an important putt in an important tournament. And it cost me the lead. For Billy coolly tapped in his three-footer for his par; I nudged in the one-incher for a bogey 5. And we were all tied.

Now there was no doubt about my goal: The record was gone (I'd have to get a hole-in-one on the last hole in order to break it), and the tournament might go after it.

The eighteenth was essentially a drive-and-pitch-onto-the-green hole. If you got on the green in good position, you could one-putt for a birdie. But the key was the tee shot—and I blew it. I pulled my tee shot off to the left into a particularly thick, matted patch of rough. Casper put his tee shot right in the middle of the fairway. At that moment, it looked like he could win it all. For he put his second shot, a soft lofted wedge, right into the center of the green. It looked like it would take me two shots to get to the green. For my ball was caught deeply in the tangled rough, and it would take a high-lofted club—the nine-iron—to dig it out of there. And the way the ball was sitting, it figured that I wouldn't hit it much more than halfway to the green with that club. But I put everything I had—every muscle that could be brought to bear—into that nine-iron shot, and I not only reached the green, which seemed impossible, but dropped it on the rear part of the green. ["*A tremendous shot . . . a fantastic shot,*" *said Casper later.*] I two-putted from there, with the second a testing, tricky down-hill putt. And Billy, who might have won with a one-putt, allowed for a shade more break than necessary on his 14-foot effort. The ball stopped a foot to the left of the cup. But I don't think he was deeply disappointed: I felt he was playing conservatively for the tie, not the win, and that he was interested most in making sure he wound up in a position to sink the second putt. He did. We both took a par 4 and went out for the playoff the next day.

It was virtually a reprise on the final day's action. I had a wonderful front nine. Billy had a wonderful back nine. In these last two days, he'd played to a 66 on the back nine, while I played to a 79. Billy won the playoff by four strokes, finishing with a 69 to my 73.

So I'd cost myself the U. S. Open victory. And I did it for the same reason that I'd lost the Masters in 1961: I forgot the reality of the situation—I assumed I had the tournament won when that was not yet a fact.

There was an interesting dénouement to the whole matter. And—for me—an ironic one.

The next year, Jack Nicklaus and I were locked in a head-on-head duel for the U. S. Open title. It was at Baltusrol, and this time I was chasing the leader. Jack had a four-stroke lead on me and, as we approached the eighteenth hole on the final round, he also had a chance to break Hogan's record. All he needed was a birdie 4 on this par-5 hole.

But Jack wasn't going for the record—at least not obviously. He was still going for the win. He remembers that it was on this hole, back in 1954, that Dick Mayer had come, with a big opportunity in the U. S. Open—and that Mayer had taken a seven on the hole and wound up losing the tourney. Jack decided that the first priority was to beat me and win the tournament. "If Arnie got a three here and I got a seven," he said later, "we'd be tied." One thing he could be sure of: I'd be going boldly for that eagle 3.

The eighteenth at Baltusrol is a fine and challenging finishing hole, some 542 yards long with a pronounced but not terribly acute dogleg left. The fairway is downhill from the tee. But the green is elevated and slopes from left to right before flattening out somewhat on the right. It is trapped left, front, and right, and—though there's a tree to the right rear—there are no nerve-shattering hazards on the back side of the green. The opening to the green—to the extent that there is one—is to the left of the sand trap in the front. (Because the green is so elevated, it sets down below a steep wall reaching up from the trap to the green.) The gap between the front and left bunkers is wide enough to play through, and the angle of the dogleg tends to bring that side of the green naturally into play. But there's a stream cutting across the fairway, perhaps 400 yards from the tee. It is narrow enough on the right, but on the left it widens and then becomes the juncture of a Y-shaped stream whose other legs—other than the one crossing the fairway—run roughly parallel to the fairway on the left. Thus to take the short route down the left side to the opening to the green meant accepting the stern threat of the water—as well as the encroaching rough from the dogleg left—on that side. It was a gamble, and one that I found most compelling.

For the safe player, there was plenty of room to go meandering down the right side, turning the corner, and laying up short of the water on the second shot to make sure there was no danger of getting into it and taking a penalty stroke to get out of it.

There was no doubt about what I'd do: go for the bold shot. I was sure I could make it. I was also sure that there was no other choice: I couldn't win the tournament by getting a par. And the only way to go for the eagle was to try to make the cut to the left and be so far out in the fairway that the green could come into play and the water would be no factor on the second shot.

But Jack decided to play it safe off the tee—to go right and, apparently, play up cautiously to the stream to make sure it never could quite offer a threat. So on the tee he pulled out a one-iron, not a driver, just to make sure he couldn't get into trouble. It was a startling decision: Here was one of the strongest hitters in the history of golf—playing with a four-stroke lead on the last hole of the tournament—deliberately deciding to bump and nudge the ball up to the hole. You just can't get much safer than that.

"I felt like an idiot, pulling out an iron," Jack said later. All the more so because, with a little risk-taking, he might go for the birdie and not only win the tournament but break Ben Hogan's record. But he'd faced the harder reality: He was more afraid of what I might do than what Hogan did do. And he knew what happened to me when I went for the record, instead of the tournament win, the year before—when I chose to go boldly off the tee with a driver on the sixteenth hole at Olympic while Bill Casper played it safe with his one-iron.

Some day, in some distant, as yet unrealized incarnation, we will all be able to look back at our times and perceive that life is not a neatly balanced procession of justices vs. injustices: It is a confusion of intolerable ironies.

For—playing it as safely as possible—Jack promptly got into as much trouble as possible.

On his tee shot, he sliced his one-iron off to the right, not quite far enough to reach the bushes and trees far down on that side but enough to end up a few yards in the rough, on a patch of bare ground hard by a television cable drum.

He got a free drop because of the obstruction and found himself in a tight little lie on crusty ground. The stream—narrow on the right—was about 120 yards in front of him. He decided to play it safe and lay up short of the stream. Again: Here is a great golfer with as powerful a shot as there's ever been in golf, and he decided not to try to go over a narrow hazard 120 yards away!

He took out his eight-iron—and he blew the shot. His club hit the ground a good two inches behind the ball. He pulled up his head, like any duffer, and looked for the ball in the air. So he didn't get a follow-through. And he moved the ball barely 50 yards. [*As the Greeks said: "Whom the gods would destroy, they first drive mad."*]

Jack wound up in a lie about 230 yards from the green. The carry from that spot would be slightly against the wind, and the green was, from that spot, elevated and guarded by a trap with a very steep wall.

He'd used two shots in playing it safe, and he was only a little bit farther along in the fairway than I was with one shot.

For I'd taken out my driver—not scornfully, you'll understand, but perhaps a little pointedly—and had smashed the ball 285 yards down the fairway. I used a three-wood on my second shot, cleared the water without trouble, and got close enough to go for the eagle.

Now Jack had an interesting problem. He had the bunker with the steep wall in front of him. He could hit his next shot short of the trap and then use a wedge to go over the sand trap onto the green. Or, alternatively, he could go for the green with his one-iron or a wood; even if the ball went over the green, he figured to chip back and still be on the green in four strokes. But either way, if he got into trouble along the way or if he three-putted, he might find himself in a tie for the lead—assuming I got the eagle.

So *now* he decided to play it boldly. He took out his one-iron. He didn't know whether—with all his strength—he could get the ball to carry over 230 yards (to the pin) against the wind with a one-iron. And at the same time clear the bunker wall in front of him. But he's got more confidence in his one-iron than in his three-wood. And it gave him a certain amount of much-needed control—more than with a three-wood—for it allowed him to try to fade the ball in from left to right, hoping to take advantage of the opening to the left and the slope of the green down from left to right. It also pretty much eliminated the danger that he might fly over and off the green on the far side. As Jack was to say later on, he wasn't chasing a birdie 4. He wanted to make sure he didn't wind up with anything more than a 6.

But the big problem was whether he could get the ball up

high enough, with a one-iron, to clear the bunker wall to the elevated green (since the likelihood was that it might fall within the range of his fade). Jack normally hits his long-irons high —higher than most—but the one-iron has so little loft to it that even *he* must have given some consideration to the height and trajectory of the shot. For the bunker was at the extreme end of his one-iron range, and the ball would be sinking in its trajectory as it approached that wall. He could hit the ball as hard as he wanted, but if he didn't keep it up high enough, he'd simply bury it a foot deep in the wall of that bunker. Or in the wall of the elevated green around it.

And by the time he got out of that spot, he might use up enough strokes to give me a chance to make off with the tournament.

But it was not to be. Jack hit the ball hard and high enough. It carried the bunker, skimmed onto the green, hopped once, and stopped. Just 22 feet from the pin.

It was, by any measure, a magnificent golf shot.

All I had to do was surpass it. In a bid for an eagle, I chipped the ball up and on the green and in a direct line for the cup. It stopped three feet short of the cup.

I dropped the putt for a birdie.

Now the hard reality was that Jack—who was on the green in three—would have to five-putt to give me a chance to tie him.

He didn't. He dropped the first putt to get his birdie—and to get out of what had been a bad situation.

It gave him the tournament.

And it gave him a 275—for a new U. S. Open record.

There's a moral in there somewhere—but it demoralizes me to think about it.

Actually, that was one of the important lessons of golf: You've got to learn to live with trouble—and you've got to learn how to get out of it. In golf, as in life, you get some good breaks and some bad breaks, but if you're going to depend on the breaks always to go your way, you're in for a surprise. An unhappy one. Because you've got to *make* the good things happen. You can't stand back and expect them to roll over you; you've got to make the breaks work for you. Just as Jack did when he quit playing safe and took out the one-iron to fight his way over that bunker wall.

In every aspect, golf is a game of compensating balances. One thing works, another doesn't: In the 1962 U. S. Open, I played perhaps the finest game I've ever played from tee to green. The balance was that I couldn't putt worth a lick: I three-putted eleven times. The result was that I wound up losing a playoff to Nicklaus.

Another time, in the 1964 Masters, I got into bad trouble on a couple of shots: Once I hooked a ball into the water at the eleventh at Augusta, then at the thirteenth I duck-hooked into the woods. But I came out of the trouble both times: On the eleventh, I took the one-stroke penalty and dropped the ball, and then chipped up to within an inch of the cup; on the thirteenth I used a wedge to loft the ball out through a pine-cone-sized opening in the trees and managed to salvage my par. After that, I earned three straight birdies. All in all, because I didn't let the trouble trouble me, I managed to put together as fine a series of rounds as I've ever played at the Masters. By the eighteenth hole, I had the tournament won—for a change—and I turned to Dave Marr, a good friend, who was struggling to come up from behind.

"How can I help you?" I asked Dave.

He glanced at me, then studied the leader board for a moment.

"Shoot a twelve," he said.

The fact is that experience on the pro tour has deepened my perspective but not changed it: If you're going to play boldly, the reality is that you've got to expect trouble—and know how to get out of it. Ninety percent of the time you can do it—if you know how. And have the discipline to try. For scrambling out of trouble isn't a matter of compounding error with recklessness in the "miracle of the mind." It's a matter of developing an awareness of reality that can expand your horizons instead of contracting them with fear or apprehension, or even with a resigned sense of defeat. My effort is usually focused on increasing my concentration on the next shot. On looking for the escape routes out of trouble and deciding which ones will serve me best. (I usually look for the escape route to the green, but it may not be there, and I may have to settle for something else. If so, I look for the escape route that will improve my position—there's no sense in taking a shot out of trouble that is going to leave you in worse trouble.) I've played some rounds that were absolutely wild, and yet managed to salvage something respectable out of them. In the 1970 Heritage Classic I was all over the place with my tee shots—I found some places that Columbus never imagined!—and I had to spend the entire tournament scrambling desperately to keep in contention. Yet when it was over, I tied for second-place money and picked up $7733—for four days of golf that could only be called chaotic.

I've also had the opposite happen: In the 1964 PGA, I played four rounds in 68–68–69–69. It was the first time in pro golfing history that all four rounds in a major tournament broke 70. As you know, it fit into a certain pattern for me: I'd been trying to win the PGA ever since I went on the tour, and I never succeeded. I didn't succeed this time, either—because of the success of Bobby Nichols in handling and overcoming trouble.

It may be that Bobby has the singular nature of a "comeback kid." For he'd had some experience in these lines when the stakes were greater than a golf championship. He'd been in an auto accident when he was sixteen years old. He suffered a brain concussion, a broken pelvis, back injuries, and internal injuries. He was unconscious for thirteen days, and he was hospitalized for ninety-six days. Yet he not only survived but emerged to become one of the "pros of the pros."

The reason is reflected in this sharpened focus on the third round of the 1964 PGA.

Bobby was in bunkers on the first two holes. He got out of both with pars, sinking putts of 10 feet and 20 feet. On the eighth hole, he hit a tree and had to play down one of the adjoining fairways, but he still got par for the hole: He hit a wedge shot up a foot from the cup and sank the putt. On the twelfth hole, he put his tee shot in the trees and his second shot in a trap, but he still struggled through to a par. On the fifteenth, he hit a tree with his tee shot, hit another tree some 50 yards farther down the rough with his second shot, then ventured to hit an intentional slice with a six-iron. He wound up 25 feet from the pin and made the putt from there for—par. On the sixteenth, he drove off the fairway into trouble; then he took a six-iron and dropped the ball 18 inches from the hole for a birdie. On the seventeenth hole, a par-3, he half shanked a two-iron into some trees; then he all but holed out his recovery shot with a wedge—the ball hit the pin and dropped a couple of inches away, and he sank the easy putt for par. He finished the round with a 69 on what could have easily been— as he admitted at the time—an 80.

What did he do for an encore?

The next day he sank a 50-foot putt on the last hole for a round of 67. To beat Palmer and Nicklaus by three strokes.

Probably the classic example of not getting rattled by trouble comes when two nonrattling types meet in a series of troubles. In the 1968 PGA, Julius Boros and I wound up in a struggle for the title. You know how Julius plays—he just goes up and hits the ball, waits for it to come down, then he goes up and hits it again. No sweat, no pain. When things go wrong, he doesn't exhibit any emotion. He just stands there like a man caught under a storefront awning in a thunderstorm, waiting for the rain to stop.

We both got into trouble in the closing moments of the 1968 PGA at Pecan Valley Country Club in San Antonio. My trouble came first. On the last hole, I hooked my drive into the rough, near a tree that was 230 yards from the hole. Now I had to get out of the harsh rough, sail over a creek and up a long, brutally narrow opening to reach a rolling, grainy green. It looked like I was too deep in trouble even to reach the green, much less to get up close to the hole. I needed the birdie to tie. And I knew that Julius was back there behind me, able to see that I was in trouble with my second shot. And that maybe things were suddenly going to get very easy for him. On the whole, there was more than a little pressure there.

But instead of cursing myself out for having hit a bad tee shot, I went after the shot that had to be made *now*. I took out a three-wood—a tough club to dig down and get the ball out of that grass. But I hit the ball hard, and gave it a slight draw so that it would pick up overspin and roll a little farther. The ball cut out of there, over the creek, up the fairway, bounced in front of the green, and surged right up onto the green, 8 feet from the hole.

An easy birdie putt away. Or so I hoped.

It was a classic example of keeping your nerves—of not getting rattled by pressure—in order to find your way out of trouble. With one shot, I'd been able to turn a tormentingly bad lie into a potential birdie and a tournament win. [*Mark McCormack has said: ". . . Palmer hit what would have to rank as one of the fantastic pressure shots of his entire career— in fact, it might have been his finest shot ever, considering the circumstances."*] Certainly the crowd was churning with excitement as I strode up to the green. For by now we could all look back and see that Boros hadn't hit a particularly long tee shot and that perhaps he wouldn't be able to get to the eighteenth green in two. If it took him three to reach the green, and two putts to get down—one over par—then maybe a birdie would win the tournament for me, not tie it. All I had to do was sink that putt.

That was the impossible dream. The grass on that green was

a particularly tough hybrid of Bermuda grass that was tougher and grainier than the customary Bermuda. It was grown to be long and strong in hot weather—and it had been very hot that week in San Antonio. I hit the ball just the way I wanted, but it didn't break a fraction of an inch. The grass just didn't give. The ball hung hole high while I saw the ultimate chance for this one title that so long eluded me—the PGA—slip just a little farther away.

But I had to pull myself together, despite my own despair, and sink the remaining putt. If I wanted to harbor any hope.

I sank it. And then I turned around to wait for Julius.

He had trouble of his own: He didn't make the green in two. He'd wound up short of the green in a lie where a hogback screened his view of the pin. Nevertheless, he *had* to get down in two shots to get his par—and to win the tournament. Anything less and he'd be in a tie and a playoff.

So the pressure was on Julius. He could see that I'd missed the putt and that getting out of that grass onto the green and in good position would mean winning or tying.

You know Julius. Nothing rattles him. He just took a look at the situation, barely hesitated over the ball, and then flicked a perfect chip shot that came over a hump in the green and settled down about the length of a putter's shaft from the hole.

A neat—and calm—recovery. For he quickly dropped in the putt that won him the tournament.

Once I accepted the reality of "in trouble, so work out of it," I picked up the added asset: You can make the trouble work for you. One time that stands out in my own memory was when I got into a magnificently bad lie on the second hole at Augusta National during the 1960 Masters tournament.

The hole is 555 yards long, a par-5 with a dogleg to the left. The rough was not heavy—it never is at Augusta—and the trees were set well back from the fairway. Thus it was—and is—my considered opinion that I could boldly cut the corner with a tee shot on this hole and wind up in an excellent position for a birdie or even a two-under-par eagle. But on this particular occasion I hooked the ball sharply off the tee into the woods at the left. When I went plunging into the woods to look for it, I found it on a dirt road under a low tree. There was no particular problem in finding my way back to the fairway—there were no obstructions in that direction. But there was an obstruction in another direction: above me.

As I stood in the woods, tentatively taking my club back, I found that I kept hitting a low-lying branch of the tree. My backswing was restricted to only slightly more than shoulder height. That could have been quite annoying, even defeating. But I decided not to let it defeat me. Indeed, I figured that I should turn it into an asset.

I tested it a few times with a four-iron until I knew exactly where the branch was when I brought the club back. Then when I was ready to swing, I knew that when I felt the branch was the instant to begin turning into the ball. So the branch acted not as a restriction but as a signal to bring all my muscles into a particular concentrated effort. The result was that I managed to hit the ball out of trouble some 200 yards down the fairway. And later go on to win the tournament.

Another time, I found a thoroughly frustrating obstacle in front of me that—by a little cunning—I turned into an asset. The hazard was an incline to an elevated green that was so close I couldn't possibly pop the ball up sharply enough and high enough to get onto the green. The way it looked, I'd either spend a countless number of strokes pounding the ball into the wall in front of me, or I'd have to dribble backward for a while —away from the green—to get the range I needed to loft the ball up high enough to reach the green. But there was one detail that was to prove pivotal: The wall has a slight forward incline, and I thought I knew a way to hit it—without losing ground. In fact, I thought I could use the lip of the barrier as a "skid plate" against which the ball could be hit sharply and then—

through the momentum of overspin—spin up and over the top of the wall.

It was in the Thunderbird Classic at the Westchester Country Club near Rye, New York, back in 1963, that I got into exactly this kind of trouble. Going into the seventeenth hole—a 346-yard par-4—I was tied with Paul Harney. Paul hit his second shot into a trap on the left of the green. I hit a wedge shot over the green. The ball bounced down a sharp incline back of the green. At the time, I figured Paul had the advantage. Usually it's easier to handle a shot out of a trap than up a steep incline back of the green, particularly if the pin is set—as it was in this case—toward the rear of the green.

There was little chance, as I saw it, of popping the ball up and over the top of that incline onto the green and stopping it near the hole. But the incline was leaning "forward," of course, and I figured I might be able to bank it off the incline and over the top. You don't want backspin on such a shot; you want the ball to have a powerful forward momentum. Choose a club with a loft that will lift the ball to the desired height on the incline. Usually it's going to be a middle iron, in this case a five-iron. Pick a spot where you want the ball to bounce on the incline, preferably one where there is no long grass or one that's not bare. Both surfaces are likely to throw the ball off its up-and-over course. Then line up with the ball played back in your stance, closer to the right foot than the left. Square the clubface to the target or even close it ever so slightly to discourage backspin. Swing with a punching action. Thus the backswing for this particular shot doesn't have to be as long as for a normal chip shot from this distance. After all, you are going to make the ball hit sharply below the top of the incline. The ball must be hit smartly, with the hands ahead of the clubhead at impact. The follow-through is chopped short. The swing is made with the arms and shoulders with the weight kept on the left foot throughout the swing. Finally, you must keep your head down and your eye looking at the ball's position where you hit it, until you hear it hit the incline above you.

Now, it doesn't take as long to think all this through as it does to execute the shot.

But thinking it through sometimes is more successful than any other way.

In this case, my shot hit near the top of the bank but ran out of gas and never did make it up and over. It just sort of died, then rolled back down and lay against a small tree that had been planted there a short time before. The ground around the ball was still dug up, so I got a free drop under the "ground under repair" rule. Now I was still attacking a par-4 hole—and I already had used up three shots.

I went right back to the bank shot—the over-and-up—that I'd missed before. This time: success—I laid the ball up on the green within easy putting range.

Paul got out of the trap neatly and left his ball six feet from the pin. If he sank the first putt, he'd have a one-stroke lead on me. He didn't; he sank the second one. If I missed my first putt, he'd still have a one-stroke lead. I didn't; I sank the first one. So we continued the tie through seventeen and then through eighteen and finally I won the match—and $25,000—on the first hole of the sudden-death playoff.

But the reason I even got into the playoff was:

I knew how to get out of trouble via the up-and-over shot; and I didn't get rattled when I got into trouble or when my first up-and-over shot failed. I just hung in there and did the best that I was convinced could be done.

It's because I practiced so much in the rough when I was a boy that I developed a realistic attitude toward getting out of trouble. I learned the intellectual process—of looking for the various escape routes, of choosing the route that would best serve my purpose, of picking the club that would help me execute the shot I chose. But something else happened that is harder to explain—and yet is vital to continued great play whenever trouble looms. That something was visual, not intellectual; I could literally *see* the shot that had to be made. Perhaps that is what removes art from craft: The great artist can literally *see* what must be done, not merely intellectualize about how it can be done.

This is not to say that golf is an art or that I'm a great artist. It is only to say that—in certain moments of everybody's career—he can see exactly what must be done. Not always. But at least often enough so that he'll remember the experience when it takes place.

I can remember almost all of such shots—the 1961 British Open, the 1968 PGA, the many others I've cited. But I can also remember them from years before I turned pro. Perhaps one of the finest shots I ever hit was seen by almost nobody. It took place while I was in college—around 1950—and competing in a college meet which, considering the times, didn't attract much attention.

On one hole I was off in the rough and screened from the green by several trees and a bunker. I was lying a four-iron distance from the green.

As I saw it, that shot had to be a number of things. It had to be low to get under the tree branches. It had to be strong to get through the high grass of the rough, in case it hit the ground. It had to be straight to get through a small opening between two trees, through which I could just see a piece of the green. And finally it had to hook to get onto the green over the bunker.

Now, nobody *knows* how to make a shot like that. You have to have a feel for it. Fortunately, I'd practiced by the hour—sometimes by the week and month!—on shooting out of the rough and through the bushes and trees, and I could see, in my mind's eye, how that shot should look in flight. It never occurred to me that it couldn't be done; it never dawned on me that the ball would do anything different than I intended. So I just took my iron, split the opening between the branches, and hooked the ball onto the green—one putt away from a birdie.

That shot reflects much of the substance behind my philosophy of boldness. It is not wild bravado that characterizes boldness. It is preparation and discipline that count—a discipline that reaches for the total and forward-looking relationship between the mind and the challenge.

VII

Dealing with Change

[*On the attaché case that Arnold Palmer picked up from his secretary's desk was taped a white sheet of paper with a reminder lettered in bold black ink:*

"*Entry deadline—L.A. Open*
5 P.M. Thursday"

It was a suggestion of the many dimensions of Arnold Palmer's mind and personality.

He is, in one side of his nature, a most conservative, even cautious man with a gift for procrastination: he didn't forget to enter the Los Angeles Open; he knew, and everybody on his staff knew, that he would enter the tournament. But the entry deadline is earlier at L.A. than at most other tournaments—and Arnold Palmer just didn't want to be committed that deeply that soon. He would rather wait and wait and wait until he was forced—by events or a deadline—to do what he was going to do anyway. Or until he'd resolved to make a sig-

nificant change—and skip the early-season tournament he handled best.

This is, to be sure, in contrast with the popular "image" of Arnold Palmer. The popular image emerged from the brisk, uncompromising, even elated manner in which he strides about a golf course, confidently tackling every decision as if there were no problem too awesome to behold. In golf, there isn't. His capacity for hard decision-making is astonishing. His sense of reality is unswerving. His recall is phenomenal. Here is a literal transcript of the tape in which he described the first golf game he ever played in high school: ". . . was with a boy who is now a doctor in Los Angeles and his name is Bill Dankow. From Jeannette, Pennsylvania. It was a cold March day and we tee off and, of course, the course was just a nine-hole par-34 which we'd made into a par-68 for the total round. I topped my first tee shot because I was nervous, first match and everything. Still made a 4 at the first hole and ended up shooting 71 in that match and the kid I was playing—he was a left-hander—I think he shot an 85. . . . " That was a match he played thirty years ago.

But Palmer is not merely a golfing machine. He possesses all the ripened ambiguities of human nature. If he is quick in some decisions—as in golf—he is slow in others. If he is unsparing in his assessment of himself, he is flexible, and usually generous, in his appraisal of others. He is sometimes abrupt or gruff with those closest to him—his wife, Winnie, says that she is amazed at his unflustered patience with all the public pressures he suffers, "because at home the one thing he is not is a very patient man." One friend and sometimes business acquaintance says, "he's been hardened by circumstances in certain human judgments." Yet he is unlikely ever to express a hard judgment. The reason, I suspect, is that he is a genuinely open, trusting, and buoyant man who has found—to his utter astonishment—that not everybody is like him. Given time, they will be. In the meantime, he won't pass judgment on them.

His "giving nature" has, I think, given an enormous substance to his career. He can—like most of us—be puzzled, abrupt, outraged, and frustrated. He can gnaw and worry at certain problems. But he is never anguished, never defeated, never made mean or malicious by a problem. He has a total sense of identity: He does not blame others for his failures, and he is not bedazzled by his own successes. He knows whereof they stem: Golf is a game of compensating balances—as is life—and when it is played completely, it must be played without remorse or recrimination.

This is what has elevated him personally as well as professionally. You and I might be dazzled by his success and lacerated by his failures: If he could eliminate just three selected strokes of the 120,000 or more strokes he's taken through his professional career, he might now be the holder of four U. S. Open titles, not one title and three or four near-misses. But Arnold Palmer is aware of the thin connective tissue of life that links success to failure. He is a multidimensioned man who understands that life is filled, properly, with a heightened anticipation. But not of surprises. Or of despair.]

In golf, the easiest decisions for me are the hardest ones for others: whether to play the bold shot.

The hardest decisions for me are the easiest ones for others: whether to change one's golf style.

The fact is, I'd rather face the hard shot all day long than face the need for constant change. And yet there are many golfers—weekend golfers, perhaps—who feel that they need to change their whole style every time they flub a shot. You see them often, working out with the pro, seeking the secret of improving their game by changing their style—because they had a bad round or executed a few bad shots.

But for me, it is the challenge that is easy. And the change that is hard.

For it takes many, many years to shape a golf style to your

philosophy and ability. I put perhaps a quarter of a century into developing the style that brought me to success. When I finally had it honed to the best that I could do, Henry Cotton, one of the finest golf stylists in Great Britain, analyzed it this way:

"Palmer has little style. . . .

"He often hits with no follow-through at all. . . .

"He rarely finishes two swings the same way. . . .

"Sometimes he finishes almost on his knees. . . .

"Even with his crouching putting stance, he stands rather oddly: very knock-kneed. . . ."

And when you stop to think of how many years it took me to get *that* good . . .

Actually, Henry was not being malicious. He was being analytical and balanced. ("Palmer drives as far and straight as anyone playing. . . . Arnold hits his iron shots to the pin like Sam Snead and putts as well as, if not better than, Bobby Locke." That was quite a compliment: Bobby Locke was perhaps one of the two or three greatest putters in golfing history.)

The reason I bring it up is to suggest that perhaps it's not so accurate today.

It's not necessarily that I've gotten better. It's that I've gotten different.

And the difference was harder to achieve than some of the boldest shots in my inventory. For it defines the difference between challenge and change. Challenge involves only one person—me: Nobody else needs face the hard shot, nobody else can be hurt by it. But change—any kind of change—involves many people. And some of them can be hurt—or puzzled or chagrined—by my change.

And so the way I think about change is different in degree, but not kind, from the way you think about challenge. Which is to say: It is done more slowly. And cautiously.

To understand all this, you must understand that boldness is a *philosophy* of play, not a style of play. There are a good many styles that can fit within the philosophy; I've used several different ones myself.

Yet you find people who feel that a "bold" player is, by definition, a power hitter. That's not quite true. A very modest hitter can be quite bold as a player. The fact is that some of the boldest shots in the game are the putts, the chip shots, the short approach shots. For they determine the skills and attitudes of the player: Is he willing to go for the pin, to get a birdie or an eagle, instead of going for the fat part of the green and taking, safely, a par? Is he willing to go boldly for the cup on his first putt—a long putt, let's say—with all the risks involved in putting past the cup and into disaster? Or will he nudge the ball up to the cup, in an effort to protect his par?

Boldness is a matter of attitude, not of power. It is a matter of shaping the tools you have to your philosophy of the game, rather than shaping your philosophy to your tools—boldness to power, caution to lack of power.

My own feeling is that boldness should be a liberating philosophy, not a confining one. I certainly haven't felt compelled to stick with one style of golf, even though I've stuck with one attitude toward it.

When I first went out on the tournament trail, I heard a lot of criticism that all I could hit was the low, hard-punched shot. It was true—but then there were a lot of golfers who couldn't do *that*. It had its drawbacks, of course: For one thing, it gave me a lot of roll on the ball after it hit the ground. That added yardage to the drive—but I never could be sure where the ball would roll to. There are a lot of golf courses where added roll means added trouble, because the fairway grass is so thin that the ball never quite stops where you want it to stop: It rolls on and on into a sand trap or water hazard or skips into the rough. There are other courses where you don't get the added roll. The grass is so verdant and strong that the low line drive with high momentum tends to come quickly to a stop. Augusta National is an example: The grass is so rich, even in the spring, that you get very little roll on it. You get greater distance by keeping the ball in the air as long and as far as possible—i.e., with a high-trajectory drive—because you can't expect any longer distance from a ball that flies low and hits early; the grass just won't let it get that extra roll. Yet I won two Masters tournaments at Augusta with the low, hard-punched shot. And I won two British Opens. And I won the U. S. Open.

For six or seven years after I joined the pro tour, I stayed with that shot. But bit by bit, as I came to understand the magnificent vagaries of the golf courses on the pro tour, I came to feel that this shot was not enough. I had to face the hard fact that the world out there on the pro tour was different from the world in which I'd learned the game of golf.

Not all the tournament courses were so deliciously free of fairway bunkers as the one at home: I sometimes found, on the tour, that a low, hard-punched shot would hit safely short of a bunker and then roll and roll and roll until it nestled in the sand. Nor were all the greens as soft as the ones at home, where I'd learned to hit a low, hard-punched shot with a one-iron, knowing that the green would slow the roll. When you get to a course with small and sometimes elevated greens—like Merion, the site of the 1971 U. S. Open—you're really in trouble if you've got an approach shot that has a lot of roll. For each time they cut the grass they do it three times on those greens —and from three different directions—and any way you hit a low-punched shot onto those greens, you've got a good chance not only of rolling past the cut but of rolling over and off the green and down into some deep trouble.

The lessons were sometimes learned hard—through experience—but the alternative was so difficult that I came very slowly to the conclusion that I was going to have to make a basic change in my game.

It would be a change in style, not in philosophy. I would not play less boldly than before. Nor would I hit the ball less than hard. But I would hit it high as well as hard. I'd get considerably more loft on my tee shots and fairway shots, and I'd learn to feather them a bit here, nudge them a bit there, and get the ball to bounce once and stop. No roll, no trouble. By developing just the right touch, I could get the ball to drop on a sharp trajectory onto a specific piece of the landing area, not generally in or around it. Still . . . change meant a significant break with the past. For I'd played the way Pap played. Now I was going to have to shake loose from that style, which also meant shaking loose from Pap's play. He didn't much agree with me; my father would never buy my argument that you had to learn to hit it every way. His attitude was understandable: He'd learned to play—and play well—with hard-punched little iron shots that rolled dead on the green. I'd learned to play and play well the same way. So why change?

The reason was that he'd never had to play thirty or forty different courses a year. And I did. And I needed to have a variety of shots in my arsenal to conquer the great variety of conditions that I met on the tour.

That's why, late in 1961, I had to begin thinking about developing another shot. And—if you will—another style. It was a long and slow process: It took the better part of an off-season and a spring to gain any credence with it. Until then, I was teeing up my ball about a quarter of an inch. And I was placing it slightly more to the right, as I faced it, thus making contact with it while the clubhead was still descending. Sometimes I hit the ball and the ground at virtually the same instant; sometimes—because of the trajectory of my swing—I was hitting the ground first. The ball did not go high but it went far, and it got a roll that carried it farther. In short, it had greater impetus than height; it had considerable momentum after it hit the ground, which gave it that extraordinary roll.

Would more accuracy be worth the loss in distance?

I thought so. And I knew how to go about seeking it.

I began teeing up the ball a little higher—about an inch

higher. Then I began planting it a little farther forward, closer to the line of my left heel. So instead of hitting it while I was still in the downswing I'd be hitting it exactly at the bottom of the swing, or even a shade beyond it. The idea was that by moving the ball to the left a little, I'd be lengthening the distance over which the clubhead was traveling in a straight line —not much, perhaps only an inch. But that, I felt, would give me a little more accuracy—just as you get more accuracy from a rifle than a pistol.

By raising the ball on the tee, I'd get more loft into the drive, which would cost some distance. It would reduce the roll— but it was the roll after hitting the ground that was getting me into deep trouble. The loss in distance was not what would make most men weep: I could still average 275 yards off the tee. But there was a distinct advantage to it all: I'd avoid hitting the ground with the club at the instant that I hit the ball, as I had under the old system. By teeing the ball up higher, I'd avoid that jarring dislocation of the clubhead that could alter the whole flight of the ball.

But if I raised the ball, what happened to the impact-point on the clubhead?

Woudn't it—the "sweet spot" on the clubhead—now be coming through the impact area lower than the center of the ball?

Possibly.

To compensate for that, I went to a driver with a deeper clubface: It was thicker from top to bottom. My drivers now measure about 1¾ inches in depth at the "sweet spot." In that way, I felt that I'd get solid, continuing contact with a ball teed an inch off the ground.

It was not an immediate success. I had a great deal of trouble with it in the winter tour of 1962, notably at the Bing Crosby Pro-Am and the San Diego Open. It seemed to come around during Lucky International at San Francisco that year and then it sustained itself well during my victory at the ninety-hole tournament at Palm Springs.

I was aiming to get it in shape for the Masters; the Augusta National course places a considerable premium on accuracy off the tee. The fairways are wide enough so that you don't get into the rough often but accuracy is needed so that you can get position on fairway shots that will open up the green for you. I was relaxed about it all; I figured to have ten weeks to get everything into shape. But I got the message at the Phoenix Open in 1962 at the Phoenix Country Club. (It alternates between there and the Arizona Country Club.) In the past, this had been a difficult course for me, if only because it had narrow, tree-lined fairways that tended to inhibit my long game. This time I found myself curiously eager to attack the course, to try out my new driving procedure on it.

The eagerness was well founded: Everything I hit stayed in the fairway, and I went on to win the tournament by twelve strokes—the biggest margin of victory by anybody anywhere that year.

Later on, I was to go on to win the Tournament of Champions at a course heavily edged by rough that somehow had kept me from winning before. And I would win at the Colonial Invitational, and at the Texas Open and at the British Open—at nine different tournaments. The most delicious of them all: my third victory at the Masters in Augusta.

There is another element in which I've changed my golf somewhat.

When I learned the game, I learned to hit the ball in a particular way—i.e., so that it would move from right to left while in flight. That means that I hit the ball with a "draw," or a slight and well-controlled hook. (At least I *figured* it would be controlled. Every once in a while, I'd get off a hook that would cut so sharply you'd think it turned a corner—the immortal duck hook.)

The reason was quite simple: the course I learned on was designed to make the most of such a drive. In fact, I might say that most of the courses designed and built from the turn of the century into the 1930s were essentially built to accommodate a right-to-left movement of the ball. Augusta, Oakmont, Winged Foot, Brookline. And Latrobe Country Club.

The difficulty is that the "draw," or right-to-left shot, possesses a pronounced sidespin. That's why it gets out of control so easily: A little too heavy sidespin and that ball is heading sharply into the rough—or the next fairway. It snaps off sharply, almost like somebody signaled a left turn.

The opposite movement of the ball—from left to right—is called a "fade," and it's the well-bred brother of the slice. It has much less sidespin than the draw or hook and so, though it can grow into a slice, it never grows quite so ugly or suddenly as the draw grows into a hook. You can, in short, duck hook a ball, but you cannot duck slice one.

The result is that the ball is under a lot more control in a "fade," simply because it has less sidespin. A great many golfers have decided that the control is most important. In his forties, Ben Hogan went to a fade, or left-to-right movement. From his youth, Jack Nicklaus made the fade the fundamental movement of his drive. And the time came when I had to decide to bring the fade, or left-to-right movement of the ball, into my repertoire. It simply is necessary when you find that the only way to reach the pin is by coming in from the left side and dropping the ball on the right side of the green or the fairway. The eighteenth hole at Augusta is such a hole. Though the course is generally sympathetic to the "draw," not the fade, the most useful way to play the eighteenth hole is with the well-controlled fade—bending the ball muscularly, but precisely, around the trees far down on the right.

The technique of hitting the fade demands delicacy and discipline. But it is not really hard to figure out. All you have to do is open your stance just a trifle—i.e., place and anchor your right foot in the proper stance and then place the left foot so that it is slightly behind a line drawn straight across from your right toe. That leaves the front of your body inclined slightly—or "open"—so that it faces the green. (On a draw, the toe of your left foot will be in front of the line drawn across from the toe of your right foot. Thus it will be the heel, or blade, of your left shoulder that will be facing the green.)

The effect of opening the stance is about the same as plotting an entirely different swing: On a fade, the clubhead must come at the ball from the outside—the far side—before squaring off at the instant of impact. You are slicing the clubhead from outside to inside, so to speak, and the sidespin thus given the ball is clockwise. It sends the ball moving out gently, grandly to the right. That is, if you haven't overdone it. And hit a slice. (The hook is obviously executed in the opposite manner. The club is moving almost imperceptibly from inside—close to the swinger —out, so that at impact it imparts a counterclockwise sidespin to the ball, sending it careening to the left as it rises over the pollen. The hook is quite easy to execute, in its more aggrieved form. Anything less than an aggrieved hook can be considered a triumph of the art form.)

In learning the fade, I didn't abandon the right-to-left shot altogether. I simply added to it. There are still times when it is more useful than the fade.

Jack Nicklaus will testify, I think, to the difficulty of using a fade on the 449-yard par-4 tenth hole at Baltusrol, at the 1967 U. S. Open. There's a clump of trees about 300 yards down on the right-hand side of the fairway. You can't outdrive them—and you don't want to drive into them. Yet that's where a fade will carry you. As it happen , there's a trap on the left side of the fairway—roughly the same distance out—if you're the opposite, a strong right-to-left hitter. So the pressure on this hole is to come up a little short of the hazards with your tee shot.

The question is: Which side is the best side to be a little short on? On the right side, if you come up short on a left-to-right shot—a fade—you're likely to land behind those trees. In fact, the fairway and rough angle in such a way that you can't even see the green from the right-hand side. Normally I would consider the sand trap on the left a more demanding hazard, but if you come up short of it, at least you can still see the green. You've got to sacrifice a little yardage either way, but going left—with a draw, not a fade—you keep the green in view.

The reason I bring it up is that in 1967, when he won the U. S. Open there, Jack faded right on all four rounds. Twice he tried his driver; twice he went to his three-wood to get control at the sacrifice of some distance. All four times he faded the ball right. All four times he wound up in the rough, with those trees blocking his line-of-sight to the green. Three times out of four he bogeyed the hole (he got a par on his first try).

In the end, it didn't exactly hurt him, as we've already seen. But the point is a significant one: The ability to hit right to left—and control the tee shot—would have been useful to any golfer on this hole. Including Jack Nicklaus. And it might have set Jack's U. S. Open record significantly lower.

It is versatility, therefore, that I sought in adding the left-to-right shot to my weaponry. With it, I can go in either direction, not just one. Off the tee, I may lean heavily one way or the other, depending on what the course demands; there've been times when I went left to right off the tee all through a tournament. But once I get out onto the fairway—or the rough—I'm ready to go either way. There are a lot of times when I'll choke down on the club and hit a little low hook shot in order to get around a particular hazard. The seventh hole at the 1971 Masters—where I shot through the trees and hooked onto a green I couldn't see—is an example. The point is that I purposely added another tool—one that wasn't "natural" to me—in order to strengthen my game and give it greater versatility. Which meant that in attacking a golf course boldly, I could attack in any of several directions.

That's not the reason I changed my putting style—actually, I changed it twice in 1971 alone. For there's one thing I hold in common with almost all other golfers: There are very few absolute truths in putting. You get the ball in the hole, and it doesn't matter how. Orville Moody uses a cross-handed grip, with his left hand well below his right hand; he won the U. S. Open with it. Sam Snead tried a croquet shot and, when that was outlawed, he developed a side-saddle technique— he putts with the stance of a surveyor lining up on an ant hill and the grip of a matron wiping away bread crumbs with a napkin. But he gets the ball in the hole. And out on the West Coast, there's an amateur named Kent Meyers who turned up in the 1971 Pacific Coast Amateur championship putting from behind his back: he'd put his hands behind him, grip the club, stick the shaft between his legs, and stroke the ball. He said it stabilized the arms and stiffened the legs—and I'm not the man to say him nay.

My own experiments are somewhat less exotic. I went for years putting with an extremely knock-kneed stance, in which my knees almost touched above the ball. It was not terribly comfortable, but then I'm not sure that you *have* to be comfortable in order to putt accurately. Also in the past, I used what was called a reverse-overlap grip. What it meant, quite simply, was that I didn't wrap the left forefinger around the club. Instead I kept it stuck downward, toward the bottom of the shaft, so that actually it tended to touch the right-hand fingers curled around the shaft. The result was a very "wristy" stroke, one that gained its movement from the break in my wrists instead of—as in the classic manner—by a somewhat stiff movement of hands and forearms, as if all were connected to the putter in a single inflexible movement. But I found that I could keep my head and body immovable more easily with the "wristy" putt.

But there are changes involved in the body as one ages that profoundly affect your putting. It's not "nerves." There is a change in muscular sensitivity—in "feel," so to speak. And there's a change in the discipline that the muscles can accept. For instance, I found that I was moving my head and body more as the years went by, and I felt it was because of my putting stance and grip.

So early in 1971, I went to a much less knock-kneed stance. And I changed my grip: I shifted my hands so that I had all ten fingers on the club—no longer was the left forefinger laid along the right fingers; it was curled around the shaft. And I reduced the "wristy" motion of my putting, going instead to a firm-forearm—it was a little less snatch in movement.

At first, I had considerable success with the new style. It was beautifully suited to the less-grainy greens of the Southwest. In fact, I putted very well in the Bob Hope Desert Classic and won it in a sudden-death playoff by dropping a 20-foot putt as smoothly and easily as blinking. But when the tour got to Florida, with its grainier greens, my putting fell off. In the 1971 PGA in Palm Beach Gardens, I putted very, very poorly. In fact, I putted myself out of contention in the very first round, when I came in with a 75. Nevertheless, there were times when I felt I had the touch again: I won the Florida Citrus Open by putting together four rounds under 70. But I was not consistent, and I began getting the feeling that this putting style was a little too selective for me. Some extraordinarily fine putters have been "arm putters," but I came to the conclusion that it wasn't for me.

Gradually I went back to my knock-kneed stance. My reverse-overlap grip. And my wristy motion. I concentrated on keeping my head and body still. I worked hard to keep my hands out in front of the ball. I took out some old putters from the stacks in my basement and changed the grips so that they were thinner than my other recent putters. I felt you can't overestimate the importance of feel. And by the summer of

1971, I'd put it all together: I won the 1971 Westchester Classic with the new/old-style and teamed with Jack Nicklaus to win the National Team championship.

I'm not sure what Henry Cotton would think of my style today: I have the uneasy feeling that he might not be so flattering about my putting. But I think it's important to change as the game and its demands change. The longer one plays golf, the more one understands some of the compensating balances of golf—and of life. In terms of strategy. In terms of weaponry. In terms of muscular control. If I've changed, it's in an effort to tip the balance—toward boldness and toward victory.

VIII

Dealing with Yourself

IN MANHATTAN, there's a magazine vice president who has an exotic way of getting himself set for a tough shot on the golf course.

He imagines that he's already hit the ball and flubbed the shot miserably. Then he convinces himself that *now* he's working on his second shot and that he must make it. With that heightened sense of urgency he brings his concentration together and focuses so intensely on his shot that he manages to get it off the way he wants—most of the time.

This suggests the extent that people will go to in order to bring themselves "up" to the demands of a good golf game. And it's one of the most important things I've learned in all these years on the pro tour: It's not enough to have a philosophy of golf; you've got to be physically and psychically ready to play. Anything less will leave you so weary, mentally or physically, that your concentration will falter; you will not be able to determine precisely what you need to do, and then you won't be able to execute the shot precisely.

The psychic problems are the most commonplace. For golf is more than a physical game—more than an elaborate ritual of gripping the clubs just so, of keeping the left arm straight, of keeping the head still, of shifting the weight on the feet, and so on and on. It is also a mental and, most of all, an emotional game. It is a test of the self—of the ability to put oneself altogether. The golfer, good or bad, exists in an environment of constant turmoil—a turmoil within himself. We all know how a bad shot plunges many a golfer into such depths of disgust and self-recrimination that it destroys his next shot or his entire game. Or how a good shot will lift him to such heights of exultation that—carried away by his excitement—he'll go on to flub his next two or three shots.

The golfer who plays the game with boldness is more likely, I think, to feel the extreme ranges of these emotions than the more cautious or conservative player. It is not that the conservative player won't hit great shots. It is that the drama of his golfing experience is not so extreme—he does not move so regularly from the improbable to the impossible. Thus the exercise of his emotions is not so continuous or played out over so broad a spectrum.

To be successful, therefore, the bolder player must be ready to accept a more difficult self-discipline than the conservative player. He cannot allow himself to succumb to the wide and remorseless torrents of emotion—to get to the point where the whole golf course explodes into a welter of obstacles and perils. He must have an attitude toward his game—and his philosophy —that brings him pleasure as well as success.

The sense of self-control must be at its best when the pressure within oneself is at its highest. I can remember the Heritage Classic at Hilton Head Island in 1969 when I invited myself to blow sky high.

I'd taken a three-stroke lead into the final round, and my spirits were so high that I felt the same élan as in the first tournament I'd ever won. I was happy, confident, eager to be playing, ecstatic at being challenged.

In that final round, I *was* challenged. By myself.

I bogeyed the eighth hole. I three-putted the ninth. I saw my lead cut to two strokes by Dick Crawford, my playing partner in that final round.

And then I drove the ball into the water on the tenth hole.

"Now hold *on*," I told myself. "You know what it takes to beat this course." I knew—par after par after par. This was a course where you weren't going to get many birdies. That meant all I had to do was not lose control—to go for the par when the birdie was impossible.

It was a struggle. After taking my drop beside the water, I managed to loft the ball onto the green about 15 feet from the cup. So I was on in three and needed to one-putt to make my par. I got it—the putt and the par.

It wasn't altogether over. For Dick Crawford was ready to make his own challenge: He sank a 30-foot putt for a birdie on the thirteenth hole. That put the pressure on me. If I got a par, my lead would be down to one stroke, and Dick would have all the momentum. So I stepped up and tapped a 25-foot putt right into the hole—to keep my lead intact. That was really the decisive point in the tournament. I'd resisted the opportunity to fall apart; I'd kept my mental attitude not only sharp but on what the course demanded—par—and I'd kept it all together well enough to fight off the challenge of an exceptional young golfer.

The next week involved the same effort in a different dimension.

We were at the Diplomat Presidential Country Club in Hollywood, Florida, for the Danny Thomas Diplomat Classic. The course is 6964 yards long, 309 yards longer than the one we'd just played at Hilton Head. But it was not nearly as complex. You really had to make birdies to stay in contention. And Gay Brewer was making more than any of the rest of us: He finished the third round with a total of 199, some seventeen under par. I was second, six strokes behind, at 205.

When we started the final round, it was clear that I was going to have to collect some birdies in a hurry if I was going to make up those six strokes on Brewer. The first hole was a good place to start; it was a par-5, on which a birdie is invited.

So what happened?

Gay got a birdie. I got a par. And I was seven behind with seventeen holes to go.

On the next two holes I missed putts that would have given me birdies. So I came up to the fourth hole, the only other par-5 on the front nine, thinking that this is the place to get that birdie—or an eagle, if possible.

On the second shot, I pressed to reach the green. But the shot was a little off line, and the ball dropped into a trap just off the green, buried under the lip.

I was annoyed with myself as I went up to the ball. I always get upset—more than a little disgusted—if I don't play a hole perfectly. It was one of those moments when the emotions can overcome the mind and completely destroy your game. And I knew it. So I just said to myself:

"All right now, Arnie, just take it easy. All you have to do is get the ball on the green. You still have three strokes to get your par. Don't lose it all here—there's still time down the road."

So I blasted out of the trap and got the par.

And the time came—just down the road.

On the next three holes, I made up five strokes. I went birdie-birdie-par while Gay collected three straight bogeys. By the ninth hole, I was three strokes behind—and gaining.

On the ninth, I almost made a hole in one. But I had to settle for another birdie. My spirits were rising and—though Gay wasn't giving up without a struggle—I knew I could go into the closing series of holes quite strong. At the same time, Gay's concentration eased off a little. "I birdied the first hole on the last round," he said later. "And then I relaxed. I felt that only a 66 or 65 could beat me. I figured I could shoot par or one over. I relaxed too much." I didn't. I got birdies on four of the last five holes to shoot the 65, to overtake Gay, and win the tournament.

Just by keeping control, by keeping my mental attitude well focused on the job at hand, I managed to pick up my second straight win.

Those two victories—at Hilton Head and the Danny Thomas Classic—meant $45,000 in winnings. And a certain sense of stature: No other pro on the tour won two major tournaments back-to-back that year.

At the heart of all this is the need to eliminate all distractions to concentration, emotional or otherwise. When I was a boy, I didn't like to be distracted by the gold-lettering of the name of the club manufacturer etched into the varnished head of my woods as I stood over the ball. So I'd sand it off and lacquer it over in order to get a blank wood. Today I manufacture a brand of golf clubs and I have come to accept the vast wisdom and higher insight of having the name on the clubhead. But I insist that the name be etched in with extreme precision so that it will point in the exact line of flight to the target area, so that I've managed to turn a distraction for me into an asset for others.

Similarly with the ball: When I stand over a putt, I don't like to see anything but those dimples staring back at me. Over the years, I've learned not to be so puritanical about this as to order my name off the golf balls. But I do set the ball up so that I don't see myself in it: I put it on the green so that the name faces the rear; then I jut pat it on its "Palmer."

Ultimately, though, the secret of concentration is the secret of self-discovery. You reach inside yourself to discover your personal resources and what it takes to match them to the challenge of the game. It involves a tautness of mind but not a tension of the body. It has various manifestations. One is the concentration on the shot at hand. The other is the heightened sense of presence and renewal that endures through an entire round or an entire tournament. There is something spiritual, almost spectral about the latter experience. You're involved in the action and vaguely aware of it, but your focus is not on the commotion but on the opportunity ahead. I'd liken it to a sense of reverie—not a dreamlike state but the somehow insulated state that a great musician achieves in a great performance. He's aware of where he is and what he's doing, but his mind is on the playing of his instrument with an internal sense of *rightness*—it is not merely mechanical, it is not only spiritual; it is something of both, on a different plane and a more remote one.

There is only one danger: You must be ready to meet the interruptions to concentration in a way that won't destroy you or your game. For you're not in a spectral world or a spiritual one on the pro tour; you're in a real one that demands real responses.

I remember back in 1962 at the Colonial Country Club near Fort Worth, I was in a playoff with Johnny Pott for the Colonial National Invitational. I was in a sand trap off the ninth green, and I had to get down from there in two shots in order to protect my lead. The crowd around the hole was immense, and just as I was over the ball, I heard a voice speaking quite clearly behind me.

I backed off from the ball, heard somebody shushing the speaker, and turned around to see who it was. It was a small boy, and he had such a chagrined look on his face—as if he'd just been told that he'd altered the course of Western civilization—that I began laughing. The crowd laughed and everybody relaxed, and I went back to the ball.

Now the little boy began crying because of the stern shushing he'd gotten from his mother. So I just backed off again and laughed a little over the boy's predicament—and that of his mother. Then I went back to the ball.

Now I heard the sound of a small boy strangling. So I backed off a third time and looked around. There was the little boy, smothering and turning red because his mother had clamped her hand over his mouth to keep him quiet.

He was more upset than I was. I just grinned up at his mother and said, "Hey—it's okay. Don't choke him. This isn't that important."

Then I went back, blasted out to the green, got down in two—and went on to win the playoff.

[*Mark McCormack, Palmer's attorney and long-time business manager, had observed ". . . I could not help but think that his finest hour came on the ninth green with that mother and child. I could not help thinking at the time what so many other pros would have done in the same situation. I can picture them staring up at the heavens as if to ask the Lord why oh why He had placed this mother and child on earth for the sole purpose of keeping him from winning a golf tournament."*]

Naturally there are extraordinary times and events when it is difficult to keep your cool—and your concentration. I've encountered a few of them—beyond the sense of "pressure" on important shots—and the only thing I can conclude is that I tend to be more bothered by internal furor than by an external furor.

Take the time my caddy lost my watch—a $1200 loss.

It happened in 1972 at the Danny Thomas Golf Classic—by this time in Memphis, Tennessee, where Danny's favorite charity, St. Jude Hospital, is located.

As I started my opening round, I took off my wrist watch. I don't like to play with a watch on; it's just one more distracting element when you're addressing the ball, it's just one more inhibiting element to the free play of your wrists and forearms.

Sometimes I give the watch to my caddy, sometimes I give it to Doc or Darrell to hold. [*Says Doc: The caddy can hold it on his wrist. And so can Darrell—he just puts it on above his own wrist watch. But I've got averaged-sized wrists and forearms and I can't keep it on my arm without it sliding around. So I usually tuck it in my pocket.*] On this occasion, it was my caddy who took possession of the watch. He is a New Yorker who makes it his profession to travel around to certain golf tournaments to caddy for me. (In some tournaments, he's not eligible; at the Masters, for example, the caddies come from the club's own caddy pool.) But in the tournaments where he is eligible my "traveling" caddy tries to make himself particularly valuable: He arrives early at tournaments where I can't play a practice round and goes around the course so he can draw a chart of it and mark off the distances from specific landmarks to the hole—or the front of the green. And sometimes he gets up at dawn to go out and scout the first nine holes of a course to see where the holes have been placed for that day's play.

At this tournament, the course was brand-new. I'd never seen it before, and I barely got to Memphis in time to play one round the day before the tournament opened. So it was a tournament in which the caddy was already proving his worth. The matter of handing him my watch before the first round of the tournament was strictly routine. I didn't even notice where he put it. But it was probably on his wrist. The truth is that it would be easy enough to slip off his wrist—the band wasn't an elastic one. And it didn't have a tongue-in-hole fastener. It had a jaw-type band, with the two leaves closing over the wrist —free of a fastener, held in place by the internal dynamics of the hinge pressure. It's not easy for the jaw band to open accidentally. But it's not impossible, either.

In any case, as I finished the third hole of the first round, the caddy came to tell me that he'd lost the watch—a $1200 watch, and he didn't quite notice what happened to it!

It wasn't on his wrist—that was for sure. We took a quick inventory of my pockets and his, of the pockets in the golf bag —any of the unlikely places that we *never* put the watch. Those were the only places we could check, but quickly. But if the watch-jaws had opened and fallen off the caddy's wrist—well, it was gone. We couldn't hold up the tournament while we went tramping back over the first three holes, looking for a lost watch.

So I did what anybody else would do in the same circumstances. I went up to the thirteenth hole—and triple-bogeyed it.

It wasn't hard: My tee shot went out of bounds, and things got worse after that.

But the significant thing is that it was all very fleeting—that it really didn't intrude permanently on my concentration. For it was an external matter, a material problem. And material problems just don't bother me as much as other problems— such as the interior ones of golf. There was a brief furor and a sense of aggravation—and then it was time to play golf again. The reason my tee shot went out of bounds was because I was trying to steer it away from a water hazard. This was the second time I'd seen the golf course—as I've said—and so I wasn't quite as precise as I should have been: I let the ball get away from me, out of bounds on the right. So I took a one-stroke penalty and went back to the tee to try again. The tee shot now was scored as my third shot, of course, and nettled as much by my loss of concentration as by the loss of the watch I struggled around that hole—and with my lapse in composure—for five strokes before concluding with a triple bogey seven. Fortunately, that momentary lapse did not bother me after that. In fact, I rallied on the last few holes of the round, went birdie-birdie on the seventeenth and eighteenth holes—sinking a 25-foot birdie putt on the eighteenth green—and came in with a 71. That was two strokes behind the leader. I would have led the tournament if I'd parred the thirteenth hole instead of going three over par. But there was no inclination in me to engage in weeping and gnashing of teeth. For however upsetting the incident of the lost watch was, it didn't reach so deeply into me that it marred my concentration permanently.

There was another cool-smashing episode in 1972, and this time it was internal. So it really bothered me. In fact, it cost me at least five strokes—and I don't know how much more because of a shattered concentration.

It took place in the second round of the Masters tournament. On the ninth hole of that round, I put my second shot into a depression caused by a chair by the green. The chair had been occupied by a tournament official until seconds earlier. In fact, he got up and scooted off when he saw my ball coming toward him. He hadn't been sitting there casually, at least from my point of view. That particular area was occupied by officials and tournament workers; it had metal tables and chairs and a copying machine, and so forth—it was a sort of official outpost set up, quite logically, at the end of the first nine holes. So I just figured that I'd get a free drop out of the depression, as is customary when a ball lands among the impedimenta of the tournament—the TV towers, officials' tables, and so forth. Usually, the PGA staff makes an inspection of the tournament grounds before play begins and marks, or ropes off, these areas so it is immediately clear that it's an area where all players will get relief, should their ball go in there. But the Masters is not run by the PGA; it's run by its own committee. And somehow, this area was not officially roped off as—in the lexicon of golf—"ground under repair." Nevertheless, I figured to get relief —a free drop out of the depression caused by the chair—because it *was* clear that the area was being used by officials and the tournament staff. But an official disagreed. We discussed the matter for a brief while and then agreed to refer it to the rules committee.

While the committee studied the matter, I continued to play the round. On that hole, I played out with two balls. With the ball already in play, I shot out of the depression in the grass and eventually wound up with a bogey 5. Then I played a "provisional" ball—which would count only if the ruling was in my favor—and I took a free lift out of the depression. With that ball, I shot a par 4 on the hole. So whatever the rules committee decided was going to count for one stroke.

By the time I was approaching the twelfth hole, I was one under par for the tournament, or even par—depending on which score you counted for the ninth hole. That was when I got the news: I lost the appeal, and the bogey 5 would stand as my score on the ninth hole. That burned me up—that *really* burned me up. And it was a bad time to lose my cool. For the twelfth hole at Augusta is regarded by many as one of the finest and most challenging par-3s in all of golf. You must be quite precise with your tee shot to land in a particular spot on the green. Or you've got to be able to chip or pitch up to a precise spot on the green if your tee shot misses. For there's a bunker in front of the green, and Rae's Creek runs in front of the bunker. There are, in addition, two bunkers and some long grass behind the green, with a wooded area rising up somewhat behind them. The hole is 155 yards long and the green is narrow from front to back, so it demands a rather delicate touch—not power, but the deft skill to get the ball up in the air and then drop it in a rather specific spot on the green. A few yards one way or the other and you're in trouble.

I was in trouble right from the tee. For I lofted an eight-iron off the tee into the bunker in front of the green. Then I played Ping-Pong with myself back and forth across the green. I blasted out of the bunker in front of the green and hit the ball into the high grass in back of the green. Then I chipped out of the grass in back of the green into the same bunker in front of it. Finally I blasted out of there—and not only managed to stay on the green, but dropped the ball three feet from the hole. Then I missed the putt. The result: I took a triple-bogey 6.

Now I was madder than ever. It wasn't just that shattering triple-bogey but also the attitude of one of the officials in reporting the judgment. He told the press that "we'd be forever marking courses if this would be considered ground under repair." That sounded a little as if I were copping a special plea. But that wasn't the case. In *most* tournaments, areas occupied by officials and the paraphernalia of the tournament work are marked off as "ground under repair," and all players are given relief. That this particular area hadn't been marked off was, I'm sure, merely an oversight. But I felt that—in fairness to all the players—it was an oversight that could be corrected. It wasn't, and—well, I've got a stubborn streak in me, and when something happens that seems to go against all obvious logic, not just against my good fortune, I tend to escalate ever so slightly. . . .

As you can guess, I had not quite recovered that sublime sense of concentration that is vital for success in golf. In fact, I was still so outraged over what had happened—the rules interpretation and then the triple bogey—that I went up to the thirteenth hole . . . and bogeyed it. Now I'd gone five strokes over par on just three holes—the ninth, twelfth, and thirteenth. The irony was that I'd been playing acceptable golf, except for those holes. And maybe I might have even done better than par on one or two of them—if it hadn't been for that unnerving episode at the ninth hole. But one thing about the thirteenth at Augusta: It's a long-enough hole—a par-5 dogleg left that runs 475 yards—that I was able to walk off, or stalk off, some of my anger. I got control of myself and appreciated an enduring truism: In golf, the only person that anger hurts is yourself. For in my own period of anger, I'd dropped from third place into a tie for twelfth.

So now I had to begin making up ground. I got hold of myself, focused down sharply to the needs of the moment, and began playing the kind of golf that I know I can play: I birdied the fourteenth hole, and on the fifteenth—where Jack Nicklaus was to get a double bogey that day—I got an eagle. But Jack was not about to lie down and get beaten. He just went on playing his game, and let me know the terrible truth: that I'd given away too many strokes in my anger. Jack was two strokes up on me when the round began, and he was six strokes up on me when the round ended. Except for those bad holes I might have narrowed the margin instead of seeing it expand—if only I'd been able to maintain my cool, in the face of severe nervous tension, on a few critical holes.

*

Given enough time on the pro tour, we all build various defenses against nervous tension and its threat to concentration. Some of them are reflexive, done without thinking. Like my hitching up my pants.

At the Florida Citrus Open in the spring of 1971, a high school junior named Mike Bradley followed me around and kept count of the number of times I hitched my pants. He said the grand total for eighteen holes was 345 hitches. He counted 50 hitches on the first hole. I got a birdie. He counted 24 on the second one. I got another birdie. He thought that I had two or three different hitches—sometimes just one side of my waist, sometimes both sides, and sometimes both sides and the front. (He called that the "triple hitch.") Mike made a correlation between hitching and shooting. "I'm not sure," he said, "but it seemed to me maybe he hitched most whenever he had a tough putt to make or some hard shot. The easier the shot, the less he hitched."

My belief is that there is something in that—that hitching my pants is a nervous release, a way of preventing tension from growing. On the other hand, there *is* a reason that my nervous release involves hitching. I've always had narrow hips. They're not much thicker than my waist. When I was a boy, my pants always kept sliding down and my mother was always saying, "Arnold, pull up your pants and tuck your shirt in." So I started hitching them up then—and I've never stopped.

There are times when tension can build slowly in a golfer and when he must give considerable thought to offsetting it. Consider what happens in waiting through the night and morning to tee off before an important round. It's not only occasional golfers—those pursuing honors at their local club—who experience this problem: I've known at least one accomplished pro who takes sleeping pills at night in order to get his rest and then, if he wakes up very early before tee-off time, he'll take another half pill to get more rest before going out to compete. He's like most people: He doesn't want to be tossing and turning all night—and letting tension build within himself—then wait around all morning in a tension-bound situation for his tee-off time to come. On the other hand, I know some superbly controlled pros who can regulate their lives so completely that they defeat tension by their very regularity. Charles Coody, the 1971 Masters champion, has long been renowned on the pro tour as a man who can go to bed exactly twelve hours before his tee-off time—he falls asleep at midnight if he's got a noon tee-off—and have no trouble coming up to his peak of concentration at just the right moment.

My own problem is how to control tension through the morning hours. Like most people who "charge" through life, I tend to wake up early in the morning, ready to go. I don't lie around in bed, groaning at the fate of an early call. I enjoy the mornings. I always have.

At one time, I could stay up half the night and still get up early in the morning and it didn't bother me. At least not much and not often. But now I find that I need eight hours' sleep to feel exactly right in the morning. And there've been many nights when I'll doze off in front of the television set at nine-thirty or so and Winnie'll have to come along and wake me to get me to come to bed.

All this is related to the circadian rhythm of the body [*from* circa dies, *Latin for "about the day" or—more freely—"around the day"*]. There are many, many golfers who have the same problem; on the whole, it serves them well if they have to get up at six o'clock in the morning to get a tee-off time at a public course near their home. Fortunately, I'm not entirely a slave to all this. There've been times when the tournament was in Las Vegas that I was known to forget the clock—they don't *have* many there—and stay up until well past midnight. And there've been other times when—to make a business appointment —I'd fly all night to get there (although my pilot, Darrell Brown, might be at the controls most of the time). And my wake-up mechanism isn't so pronounced that I can't drowse in bed until nine o'clock in the morning if I have to, to get my eight hours of sleep. But that morning in 1969 when I had to get up at 4:50 A.M. to go to qualify for the U. S. Open wasn't as difficult for me as you might think. In fact, I was tossing and turning for an hour before that, so I was ready to get up and start puttering around the house, working myself into the proper mental attitude to do the best I could that day. Besides, it was a morning in spring, and the velvet night was lovely in the pre-dawn hours in our little corner of Pennsylvania.

The trouble in all this is that a professional golfer doesn't get to choose his tee-off times. He can't go out and start playing at seven or eight o'clock in the morning just because he feels good and is going to play his best game at that hour. He's assigned a time to tee off. In the last two rounds—on weekends —the leaders usually start late and finish late. That's because the crowds will, hopefully, be thickest at that hour and, on weekends, television will come on late in the afternoon on many of those weekends and relay to millions of homes what the leaders are doing on the last few holes of the course.

The corollary is that players who are trailing the field usually start early and finish early on those days. On the last day of the tournament, they rarely even wait for the final results; they just go out to the parking lot where the wife and family are waiting in the car or station wagon—the wife has usually packed and checked out of the motel while the pro was playing his final round—and get in the car and start driving to where the next tournament or pro-am will take place. They know that the tour officials will pick up the check for any winnings they have and bring it along to give to the player when the next tournament starts.

In general, though, there is an irony to being a "morning person" on the pro golf tour. The pro who's a morning person finds—because of his success—that he's usually playing the most important of his rounds at precisely that time of day when his nervous and physical system is at the very bottom of his daily cycle. He may not notice it physically too much: The physical activity disguises the fact that he's at a low ebb. But he will find that it is considerably more difficult to concentrate on his shots and on his over-all game. *Any* labor that demands concentration suffers when the individual is weary or distracted. He'll also find that he does not have the serenity and certitude that he had in the morning. His nervous system is not giving him the same kind of support; he becomes edgier and terribly impatient, and he's more likely to hit just any kind of shot, if only to get along with the affair. That means he is not examining or thinking his shot through carefully—and that he is much more likely to fudge on the realities and hit his way into incredible difficulties. Thus the self-discipline on a morning person must—at such times—be more profoundly effective.

There is another problem with such a circumstance: It is that the golfer must wait . . . and wait . . . and wait . . . just to get started on his crucial round of golf. That can be a difficult problem under any circumstances. It becomes a real test of self when the golfer is in that special state of "aware reverie" when he is functioning in the real world but has part of his mind always on the success of his game.

There are times when the leaders might not tee off until one or two o'clock in the afternoon and might not start their final nine holes until after four or five o'clock.

How do I handle the tension buildup in all this?

On some mornings, when I have a late tee-off time, I'll get

up and start reading business reports, either for the business world at large or for the various parts of Arnold Palmer Enterprises—the golf equipment plants, the driving ranges, the string of franchised laundries, the "academies" where a boy can go to spend a few weeks in the summer to learn about golf as I learned about it. But there has to be a limit on this. You can't maintain a peak attitude toward competitive golf when you're consumed in business details. The deep test of the pre-tee-off or noncompetitive hours is in how I can bring myself around to concentrating on the game without building tensions about the round I'm about to play.

Usually I go out to the club fairly early, not just to practice but to use it as a sort of decompression chamber between the outside world of business and the interior world of golf. I'll head for the locker room or—if I need more solitude—I'll head for the workshop of the local pro.

The locker room is a place apart. The press is allowed in— I enjoy sitting down and shooting the bull with them—but the club members themselves usually are not. (One notable exception: at Augusta during the Masters.) In many a clubhouse, there'll be a table with fruit juice and Danish set up in the locker room with white-jacketed waiters to help serve them. (In the late afternoon, the helpings change to beer and cold cuts. Most of the pros come in famished after a round. They head for the food even before they stop to have a beer or a cold drink.) The action is desultory in the locker room in the morning. Some pros come in and open their lockers tentatively; they keep their most treasured possessions in there. Usually their "hot" putters. (When you've got a "hot" club, you can't help worrying about loss or theft. From time to time, a pro will pick up a club to practice a few "take-aways"—swinging back from an imaginary ball on the carpet—in the rows between the lockers. Sometimes the mail comes in while you're there, and you can while away the time reading it. Most of the time, a few newsmen looking for leads for the afternoon papers, or columns for the next day, drift in and out. Just talking with them helps me focus on golf and on the round at hand. And yet talking with them arouses no tensions, at least in me. They're good friends and old friends, and what they contribute to golf goes far beyond what they print in their papers.

But there are other mornings when the inner imperatives draw me to the pro's workshop instead. It's lonelier but, in its way, it's more gratifying. I feel completely at home in the pro's workshop—it's my turf, so to speak. For I didn't just grow up on a golf course learning how to hit a golf ball. I grew up under a golf pro who taught me every detail about how to work in the shop, building and rebuilding clubs, adding weights under the plate in the soles, changing the shafts and grips, finishing and refinishing the ultimate product. It is a labor of love that persists today. [*Mark McCormack has said of Palmer's tinkering, "If a wizard gave Arnold a divining rod that would point to gold in the ground, Arnold would take it home and start whittling on it to see if he might get it to point to diamonds, too."*]

So I find both refuge and renewal when I enter the workshop of a golf club where the pro tour is visiting. Working there has two benefits. One is that I'm working with my hands, changing grips, filing the clubheads, straightening the face of the clubhead a little, perhaps spreading a little lacquer or clear spray on the club to help preserve it in the rain. The second benefit is that my mind is thrown deeply into the flavor of golf—not necessarily the competitive trials of the day, but simply *golf*. And I'm thinking of it in terms that I love—the deep, enduring, almost visceral terms that rose out of my childhood, the shaping of clubs as much as the shaping of the game . . . the shaping of the clubs to an ideal that I can see and feel—it's a tactile involvement that provides a mental involvement. And a nervous release.

Usually I've got an extra set of clubs along on the pro tour —something I can work on in my spare time. It's part of the inner experience that is beyond explanation: I'm improving me as I improve them. But from time to time, I'll work on a club for another pro. He may come to tell me that a particular club just doesn't feel quite right and that he needs the grip changed or reshaped or the head made lighter. And sometimes another pro will let me borrow a club to see what I can do to make it just a little bit better. Years ago, before I had my own golf company, I couldn't get the exact driver I wanted from the sporting goods manufacturer that provided clubs for me. So one day in 1960, I borrowed a driver from Ben Hogan and, as it turned out, Ben's driver was just exactly what I wanted. With just a small change here and there. I built up the grip a bit and made it slightly shorter. I put just a very little more loft on the face of the clubhead. I built maybe just a little bit of a gooseneck into it. And I sanded and refinished it, and the next time Ben saw his driver in my bag, he gave me a look of mixed chagrin and horror.

"What did you do to my driver?" he asked in astonishment. "You took a perfectly good club and ruined it!"

Not really. For I went out and won many a tournament with Ben's old driver. Even though it looked to him like a misspent retread.

Not all of my work in the pro's own shop is idle work. Many times I'm laboring over a club I've played with and that somehow needs changing. You know the feeling—maybe I've had a poor round and I think, "Well, *some*thing needs to be changed." It can't be the swing; you can't lose confidence in your swing in the middle of a tournament. So it must be the clubs. I missed a couple of short approach shots, so I take out the short irons and go to the shop and begin working with them there—maybe straightening out the gooseneck a little, raising the angle of the loft a little, or maybe giving the clubhead a little more weight in one spot or another.

In fact, I carry around a special kit of tools so that I can work on clubs during the tour. The kit has a sharp knife, a bending iron, black tape for grips, a couple of files, some lead tape for minute changes in weight, some clear spray, and maybe a few special tools I got up for myself. Then when I go out to the practice range, I can do a little more with the club, adding some lead tape here, taking off some there, to change the weight ever so slightly. It provides a nice transition into the game, working on clubs in the workshop, then going out to work on them during a practice session, then simply practicing with the clubs to sharpen my game—to improve what I'd done poorly the day before or to explore how sharp my "draw" or "fade" might be that day. Mostly I'm working on basic shots and fundamental aspects of my game—rhythm, stance, alignment, meeting the ball correctly. At most, a bag of balls a day —perhaps fifty swings—then some more time in chipping and putting. By lunch I'm ready to go play the game—without having gotten all edgy and tight, simply waiting for my tee-off time to come.

From all this, you can see that golf is not merely my job. It's also the way I get released from tension—it's my substitute for fishing or hunting or driving sports cars. For many exceptional golfers, it is only an aside to their lives. Jack Nicklaus, I would guess, would just as soon spend his days fishing. Gary Player would just as soon be back on his ranch in South Africa—he's a farmer at heart. For them, golf is a way of making a living. For me, golf is a way of being alive.

In talking about the physical aspects of dealing with yourself, it's hard to avoid the obvious. Of *course* you're going to enjoy the game more if you're healthy. The deeper question is, "How does anything but perfect health affect your game?" For there are relatively few pro golfers who aren't plagued with a health problem at some time or other.

We've long had golfers on the pro tour who were severely handicapped physically and who were still able to carve out a significant place for themselves in golf. Ed Furgol in the past and Larry Hinson in the present both played with withered arms. Both not only played fine golf but found subtle assets in their handicaps. Larry, for example, cannot really duck hook a ball because of his poor arm. And Pete Brown has done even more: He's found a way to compensate for a severely restricting—if largely unknown—handicap and still do well on the tour. Back in 1956, just before he was going to compete in the Negro National Open, he was stricken with a painful though non-paralytic form of polio. He lost control of all his senses and for a year he was confined to recovery, he had to learn to talk again and to walk again—just as my own father had to do when coming back from the same form of illness a generation earlier. The hardest part, as I understand it, was not just to learn to use his hands again but to use them with the particular skills and strength needed in golf.

"Some friends had been visiting me for months and they brought me a golf club," Pete has said about those times. "I'd been trying to grip it, even while I was still in bed. Finally, when I could walk well enough to get outside, I tried to see if I could swing the club. But I had no coordination at all. I couldn't even come close to hitting the ball."

It was a long, hard struggle for him, but he finally managed to put it all together. He not only got to the point where he could hit the ball, but he could hit it well and sharply. But he never hit it in quite the old way: "Because my back isn't as strong as it was before I became sick, I've had to flatten out my swing. It's not the kind of swing that I like, but I have to put up with it." He's shown what he can do by way of compensation: By the start of the 1972 season, he'd won more than $173,000 in tour prizes.

There are a good many other less grave afflictions that can profoundly affect any golfer's game—how much he enjoys it, whether he can apply himself to so demanding a discipline as boldness, whether he can play the game at all. Gene Littler is so deeply bothered by an allergy to pollen that he tends to get sick when he goes out on the course at a certain time of the year. (And now he's showing us all how to rebound from the menace of a more malignant disease.) Billy Casper has said that he's so allergic to the pesticides used in Florida—among a great many other allergies—that he generally avoids playing the tour when it hits that state. My problems along these lines have been less celebrated and less inhibiting: I'm somewhat susceptible to colds and inflammation of the ears, and I have a generally bothersome sinus condition—sometimes when you see pictures of me with my face all screwed up, it's not just my reaction to the shot I've made; it's my sniffles.

Now I've got another problem that is a little more noticeable: I've gotten near-sighted.

In itself, that's unusual. Most people tend to get far-sighted in their middle years. The reason is that all their muscles—including those in their eyes—begin getting a little more taut, a little tighter. The shortening of these muscles is gradual—it's something that occasional golfers notice when they find it takes a little longer to warm up and get the arm, shoulder, and torso muscles loose before playing a round. Most people notice the muscle-tightening in the eyes because it causes them to get far-sighted: They find that print or maps or other details held close to their eyes—scorecards, for example—look a little fuzzy. So they compensate by holding the print at arm's length in order to bring it into focus. Eventually they find that their arms just aren't long enough, and they know it's time to get glasses to compensate for far-sightedness.

My problem was a little different—and more complex. For I began to get near-sighted, not far-sighted. I just don't know why, and neither does my doctor. The insidious thing about being near-sighted—as opposed to being far-sighted—is that you don't know it's happening. Things fuzz out at a distance, but you think they're fuzzy for everybody—that *that* is just the way things look. At least in becoming far-sighted, you do notice that you just can't read a newspaper comfortably any more, so you do something about your eyes. That gives the far-

sighted person an alert that the near-sighted person doesn't experience.

The reason I was alerted to myopia—near-sightedness—was
because I play golf.

Bit by bit, I became aware that I couldn't quite see where
the ball was dropping on some of the long tee shots. There was
a time, I remembered, when I not only could see the ball all the
way but count the dimples on it when it landed. But now the
ball was just fading into the fuzzy distance. At about the same
time, I discovered that I couldn't always see and measure from
the fairway just where the pin was placed on a particular green.
That can be quite crucial: If you guess at the distance and miss
by ten yards or so, you're going to find yourself out of the
running in a lot of tournaments—by the end of the first or second round.

These were small, gradual, but very perceptible changes. But
because I was aware that there were changes—because I had
something in my past experience to measure against the present
—I decided to have my eyes checked. The doctor found that I
was 20/50 in my left eye. That meant that my left eye could
see at 20 feet what the normal eye sees at 50 feet. ("Normal"
vision is 20/20. The eye can see at 20 feet what is specifically designed to be seen at 20 feet—such as a particular line on an op-
tometrist's chart.) My right eye isn't quite so bad: It is 20/30.

This isn't a very serious myopia. I know people whose eyes
run 20/600 and 20/800 and they function at life—though not
in golf—as well as anybody else. But the doctor said he could
bring my eyes back to normal and then some. In fact, he
worked out a prescription that would correct my eyes to 20/15
—I'd be able to see at 20 feet what the normal eye could only
see at 15 feet.

He did exactly that, and we had a set of soft contact lenses
made up.

Late in March 1972, I began wearing them. The first tournament I wore them in was the Greater Greensboro Open, and

the change seemed dramatic: I grabbed a lead that I held up until the last three holes. In a sense it was significant, for one day of the tournament was rained out and we wound up playing thirty-six holes on the final day. That's not really a chore, but it was perhaps a little wearing on the eyes—I hadn't anticipated wearing the contact lenses for that long at one time so soon after starting to use them. As it happened, I took a triple bogey on the par-3 sixteenth hole of the final round. It was on my own "genius"—I can't really blame it on the contact lenses. Unfortunately, that triple bogey cost me victory in the tournament.

After that I wore them consistently up until the Tournament of Champions in Rancho LaCosta, California. In the first round of that tournament, my eyes felt irritated; maybe it was the wind or maybe a small grain of dust or sand got into them. In any case, I took out the contacts after the fifteenth hole and switched to regular spectacles. I had a miserable finish.

Well, you know the psychology: The next day I played without any visual help—and I played myself right out of contention. The next two days, I figured I had nothing to lose, so I went back to the contact lenses and played somewhat better.

That's the way it went. At the Byron Nelson Golf Classic I wore the contacts and got together a charge on the last day that finally petered out. At the Danny Thomas Golf Classic in Memphis—the place where my caddy lost my watch—I wore regular glasses and played acceptably if not triumphantly. But I still hadn't found my way: I played my own course at Latrobe without wearing glasses at all—and shot a 69. (But then, of course, there are some people—friends, colleagues, and critics —who say I could play that course blindfolded and shoot a 69. Which is, perhaps, what I was doing.)

That reminds me of a story that's so much to the point that I'd hate to suggest we ruin it by checking.

It seems that a number of blind golfers take part every year in a golf outing at Northmoor Country Club in Highland

Park, Illinois, near Chicago. One of the golfers became so proficient at the game—played with balls emitting a radio beep and with friends who'll set them up in an address position—that he managed to break 90 rather regularly.

So his friends decided to surprise him one day with a visit from you-know-who—Arnold Palmer.

"Palmer," says this extroverted golfer—or so the story goes—"you step on a golf course with me and I'll take you apart. I'll make mincemeat of you. You name it—I'll play you a thousand dollars a hole."

Well, I wasn't about to play him for money—but there was that nagging little challenge in there.

"Look," I said, "you're a credit to golf and I admire you. But you know I just can't ignore a challenge. What do you say we skip the money and just go around to see what happens. When do you want to make it?"

The blind golfer just blossomed triumphantly and beamed at me.

"Just any night you name!" he said.

Well, the way things were going with my eyes and glasses and contact lenses in 1972, maybe we could have made a contest of it. For halfway through the tournament tour, I didn't know which way things were going to turn—whether I'd play with specs or contacts or take my chance with neither. All I knew was that this was going to be a period of testing and experimenting. But that, in a sense, is what life is all about: It's a time of testing and self-analysis and constant effort to find something geniune—and worthy—in oneself. The most useful tests are not always in doing easily the things that ones does well. They are in doing what *needs* to be done—even if that interferes with what you can do easily.

The most obvious everyday example—for most of us—is another health problem: quitting smoking. It *needs* to be done. It not only endangers your health but affects the way you think about yourself. Yet the denial of smoking interferes with almost every kind of life on every kind of level. The way it interfered with my life—and what I wanted to do with life—got almost as much attention as the way I played golf.

In my early years in professional golf, I smoked regularly and—some might say—heavily. I was a two-pack-a-day man. Not many of the cigarettes would get burned to the cork: I'd light up, examine a shot, bite the cigarette for a little while, then flick it away and hit the shot. At the next hole, I'd do it again. Sure, there were times when I'd hand the burning cigarette to a friend or my wife in the gallery while I made a shot, but there weren't many times that a cigarette lasted through two holes.

The smoke and the flicked cigarette became sort of a symbol with me—and with one of my sponsors. For a cigarette company paid generously through the early 1960s to get my name to sponsor its brand. But there was something about it that bothered me—the cigarettes didn't taste good to me, food didn't taste good to me, and I was thinking, subliminally, that maybe the weed had a permanent grip on me.

[*Says Mark McCormack: "Knowing Arnold, I am sure that one thing which seriously troubled him about his smoking was the thought that he could not control it. His personality does not take kindly to the notion that he, Arnold Palmer, cannot govern something that he himself is doing. He shows this on the golf course all the time. If a shot can be hit, then Arnold is going to try it."*]

But as I've said, change comes slowly with me. I was waiting for the challenge. In the Bing Crosby tournament in January 1964, I was feeling miserable. The tournament is frequently played in wet, gusty, even storm-laden weather. And because it's a rather large field pro-am, along with the regular pro tournament, the pace of play is often slower than in other tour events, and you sometimes find yourself standing out in bad weather for five or six or more hours. In any case, I found myself in this tournament with my sinus flaring up dramatically. I shot a 76 in the third round and, for the first time in years, I missed the cut. I lingered long enough to finish playing in the pro-am. Then I flew up to San Francisco to have my sinuses drained.

At the hospital, I encountered a doctor whom I met again that evening while at dinner at a friend's home. During the course of the evening, he lit up a cigar, blew out vast clouds of blue smoke, leaned back professionally, and opined: "With a sinus condition as bad as yours, Arnold, I'd give up smoking."

It was a little startling. No doctor had ever suggested before that I give up smoking, particularly a doctor who issued this opinion from behind a cloud of tobacco smoke so dense that I could barely see him.

"I'll stop if you will," I shot back. He thought it over and allowed as how it was a tolerable idea. (The first surgeon general's report linking smoking and cancer had recently been published.) So we made a wager. I said that if I smoked again, I'd fly everybody in the room to the Masters tournament that spring. "What am I supposed to do—give you a free frontal lobotomy?" asked the doctor. No—but we did settle on a little side money on the effort.

So I had the challenge: I took a long, last drag and put out my cigarette. "That's it," I said. "That's the end."

"Well, if you're going to stop, I'm going to stop, too," said Winnie. "I won't smoke again until you do."

"Then you won't ever smoke again," I said—perhaps a little more confidently than I should have.

"What about in the mornings?" asked Winnie. And: "What about after a good dinner when a cigarette tastes so good?" And: "What about at parties when the room is filled with cigarette smoke?"

I had brash, breezy answers for all of them until she asked one final question:

"What about the short putts?"

Wives.

Wives and short putts.

In the next incarnation, there'll have to be a few things eliminated to guarantee paradise: smart wives or short putts.

(The way things have been going lately, I hope it's the short putts.)

The next few weeks were testy ones. I was a little jumpy, particularly over the putts. But I managed to keep myself under control; I even felt pretty good about myself—dropping the habit of the weed. By the time of the Masters, I was in great interior shape. That may be why I went on to play so satisfying a tournament—and why I won it by six strokes. It was my fourth Masters win, and no golfer had ever won so many.

But little things were happening. I was eating more than ever. Not snacking—I never have been much of a snacker. But I'd order a big dinner, and eat it all; not push the plate away and light up a cigarette and flick ashes all over the cold food as I used to do. Then at breakfast, I'd have another big meal. After a while, I found I'd put on fifteen or twenty pounds—I was up around, or over, 195.

Nevertheless, halfway through the U. S. Open in 1964, I was in great position, only a stroke behind the leader. And I was in great shape—my confidence was high, I'd managed to scramble out of trouble several times, and I was beginning to feel, and look, like a man who found it no more trouble to play the U. S. Open than to wander around the back yard looking for the crab grass. That Friday night, I had dinner with Mark McCormack, and we were both so confident of what I'd do in the final thirty-six holes the next day that we began planning various business activities, halfway based on the contingency of my win.

The next day was a torment. The temperature was around a hundred degrees and the humidity was about as bad. Just surviving was—as it turned out—going to be a triumph. For the envelope of smothering heat was to be enormously wearing on the stamina demanded for thirty-six holes.

For my part, I started out high and happy. I'd always been a good hot-weather player. The hotter the better—the heat helps the sinuses. My optimism was high and so was my level of aggressiveness. I began going for the pin right from the start. But there was one small trouble: I was missing the pin—and the green. I missed the green on the first five holes—at least in "regulation" shots—and when I finally hit it on the sixth hole, I three-putted. Suddenly I found myself four strokes behind Tommy Jacobs, the leader. I didn't get a birdie all morning— through the first eighteen holes of the final day—and my putting was miserable. I had a good start on the second eighteen that day (I got a rather dramatic birdie on the first hole), and there was a feeling that maybe the charge was coming on again. It wasn't. I faded a little; in fact, I wound up those same four strokes behind Tommy Jacobs. But Tommy had faded too. We were both passed by Ken Venturi, who was himself one of the walking wounded. Over the years his once-bright promise had faded under a series of ailments, from a back injury to troubles with the muscles in his hands to walking pneumonia. In fact, on this day, a doctor walked around the last eighteen holes with Ken, so drawn and delicate was his condition in the heavy, humid weather. Ken wavered and struggled and he walked the last few holes with the tortured stiff-legged gait of an old man determined to get home any old way he could. He got home—in the best way possible. He had the U. S. Open title with him.

It was a tribute to Venturi's regimen and his conquest over bad health. But it wasn't much help to my regimen and my conquest over the weed. For three tournaments later I played those four highly successful rounds in the PGA, but Bobby

Nichols, scrambling all the way, still won the tournament. You begin to think, "Now *what* is going on here?" And you begin to look for all kinds of causes outside yourself—like the distraction of thinking, "I do *not* need a cigarette"—and if you ever want a rationale for going back to the weed, it's a series of experiences like that.

A month or so later, Mark McCormack asked me—while we were filming some TV golf matches—whether I thought I should reconsider my policy of not smoking. "No, sir," I snapped. No weed was going to get the better of me. I was playing well, and I was never quite out of a contending position: I'd finished second or third in seven straight tournaments. But that wasn't first, and a few putts here, a little more concentration there might have meant the difference between seven straight titles and a string of so-so also-rans. And maybe a few puffs on a cigarette might have helped my concentration.

Early in the autumn, I flew to England to take part in a tournament sponsored by an English cigarette maker. (In America, I'd ended the relationship with my U. S. cigarette sponsor, and I refused to take part in a television series sponsored by another cigarette maker.) The sponsors were warm and generous hosts. They'd provided two suites—one for Mark, the other for Winnie and myself—in the Carlton Towers in Knightsbridge, and they'd been thoughtful enough to provide everything in the suites from fresh fruit to several cartons of their product.

It was Mark who started it all. We were having a casual evening on the night we checked in—Mark and Winnie and I, along with the tournament chairman (who was, not too surprisingly, director of advertising for the cigarette company), and the public relations man for the sponsor, and one or two others.

Mark—who'd never smoked before in his life—suddenly said, "I think I'll have a cigarette." Here's a man who's the ultimate business manager: He'll gladly lay down his life—or at least have a cigarette, which may mean the same thing—for his clients. "Everybody else in the world is stopping, so I think I'll start smoking," he said. The cigarette people thought that was a good idea, seeing as they had a factory load of cigarettes just down the road a piece, and every little bit helps.

There's sort of an electric quality to an approaching Fall from Virtue—to seeing Original Sin about to be played out before your eyes. Winnie and I sat around and discussed cheerfully the substance of Mark's soul and the disposal of his remains. Then somebody said, in deference to our hosts, "Arnold would never have quit smoking in the first place if he'd ever had a good cigarette to smoke." And suddenly I was talking smoking, which is the next step short of smoking.

For a while, I lectured the gathering sternly on my long and proud history as a smoker—on my high taste, deep discernment, and indefatigable devotion to the weed. Our cigarette company hosts sat around and nodded sympathetically and smiled knowingly. And suddenly I heard myself saying:

"Well, maybe just one cigarette wouldn't hurt, seeing as how this is a special occasion and all." And besides, I'd never smoked one of their products.

Well, Winnie gave me a look—one of *those* looks.

And a long, uncomfortable silence followed.

Finally Mark said, "Well, *I'll* go ahead and have one anyway, in honor of the tournament." He didn't even know how to hold a cigarette, or light one, much less how to inhale one. Beside him, one of our English hosts reached out to help him, and he returned the favor by burning a hole in the man's sock.

But, you know—you just can't sit there and let your friend suffer alone. So I finally said, "Okay, if Mark can do it, I can do it."

Everyone laughed and relaxed and congratulated me on my wisdom and selflessness and my utter generosity. Everyone except Winnie.

I had the cigarette. But of course I wasn't hooked.

"It doesn't affect me at all," I said loftily as I sat back contentedly and let the smoke play awhile in my nostrils. "If you'll pardon me for saying it," I said to our hosts, "it just doesn't even taste good to me."

And just to make sure I was right, I had another one before going to bed that night.

By the time we left England, I'd entered the rule-setting phase of not smoking—a phase familiar to millions of failed purists. My basic rule was that I would not smoke while I was in the United States, and if you think that was a harsh discipline, you have to consider the agreeable cunning of the rule: I knew I'd be going back home only briefly before heading off to a tournament in Australia and then through much of the Far East that would take several weeks.

But I did not know how things would go in those weeks.

Gary Player joined us on the tour and and it turned out that his role—informally—was as a nagging conscience. For Gary is one of the great all-time authorities on good health and bad habits. He's also a man of rich and varied humor, and on that trip he directed all of it at me and my "habit." I looked at my smoking as only an occasional fall from grace—two cigarettes after each meal, perhaps one or two in between—but Gary sort of made me feel like a laboratory specimen of noxious habits. It was all on a pretty light level. But when I got home I resolved—again—never to have another cigarette.

At least in public.

Those first eight or nine months in 1965 were as bad as I've ever had. My morale collapsed. My boldness had disappeared. Golf was becoming a labor, not a love. I finished sixty-third in one tournament, twenty-ninth in another, forty-fourth in another. And I missed the cut in the U. S. Open. (I picked up $200 in prize money for the 1965 U. S. Open—$20 more than I won in the 1955 Open.) I won only one tournament—the Tournament of Champions at Las Vegas—and my scoring average soared to 71.49 strokes a round, the highest it had ever been since I'd joined the pro tour ten years earlier. That was the time when I began wondering whether I should give up the Palmer method altogether and adopt the more cautious play-it-safe style of the conservative in golf. It was a time when I was tempted to give up being *me*.

In August 1965 I had a cigarette in public—in a tournament for the first time in eighteen months. Things immediately turned for the better. I finished second in two tournaments in a row and won $29,000 in prize money in those two weeks, or almost as much as I'd won all year up to then—on the PGA tour. So I was hooked again. I went back to smoking regularly (and I went back to the Palmer method, with its gratifying results the next year—see Chapter II).

But I never could get used to the idea that the weed had me conquered. So I'd give it up for a while, then go back—just testing myself, so to speak. Then finally on New Year's Eve before 1971, I made a new resolve: no more smoking at all. Ever. Publicly or privately.

This time the results were far happier. In that year I won four tournaments, I won over $200,000 in prize money for the first time, and I finished first in the rankings of *Golf Digest* in their "performance averages" with a .737. (Lee Trevino finished second with .641, and Billy Casper finished fifth with .529. Jack Nicklaus was not eligible because he didn't compete in enough tournaments.) There were times when I felt that my performance was a little uneven, but at last I'd proven one more thing to—and about—myself: that I could play successfully using the Palmer method—while staying off cigarettes.

By early 1972, I'd found only one lingering problem: I was gaining weight again. So that winter I began swimming every morning that I was home—fifty laps a day in the enclosed pool outside our kitchen window. At six-thirty in the morning—and Winnie never missed a workout: She went swimming in those predawn hours with me every day. (I've never been much for lifting weights—I don't even have them in the exercise room next to my office. They build bunching muscles, which—I feel —tend to bind your swing in golf.) The trouble with the early-morning exercise was that it would stimulate my appetite, and I'd go back to having a big breakfast. But you can't stay off of everything all the time, and if it's a choice between eating and smoking, I'll take the risks of eating over the slavishness of smoking.

In all this, we've been talking about the enduring problems of health—the permanent handicaps of the permanent hazards of everything from allergies to addictions (to tobacco). But there are other kinds of health hazards that can profoundly affect your game—the kind that come and go away—and I've had most of them, winning with a few, losing with a few.

Back in 1962, I was plagued by sharp and persistent pains in my back as I was playing in the British Open at Troon. It got so bad that I knew I'd experience pain every time I swung the club. It *had* to attack my concentration. Yet I *had* to go on to play the tournament: I was the defending champion, and I had that irrepressible drive of youth—and success. So not only did I determine to stay in the tournament, but I determined to do well. The result was that I shot four of the finest rounds I've ever shot in my life—and won the tournament by six strokes.

Or take another example. In the 1964 Masters, I was bothered by a skin infection on my face. It was not a terribly serious matter, as long as the infection didn't deepen or spread. But the way in which I protected my face caused some comment: I wore a cap to protect the skin from the hot Georgia sunshine, and this caused comment on the part of everybody from my wife to the "army." Neither wanted me to keep the cap on. My wife just doesn't like me in hats or caps. She went out and found a tennis visor for me; it protected my face from the sun without covering my head. As it turned out, neither the infection nor the visor bothered me: I led the tournament from start to finish and won it by six strokes over second-place Dave Marr.

Now, lest you think that all it takes for success is a really bad threat to good health, let me tell you of the other kind of cases. In the 1963 Colonial Invitational at Forth Worth, I was terribly harassed by plaguey, if temporary, problems. They were no threat to health, but they were a threat to concentration. And to my golf. For I'd turned up that week with certain nerve inflammations and a cyst located in my pelvic region. Neither was terribly serious. The cyst was a sebaceous cyst that became inflamed and caused more discomfort than deep concern. But the combination led me to a firm conviction—never to recommend even to my worst enemies that they play seventy-two strenuous holes of golf, with its forceful swing and accompanying twist of the pelvic region—while burdened with this particular combination of irritants. They are not likely to cripple you, but they *are* likely to distract you. At least they distracted me: I finished forty-first in that tournament, the lowest I'd finished in four years.

The next tournament I entered, when these problems were cleared up, I won. In fact, I won or tied for first in each of the next three tournaments, and was on top or in second place in five of the next six. Which suggests what good health can do for you.

There are ailments that you can play with, but they do profoundly affect both your concentration and the way you swing the club. I've had two very long sieges with bursitis, an inflammation of the sacs in and around various joints that are supposed to help reduce friction in the moving joints. In 1963, I got bursitis in the shoulder; then late in 1969—after fighting it for a long while—I had to leave the tournament circuit with bursitis in the right hip.

Bursitis provides an intense pain when the affected joint is used. Some adults get one form of it from other sports—"tennis elbow," for example. Even children can get a form of it—"Little League arm." It is most disturbing to an athletically active adult, particularly one who makes his living from sports. He can't help but wonder what causes it. (Medically, the causes are not certain.) I keep thinking that the shoulder bursitis might somehow have been rooted in the pains I suffered in my left arm back in 1955, when I was practicing so hard for so long on the hard surfaces of the Southwest. I wondered whether the problems I tried to overcome at the 1963 Colonial might somehow have contributed to the bursitis later that year; perhaps, I thought, I may somehow have tried to compensate for the pain by altering my body motion in a way that later aroused the bursitis.

The thought reoccurred to me when I suffered the bursitis in the hip a few years later. I'd injured my back during the New Orleans Open of 1966 and had to withdraw halfway through the tournament. The pain in my right hip began to grow sometime after that, and it flared up quite intensely over the next two or three years.

I decided that I had to learn to live with this problem. Financially, I could afford to retire, but I didn't want to: I didn't want to give up and give in. And so I learned to pamper my hip somewhat—and to cherish hope from day to day and week to week. I swung more easily; a good many of my playing partners were outdriving me 20 and 30 yards on every hole. I took it easy on the follow-through. The difficulty was that the easier swing seemed to take some of the edge off my enthusiasm for the game. I'd learned from my father to go out and hit the ball as hard as I could. Now I could no longer bring power and the zest that it offers to the game.

Beyond all that, my game was built basically on the strength of my right side. But now, when I tried to press or push to get some strength out of my right side, the pain in the hip would flare up again. And when it didn't, I kept thinking that it would.

The thing about pain is that it seems to have a will of its own. You think you can forget it, or overcome it, or compensate for it. And you *can* do all these things. But the pain has a way of being there and getting greater and of attacking you when you want most to ride it out. In August of 1969, the bursitis flared up with great intensity. The tour was then at the PGA Championship in Dayton, and of course I wanted to stay with it. I'd never won the PGA—it's the only major title that's eluded me—and I hated to quit now. But more than that, I needed a certain number of points in the PGA to win a place on the United States Ryder Cup team. (I'd been on it ever since 1961.) Twelve players are picked for the team, based on points they'd earned on the pro tour, and in this tour I stood fifteenth in points. So I'd even had a new set of irons delivered to Dayton in time for this tournament.

In the last practice round of the '69 PGA, the pain flared up again. Winnie was with me and she rubbed and rubbed Ben-Gay into the skin, just as she had so often done in the past. The next day I went out and started a round, and she said I was drawn and white with pain. I bogeyed the first three holes. On the fourth I had a putt of 18 inches. The ball never even touched the hole. On the 535-yard tenth fairway, I reached for my driver for the second shot, with the idea of going for the green. Then I said to myself, "Now, that's ridiculous. How can you use a driver on the fairway when it hurts so much just to use it off the tee?" You can see how deeply the pain was influencing not only my game but the way I was thinking about the game. On the sixteenth hole, I pulled the drive to the left, dropped the second shot into a sand trap, and couldn't blast out with my third shot. When finally I did get on the green, I missed another 18-inch putt. When I tried to total up my score on the hole, I couldn't concentrate because of the pain. Billy Maxwell, the pro who'd been playing with me, had to help me to get it right.

I got an 82 on that round. It was as bad a score as I'd ever shot as a pro. (I'd gotten an 82 in the 1957 Kansas City Open, some twelve years earlier. And once, as an amateur back in 1954, I shot an 84 in competition.) So I went off to sleep on the whole thing. And the next day, I withdrew from the tournament, cleaned out my locker, and told the press that I was going home and rest until the whole problem had cleared up.

Nothing could have been better for me. I began strengthening my whole trunk and torso: I'd do fifty situps in the morning and fifty more at night. Just a month after I withdrew from the PGA, I went out with three friends to the Latrobe Country Club and shot three eagles—two of them consecutively—and eight birdies in finishing a "casual" round in a record 60. But the most rewarding—and delightful—experience of all was the reaction of the public.

They all wanted to help, just as they did when I got bursitis in the shoulder. At that time, one fan suggested that I take twenty alfalfa tablets a day. Another suggested that I put a pad of absorbent cotton dipped in Heinz Dark Apple Cider Vinegar over the sore part. Another suggested wheat germ, and another suggested a tablespoon of Certo once a day for thirty days ("you can get it in any supermarket"). This time, the fans recommended Sal Hepatica and cod liver oil and a bottle of Squirt a day (one of my business affiliations is with Coca-Cola). One man sent me a bag of radioactive plutonium and suggested that I sleep with it, another suggested that I carry a potato in my pocket ("if the potato does calcify, you might use four or five of them by the end of the year . . ."), and a doctor in Idaho suggested that I use a cuboid pad for my foot to help my hip get better. The only trouble is that we couldn't figure out what a cuboid foot pad was.

The genuine desire to help was quite touching to me and to Winnie. Of course, none of the "cures" were medically approved: They reflected more about the spirit of the people than the facts of medicine. But there are always people who want to offer you their help when they feel you're in need. Once when word got around that I had a "sick" putter—certainly my putting *was* sick at the time—some of the salesmen in my golf-equipment company sent me a putter that had a blade shaped like a huge hot dog and a shaft shaped like a fork. They also sent me one shaped like a pickle—"for when you're in a pickle," one shaped like a banana, and one shaped like a shoe—"so you'll be a 'shoo-in.' "

Even while I was trying to rest, after dropping out of the PGA, I had to fulfill some commitments. I remember going over to Kansas to make a competitive appearance at a course that Jug McSpaden, the old-time touring pro, had built in eastern Kansas. Jug was teamed with Byron Nelson, who set golf records all during the 1940s, against the "kids"—Jack Nicklaus and myself. To be sure, we represented faithfully our different generations. But when Jack saw Jug go with Byron up to a tee-off point some 50 yards in front of us, Jack asked, "Is the handicap based on how old we are or how old we feel?"

"I don't know," I said. "But if it's on how old we feel, I'm moving up 50 yards."

When I left that PGA tournament—having given up a chance to make the Ryder Cup team as well as to win the PGA—I wasn't sure that I'd be playing on the tour again that year. But ten weeks later, in the last week in October, I was with the rest of the pros on the fall tour. I shot a 69 in the first round at the Sahara Invitational and a 68 in the third round. But on the second round, I got into trouble on the fifteenth hole, a par-5, when my second shot rolled out of bounds. I dropped a provisional ball but picked it up when the gallery up front said that my original ball could be played. I went to take a look and found that the original ball was very definitely out of bounds. Now back to the previous spot to shoot another provisional. I took a two-stroke penalty and a nine for the hole, and it was clearly my fault: The player is responsible for his own ball. But if I hadn't picked up the penalty and simply gotten a par, I would have had a 71 for the second round, not a 75, and I might have been in the thick of the fight for first place. And that tended to tell me something about the rewards of resting that painful hip.

At that point, I felt tired but satisfied. And though I didn't do much in the next couple of weeks, I did manage later to go on to win at Hilton Head and then later at the Danny Thomas Classic. To be sure, there were times when I was staggering in both tournaments. But I hung on—and got the spirit to believe that my health problems were behind me. At least with the bursitis. In the next few touring seasons, I didn't feel a hint of it.

If there are any lessons in all this, they are in the realm of reality. If you love the game, as I do, there's always the temptation to go on playing when your body is saying no. My suggestion is to measure the matter two ways:

Would playing hurt your health further? Then don't play.

Would playing hurt your game at all? Then don't play.

Just go off and relax at something else. Don't fight bad health; reclaim good health. You simply can't concentrate, or think through the game properly, if you try to play in poor health.

Part Four

ITS STRATEGY

*Ninety percent of golf is played
from the shoulders up.*
—Milfred "Deacon" Palmer
Head pro, Latrobe Country Club

IX

Where Am I? Why Am I Here?

JUST before the 1970 U. S. Open at Hazeltine National Golf Course in Minnesota I was practicing approach shots to and around the green.

As it happened, many of my approach shots went up and over the green, and I repeatedly found myself working the ball back from the far-side rough and near out of bounds onto the green and into the cup.

"Poor Arn," said some of the folks in the gallery as they gathered around the last few greens. "He's really off his game. Overshooting on everything."

That, I think, suggests the difference between the bold player and the weekend golfer.

For I wasn't overshooting accidentally. This was one of those moments—infrequent, to be sure—when I was doing it purposefully. I was playing—and practicing—into trouble, so that I'd know all the trouble this golf course could offer *before* the scores started counting.

It is part of the philosophy of boldness: You must practice

the treacherous spots beyond the green if you intend to play so boldly that you'll likely go over the green. My simple and direct intention was to learn to play the hard shots on that golf course, not to indulge in fantasies about the easy ones.

So I was not simply practicing how to play the golf course. I was practicing how to apply a particular philosophy—that of boldness—to the golf course. If I came up boldly to those greens, as I planned to do, I'd have to know what kind of trouble would confront me in that effort. And so I was finding what danger lurked in the hearts and shadows of the far side of the green.

There are encyclopedias, even vast libraries, on how to grip a golf club, or swing it, or move the feet, or swivel the hips. Some people do one thing better than another; few people learn perfection in all its conquering detail. It is in the exalted nature of their imperfections that most people find their end result: frustration.

But to me, the exciting thing about golf is that it is a continuing challenge to the mind, not just to the muscle.

It is, to be sure, wonderful to have the muscle—to be able to hit the ball hard in the direction that you choose. I, above all, am not about to decry the aspect of power in golf.

But first you must choose the direction of your shot—you must have a reason for going one way rather than another. It is the quality of thought that, I feel, evens up the competition in golf. One man may outdrive another by 20, 40, or 60 yards, but if he has not the power to think through his game as carefully as the less-muscular driver, then he may find himself consistently the loser. It is not just the long hitter but the clear thinker who triumphs most in golf.

These pages are devoted to the quality of thought. They are not an attempt to tell you how to think or to persuade you to think only my way: It is the difference in opinions—in thinking patterns—that gives a high and distinctive flavor to golf.

No—this is an effort to make you aware of the elements that

go into the decision-making of golf. Much of this is reflexive in professional golfers; they use it mindlessly the way that accountants use addition and subtraction. But the amateur—or weekend golfer—may not be aware of the subtle interplay of these elements and the way they influence the game.

By understanding these elements, the golfer on every level is not only able to "think through" his game, he is also able to think it through in a way that can conserve strokes.

For bold and aggressive play demands much of the cerebral quality in man, as much or more so than does cautious play. To choose to work on the leading edge of any enterprise takes not just daring, but insight and judgment and careful preparation.

It is to the basic strategic thinking of bold play, then, that the following pages are dedicated.

The most salient and significant question you can ask yourself, in starting to think through your game to boldness, is:

"Where am I?"

Don't laugh—the wrong answer can lead to weeping and gnashing of teeth. For the game must be and is played to the particular conditions that affect the region in which you are playing.

The thinness of the mountain air in the West will—as we've seen in Chapter I—allow the ball to carry considerably farther than, say, in the heavily humid bayou country of Louisiana or around Houston.

The closeness of the ocean seems, in certain locales—such as Torrey Pines, near San Diego—to tempt the putts to break toward the sea.

The sand used in hazards in New England is more gravelly than the soft, more compacted sand used in the South; in wet weather, the ball will sit up higher in the gravelly sand—and give you a better recovery shot—than in the quickly clotted sand in the South.

The fairways of the East, Midwest, and Northwest tend to

be thick and lush and the roughs dense with vegetation and with trouble. But in the South and Southwest, there are places where the fairway grass has been all but burned away by the unwavering glare of the sun, and the rough—which is "thick" only by comparison with the bare land of the fairway—sometimes gives you a better lie than the fairway. In Florida, in particular, you'll find rough where the grass is so tough and wiry that the ball will sit up right on top of it and you can use a driver to get the longest possible shot out of it.

In much of the Northeast and Midwest, the trees in the rough are not only dense in numbers but are heavily branched and thick with leaf cover from top to bottom. Thus they make it difficult to play out of the rough, anywhere but to the fairway. Indeed, they make it difficult to get a line-of-sight to the green, much less an opening through which a ball might be guided. That's why playing safely back to the fairway is often the only possible shot in these areas. But in the South and in Southern California, you'll find the rough scattered with palm trees or tall, high-trunked pines where there are few or no branches close to the ground. Thus you can frequently see through the trees to the green and can find a route to guide the ball through the rough to the green.

In Florida, the greens are much slower than they are in the Northeast and Midwest, so you must be much more aggressive with your putter in playing many of the Florida golf courses. The reason: The northern greens are usually of bent grass, while those in Florida are of a tougher, bristling Bermuda grass, usually thickened with an overseed of rye to give it color when the grass goes dormant in the winter.

Thus it is vital to plan your game according to exactly where you are, and what the impact of wind, weather, grass, and climate is. For it is quite apparent that you will be less venturesome—and perhaps less aggressive—about playing into the tree-thickened rough in the Northeast and Midwest than into the more beckoning rough of the Southeast and Southwest.

But you would be less upset at getting into wet sand in New England than in the central South.

If all of this is vital to planning your game on your home course, it is the more so if you are playing on different courses in different parts of the country. For it is not enough, in these days of highly mobile living, just to have the stroke. It is important to have the insight about the course you're encountering. And to remember that you need that stroke *only* for that course in that part of the country—i.e., a strong putting stroke on the nappier, grainier greens of Florida. For if you aren't aware of the changing conditions as you go from place to place, you may find your whole game thrown off: It could take months for a man who's developed a strong, confident, aggressive putting stroke in Florida in the winter to find the normal putting stroke that he needs to play a course in Westchester County in New York State.

It happens even to the pros. It happened to me in the early stages of the 1971 season. That was the period I was using to hone and sharpen my game for the Masters, to be played early in April. I played well in that period, and in some cases I played more than merely satisfactorily. In the Florida Citrus Invitational in Orlando that March, I shot three 68s and a 66 and won the tournament with a total of 270. But then the tour led us into the windy, rather cold weather in Jacksonville, and I made the expected adjustments to accommodate to the wind —teeing the ball up lower, catching the ball on the downswing in order to give it less loft and more of a low, "ramming" drive into the wind. The next week we went into windy, somewhat warmer weather in the National Airlines Open in Miami. The adjustments went on; they were as minor as you could want to make them, but they *were* different from the kind of game I'd be playing in calm weather. The feel that you get for the game goes off. Your timing becomes just a little erratic. Your stance becomes a little wider so you don't get thrown off balance by the wind. Your thinking is directed on how to play the wind, not how to play the golf course. Thus, bit by bit, you become acclimatized: You wind up playing golf that is perfectly tailored to windy conditions—but *only* windy conditions. At least that's what I did. For the wind seemed to endure even into my final preparations for the Masters tournament.

You may recall that the first part of the Masters week was quite windy and turbulent. In fact, tornadoes were sweeping through Georgia and the South that week. My driving? It was as beautiful as you'd want to see. I really thought I had it made —I hadn't driven better in months. Perhaps in years.

Then the opening day of the Masters dawned clear and sunny and beautiful. The scent of magnolia wafted over the land, the starched jackets of the waiters glistened in the sunlight, the dew looked like scattered diamonds in the sunlight.

And my game fell apart.

You may have seen the Masters on TV and noticed that I missed some short, not to say microscopic putts. That hurt— it had to hurt. But what hurt much more constantly was my driving. It had simply changed in three weeks of windy weather and—when suddenly given a few days of exceptionally nice weather—I couldn't get it all together again.

That was what just one aspect of the environment did to my golf game. It did it gradually, yet destructively. So the lesson was a valid, if painful one: to appreciate what all aspects of a particular environment can do to a golf game, in combination as well as alone.

The simplest place to start is with what the golfer stands on. And brutalizes: the grass.

For understanding how to play different kinds of grass, as it appears in different parts of the country, may make a significant difference as to how strategy can evolve from philosophy. Even knowing how weeds affect the ball can be terribly important. The *Poa annua*, a weed that appears every four or five years at Augusta, giving a whitish hue to the grass, inspired chagrin, frustration, and desperation when it came early in 1972 and struck the Masters tournament. For it made the greens very rough and uncertain and threw off the pace of the game of virtually everybody in the field. I found two greens, in particular, unsettling during the 1972 Masters: the eleventh because it had no *Poa annua* and thus was astonishingly fast (at least compared to the rest of the course) and the twelfth, which was riddled with *Poa annua* and thus was completely unpredictable. On the first round, I hit a six-iron to the green of the par-3 twelfth hole, measured the break-to-the-left carefully, hit a super putt, saw it catch some of the weed, and watched in frustration as the ball failed to follow the break precisely and rolled past the cup for a blown birdie. And at a time when a birdie might have put me into the lead or very close to it: I finished the round with a 70, only a stroke behind Sam Snead and two behind Jack Nicklaus. And I wasn't the only one with problems. Nicklaus stayed until evening of almost every day, working on the new demands for putting on the *Poa-annua*-sprinkled putting greens, yet he caught a surprising number of three-putt greens during the tournament. And I mention Jack only because he *won* the tournament. With a 286, seven strokes (or almost two per round) higher than what it took Charles Coody to win in 1971. Jack was the only golfer in the field who broke par. Nobody else even matched it. Compare that figure with the eighteen who matched or broke par in 1971—or the twenty-seven who did it in 1969—and you get a faint idea of what not only the grass but its aberrants can do to your game.

Actually, there are only two main kinds of grass in use on golf courses in the United States, and—though there are an infinite number of varieties and hybrids—that all comes down to "bent" and Bermuda.

Bent is found most frequently in the East and Far West, in the Midwest and portions of the Southwest.

Bermuda is found mostly in the Deep South and Florida, and—as we've seen—it is often given an overseed with rye during the wintertime. The rye will not only make the grass *look*

greener, but it will make the grass *be* thicker and thus somewhat more resistant to the roll of the ball. When the pros are
playing in the Bermuda-grass country in the winter, they do
not always favor the "green" green. For it is likely to be a very
thick, nappy, grainy Bermuda with the green-of-the-rye overseed giving it support. When they see an off-color or wheat-
colored green, they tend to feel that it's a Bermuda that has
gone dormant and that has not been given a thickening overseed of rye. Thus it will offer a "truer" putt, which provides
less grain resistance and a more constant speed to the ball.

Bermuda is a much tougher grass than bent. It is short and
bristly. It looks and feels like a crew cut. It is very tolerant to
drought, it is not much disturbed by saline conditions, and it
prospers in a sandy loam. Thus it is ideal for the sea-surrounded
courses in Florida—particularly those that are exposed to a hot
sun, an ocean spray, and the roughshod style of the wintertime
fanatic. Bermuda grows well in the kind of loam that percolates
well. Because the water sinks right on down through the soil,
the fairways and greens are drier than in bent-grass regions. So
it is not because the greens are "heavy" with water that they
are "slower" than in the North. It is because the Bermuda grass
is so tough and bristly—so insistent that it can "capture" a putt
unless the golfer makes a specific effort to overcome it. There
were times in the past—before some of the more refined ver-
sions of Bermuda came along—when you would have done better to avoid using a putter on Bermuda greens; you'd take out a
nine-iron and chip across the green instead of trying to putt
through it.

Bent grass has a longer leaf, but a thinner and more pliant
one. It is much more likely to bend over—it *is* called "bent"
grass—and thus provide less resistance to the roll of a tee shot
or the momentum of a putt. Quite frequently, it is planted in
areas where there is a clay underbase (where Bermuda is likely
to be planted in sandy areas). Thus it must be watered constantly in order to soften the clay enough to let the roots dig

deeply. But that watering means—on the green—that the grass will be more subject to backspin. Thus you know that you can play more boldly to the greens—taking the risk of going beyond the cup—because you'll get so much backspin that the ball will bite and hold. Or even hop backward toward the golfer.

Another thing to remember is that if the grass is bent, and the undersoil is clay, the watering might have another effect on your game. For the water will not quickly seep from the grass down through the clay; instead it will gather near the surface, keeping the grass "heavy" with water through much of the morning. That means that the fairways will be a little "slow" —and a little resistant to the roll of the ball. The fact is that not many golf courses have a system of sprinkling that distributes the water evenly all over the course. Instead, the water is spread in a particular pattern—usually by permanent underground sprinkler systems—and thus the grass remains "heavy" in the same pattern. By studying the pattern of the sprinkler system, and thus the pattern of "heaviness" in the grass, you may be able to determine certain spots on your home course where you can get the ball to hit and hold when you want it to. Or—by avoiding those spots for a specific bold shot—you may be able to drive the ball into a drier part of the pattern and thus get a little more roll. This, in fact, is more easily done by golfers regularly playing a particular course than by the pros, who seldom linger long enough to acquire that kind of insight.

In addition, you should know what special conditions involve the grass in your area. If you travel, you will find that the courses in South Africa have the grainiest Bermuda in the world. Bobby Locke came out of there with the most astonishing and successful putt I've ever seen: He had mastered the draw putt to the point where he rarely putted straight into a hole, not even on bent grass. In fact, he could duck hook a putt into the hole if need be, so thoroughly did he learn to overcome the grainy Bermuda in his homeland. There were times when I was sure he could send that putt in by any route possible short of making a full circle. (And there were times when I had the feeling he'd do that if it was necessary.)

On the other hand, don't be deceived by reputation: there is no longer any Merion bluegrass at the Merion Golf Club. It's all a disease-resistant bent that can be cut quite close. And do be alert to the character of the new hybrids that are beginning to spread around the country. For they can plague the uninitiated, among whom I would number a great many pros—including myself. At the PGA championship in San Antonio in 1968, there was a new hybrid called Tifton 328. (It was developed in an experimental station in Tifton, Georgia, and the name of the hybrid is a combination of the town and the experimental series involved.)

Tiff 328 is a tough little Bermuda that is fast-growing, even in hot-weather areas. In fact, there were pros who swore that the Tiff 328 in the rough grew three inches in the four days of the '68 PGA. The rough had been cut to three inches the night before the tournament opened, and by Sunday afternoon the pros were insisting that now it was six inches long. It was a challenge to the muscle as well as the mind. "You have to blast out of it like you would a sand trap," said Billy Casper. Don January, who was the defending champion in the tournament, said, "I never felt I could get the ball on the green if I was in the rough." Mason Rudolph suggested why: He hit a shot 15 feet from the pin, but the ball was lying in the collar of rough just off the green—and Mason approached it as if "it was almost an unplayable lie."

Once you know how the particular grass affects your game, you should know how the climate affects the grass. It may be a permanent matter of strategy: how the humidity of sea-level courses affects the lushness of the grass, how soon the hot sun of the desert areas tends to burn it down. It may be a temporary matter of self-protection: You would not go to play golf in the wet, blustery weather of the Monterey Peninsula in California in the wintertime without carrying a wet suit—

waterproof pants and jumper—in your gear. It may be a seasonal matter of total chagrin.

Take the winter before the Masters in 1966. It was an un-usually cold one in Georgia; four days before the tournament opened, the temperature dipped below freezing. To help offset the damage caused by the poor growing season, the fairways had been left unusually long. The result was that grass would get between the clubhead and the ball at impact and thus neu-tralize the impact of the grooves on the face of the clubhead. That meant that the grooves would not be able to provide an "undercutting" motion as the club hit the ball. Thus there would be no backspin on the ball, which is one of the advan-tages of using the deeply grooved clubs. Instead, there would be overspin. But the greens were firm and fast, and overspin would cause the ball to hit and run over the green instead of biting and holding in place. So difficult was it to get the ball to hold on the greens that on some of the holes—notably the tenth—the players were hitting the ball onto the rather steep banks in front of the green and hoping it would pop up and onto the putting surface—with much of its momentum gone—instead of dribbling back down the bank.

But on the whole, few of the pros were ready for the im-pact of the long-term weather conditions. On opening day at the Masters, Tommy Jacobs and Gay Brewer—who were to wind up in a tie for the title with Jack Nicklaus—got a 75 and a 74, respectively. Doug Sanders and I, who were to tie for the spot just behind the leaders, both got 74s. Nobody could break 71 that day except one golfer—Nicklaus. He got a 68 that day —and a 76 the next day. In fact, for the entire tournament, there were only two rounds below 70. The other was by Paul Harney, who got a 68 one day—and a 76 the next. When you can get the finest golfers in the world to play roughly 320 rounds of golf, and only two of them come in under 70, you get some impact of what the winter-long weather means at Augusta.

Fortunately, there are cases where the seasonal changes provide a happy surprise—and a higher sense of anticipation. In 1960, the Canada Cup International Trophy Matches were held in Portmarnock in Ireland. It lies about 11 miles from O'Connell Street in Dublin, on a thumb of heaving duneland that sticks out into the Irish Sea close by Howth Head. It is a long course (7093 yards), and, like most true "links" (which is really a Scottish word for "dunes"), it has only a few trees to bother the golfer. But it has heavy weather—wet weather with swirling winds—and a formidable rough: a thick growth of seaside grass, creeping willow, ferns, yarrow, some gorse, and innumerable wild rose bushes. The club and its members had taken painstaking efforts—even heroic ones—to make sure it was in prime condition for the Canada Cup matches. In order to make sure that the fairways would be fresh and unscarred, for example, the members of the club never used the fairways during the four months preceding the tournament. After hitting their tee shots, they'd pick up their balls off the fairway and place them in the adjacent rough and make their approach to the cup from there. Ireland may be a disputatious land, but it is a gracious and high-minded one also.

In any case, the fairways and the rough had been cut short many weeks before the matches. It was expected that the rains would come, as usual, but they didn't. It turned out to be one of the driest springs in years, and one of the calmest. Oh, sure, there was a ripple of breeze each day around noon, but it was nothing like the whipping gales that characterize so much of the Irish coast in spring. All this made the fairways agreeably fast and clean and the rough a little less terroristic than usual. The unexpectedly good weather held all through the four days of the Canada Cup matches, warm and sunny with gentle caresses from the sea. "This is typical Irish summer," said the Prime Minister with a bit of a twinkle. "It's the first typical Irish summer we've had in ten years."

The two-man United States team—Sam Snead and myself—

finished first among the thirty nations competing. The Irish team finished fourth, but that did not deeply upset the natives. They were torn, I think, between joy and dismay as each day turned up bright and windless—particularly after Gary Player, of South Africa's team (with Bobby Locke), shot a new course record, with a 65 on opening day. They were happy, I am sure, that their visitors liked the weather, but they openly confessed what a shame it was that professionals of such "foine" stature might be deprived of experiencing the true glories of Portmarnock, which could come only when it is played in a brisk cross-wind with a good belt of rain as a chaser.

There are times, of course, when you can't help but follow up the query, "Where am I?" with another: "Why am I here?"

Those moments are at their richest when "unexpected" weather occurs. Not just a sudden storm: Most golfers have the sense to stay out from under solitary trees, or to get back to the clubhouse, or simply to lie down in the lowest possible depression—the sand traps, if need be—to avoid the danger of lightning in such a situation. I'm talking abut those weather conditions that not only force you to abandon your strategy for attacking a particular course but force the tournament committee to alter their whole strategy for making the course difficult. The 1970 U. S. Open at Hazeltine National Golf Club in Chaska, Minnesota, was an example.

On the Thursday morning that the tournament opened, the wind was blowing out of the Northwest at thirty-five miles an hour, and it was gusting much higher than that—hurricane levels would have seemed a welcome relief. The wind was so strong that it uprooted TV tents around the eighteenth green and tilted a massive scoreboard that was mounted on six-by-six-foot pilings driven four feet into the ground. A truck had to be eased up behind the scoreboard, and the board was lashed to it by cables. Golfers were using irons off tees that demanded a drive in practice if the shot was downwind; others were going to drivers to shoot a normal-iron shot into the wind. ("Do you realize," said Gary Player, who shot an 80 that day, "that there's no such thing as knowing how to play out there today?") The drives on the downwind holes were fantastic. The third hole, downwind, was one of the two holes used by the U. S. Golf Association to measure driving distances in the Open. Jim Dent, who hadn't even graduated from the pros' "postgraduate school"—the qualifying school for the pro tours that's held every November—sent his tee shot off the third hole a screaming suborbital 346 yards. Three other golfers were over 340 yards: Jim Mooney, Jim Wright, and Andy Borkovich. Sam Snead, who was only fifty-eight then, hit a shot 340 yards. Tom Weiskopf hit one 338 yards. Altogether, there were ten golfers over 335 yards.

The wind even altered the "play" of the earliest man on the greens. He's Bob Howse, and he's out on the course at six o'clock in the morning—at the latest. The reason: He's the man assigned by the USGA to set the pin placements for each round of the U. S. Open. Bob is an agreeable chap with only a slightly flawed character: He can be a fiend when it comes to selecting pin placements.

Actually, he's made a close study of them. Long before competition begins in the U. S. Open, he charts four places on each green to locate the pin—one place for each round. He grades them according to difficulty and gives each placement a score: 4 for a very easy location, 3 for a slightly more difficult one, 2 for the next step up in difficulty, and 1 for the most severe location on the green. He mixes them up artfully; he doesn't want all of the most severe locations to turn up on one day (which would give him a total "pin placement score" of 18). Nor does he want all of the easiest placements to turn up on the same day; that would give him a pin placement score of 72. Normally, I'd say, he likes a score in the high 20s or the low 30s; after all, he's challenging the skills of the top golfers in the world. And he's able to regulate the pin placement scores rather

well, if only because he charts in advance where the pins might
be located as play progresses.

But on this morning, he had to throw all the charts away. The
wind was simply making a farce of certain pin placements: You
can appreciate how a pin set on the front, secluded part of a
green would become almost inaccessible in a stiff downwind—
the ball would simply be blown over and beyond the green
if any player tried to pitch sharply high into the air to go over
the hazards. So Bob simply recharted—and eased—the pin placements. They totaled 46 points that morning—the highest total
he can ever recall setting. And later on he conceded that he
should have made them easier still. "I didn't guess quite how
hard the wind would blow," he said, "or how quickly the
greens would harden in the wind. The pins should have been
more accessible in the downwind situations."

The way we played the course that day, you had to figure
that the only accessible location was on the tee. Anything beyond that—anything that took the ball into the air—turned golf
into anarchy. We were trying very fancy shots to get onto
the green, shots that we hadn't often made before. Or now. I
made 40 on the first nine holes—and that wasn't a disgrace.
Orville Moody, who is a good "wind" player, also got a 40.
Gary Player and Gene Littler got around in 39, but Jack
Nicklaus didn't: He shot a 43 on the front nine. He hit only
four greens out of the first nine in regulation play (par for the
hole minus two putts). His shots—like all of ours—were flying
all over the golf course before they hit the green. He turned
in an 81 for the first eighteen holes. Not even when he was
seventeen years old and playing in his first U. S. Open at Inver-
ness back in 1957 had he ever shot anything like that.

One pro, Everett Vinzant, out of a club near Kansas City,
pointed out that he hit downwind to the third green, using a
five-iron, and watched the ball hit the green and bound across
it into high grass some 20 feet beyond the putting surface.

With him was a very promising collegiate player named Ben Crenshaw, who also took out a five-iron—after watching Vinzant's shot—but played it more conservatively. He hit the ball to an impact area six feet short of where Vinzant did—and the ball backed up on him. Vinzant said he'd been accurate enough; he'd missed only five greens in regulation play but was close enough to all of them. "But there was no way I could club myself," he said. "It was unreal. There is no way I can describe it. It was a par-80 golf course. I hit the ball real good, and I shot an 83."

About the only golfer it didn't bother deeply was Tony Jacklin of England. He shot a 71 on a day when only 81 players out of 150 could break 80. "I try to use the wind, not fight it," he said. But he did admit that the wind had disturbed his balance as he stood over several putts. He three-putted the sixteenth green and got a double bogey on the seventeenth, and he felt he'd simply destroyed himself; he didn't know he was coming in ten strokes better than some of the finest golfers in the world.

In fact, he didn't realize how well he'd done until he encountered Jack Nicklaus at the flap of the press tent.

"I blew it," said Tony. "I had it in my hands but I blew it." Then he asked Jack what he shot—obviously expecting the worst.

"I had an eighty-one," said Jack.

Tony's eyes popped open. "You've *got* to be kidding," he exclaimed.

"Listen," said Nicklaus. "Don't knock it. I had to play great golf on the back nine to get it."

The next day, by way of contrast, came up sunny and bright and warm. Little puffs of white clouds glided lazily across the sky. The wind had disappeared and so did the grotesque scoring. I went from a 79 down to a 74. Nicklaus went from 81 down to 72. Gary Player went from an 80 to 73. (We were all tied at 153—and we all barely made the thirty-six-hole cut.) And we weren't the only ones. Dan Sikes went from an 81 to a 69. Dave Marr went from an 82 to a 69. Bert Yancey, George Knudson, and DeWitt Weaver went from an 81 to a 72. Labron Harris went from an 83 to a 73. On the wind-filled Thursday, there was only one round under par—that of Jacklin. On the serene, sunny Friday, there were thirteen sub-par rounds.

How did Jacklin do on the calm Friday?

His score went down, also. From 71 to 70. He continued to shoot 70s for the rest of the tournament, and he won it by seven strokes.

Maybe the lesson at Hazeltine was that in asking the question, "Where am I?" the answer should be, "Tornado Alley one day and Paradise Valley the next." And that you develop your strategy to embrace chaos as well as conquest.

X

Conquering the Course—An Overview

IT'S GOT to be a full generation since I took up golf seriously: Let's say I didn't get serious about it until I was in my seventh year. Yet I've never been bored by the thought of going out on a course, even one that I've played hundreds and hundreds of times. For every day it is a new course with a new subtlety—the weather changes, the rough changes, the pin placements change, the consistency of the sand changes, and the grass is a little longer or, if it's been cut, a little shorter. And of course my own ability changes.

So whenever I step out onto a course, it is with a vast expectancy. On any given day, I want it to tell *me* what it has in mind.

Is it going to be a course for boldness or caution?

Is it a course that offers mental delights as well as scenic ones?

Will it reward the good, or great, golf shot and penalize the clumsy or sloppy one?

How can I plot to conquer this course?

Knowing what I know about the grass, the climate, the design, and the deceits of the weather—now how do I go about attacking the course?

The first step is quite simple: Don't believe anything you've heard about it until you've gone out and personally examined it. For the golfer must never be neutralized, or paralyzed, by the reputation of a golf course.

Around Thanksgiving Day in 1969, for example, I was one of the pros who baptized the Harbour Town Golf Links at Hilton Head, South Carolina. We'd all heard a great deal about this course: that it did not follow slavishly the new golf architecture—it was not one of the sprawling 7000-yard marathons with greens the size of a drive-in parking lot. In fact, we'd heard it was a scenic though flinty course, that it was the most difficult thing ever seen on the tour, that it was not suited to the driving game of the "strong men" on the tour, that it had spectacularly narrow fairways and tiny greens that demanded great precision and unending finesse. Jack Nicklaus helped design the course, and he is a booming big hitter who likes a lot of roomy greens and fairways to exercise his muscle. Yet the word on this course was that it was going to demand something else of him: "You've built a course for you to practice the talent shots on," someone told him just before the first Heritage Classic there.

The course turned out to be every bit as stunning as people said: a tangle of brooding pines and dripping moss and crooked magnolias with fierce marshes guarding some of the imperceptible greens. But the rest did not go according to rumor: On the second day, Tom Weiskopf, a very strong young man and a long driver, shot a 65 at Harbour Town. ("A sixty-five on this thing," said Art Wall, "has to be one of the great rounds of all time.") I got a 68 one day that could easily—and should easily—have been a 64. And eventually I was the guy who won the tournament with a 283, three strokes better than the runners-up. If my putting had held up, I honestly feel I might have won by a dozen shots. But the point is that the big hitter did well on this course—and that the reality was different from the reputation.

What you *should* go onto a golf course with—instead of "rumors of oppression and deceit"—is an overview of the course and its potential. For a great many pros, gaining this overview is as reflexive as blinking. But an amateur rarely appreciates how useful it is simply to take a long, studied look at the course he's playing—even one that he's played often—to understand how best to use his skills on it and against it.

In short, he doesn't know how to "think" his way around the golf course, rather than just lobbing the ball around.

The first thing I'd suggest is to get a scorecard and a drawing of how the course is laid out. From the scorecard anyone can learn the obvious, such as how long the course is and what par is. On the pro tour, we run increasingly into courses over 7000 yards long that are par 70: Firestone, Preston Trails, and Colonial in Fort Worth among them. You can also see how many par-3s and par-5s there are: I'd be sure to note if there are as many of one as of the other—four of one and four of the other is the customary proportion. Then I'd check how long they are: Do the par-5s run so long that not even a pro has a chance to reach them in two and go for the birdie, or possibly the eagle? (What other use *is* there for a par-5?) Are the par-3s long-yardage—240 yards and up—or short? I'm against these long, lazy par-3s that demand nothing more of the golfer than that he hit a long tee shot. I'd rather see a shorter par-3 that's got some challenge to it—that asks the golfer to hit well and precisely with his irons instead of just muscling his way onto the green with his driver. But if the par-3s do demand more muscle than finesse, it's something you must learn before you set foot on the tee.

Then take a look at the diagrammatic sketch of the course to see what it tells you. For example, is the basic route of the holes clockwise or counterclockwise?

The choice is not always that simple: At Firestone, for example, the holes are laid out largely in parallel. At Augusta, the first nine holes are laid out in a basic counterclockwise motion, the second nine in a clockwise motion. And the East Course at Merion is counterclockwise through the first twelve or thirteen holes, then breaks the pattern—around the clubhouse—and runs clockwise for fourteen through eighteen. Perhaps because it was the only way to use well the land that was available.

What use is all this?

It tells you:

What kind of golfer the designer laid out the course for.

What kind of out-of-bounds directions he considered to be more serious. If you know that, you'll be better able to gauge how and where to place the emphasis on your bolder shots.

History is a little weak on this point, but my guess is that around the turn of the century, the golf course designers laid the holes out counterclockwise to accommodate the members. Most country club members were figured to be right-handed. And they figured the members to have played golf enough to get rid of the slice and acquire a hook. (Only truly dedicated duffers could afford to belong to country clubs in those days; the rest never got enough experience to get rid of their slice.)

The golf course designer also had to be concerned about what was around the golf course. In the old days, there were places where people either walked or rode in their horse and buggies. For in those days, few golf courses were built far out into the country, unless the members lived out there. They had to be close enough to the living areas—city or suburban—so that the members could reach them easily by horse and buggy.

So if the course was built clockwise—which is a natural kind of design and movement—the right-handed hook-hitter was likely to keep hitting the ball out of bounds on the left, out into the road or street. Even more so if he duck-hooked the ball. This was inconvenient for him: Climbing fences was not in the dignity of the times. It was costly to him: The out-of-bounds rule, with its penalty strokes, was devised in the 1890s at a course whose architect saw the problems of over-the-fence-and-out. And it was a threat not only to him and his sanity but to the people who happened to come along the road or street.

By turning the golfer around and getting him to go around the course counterclockwise, the designer didn't cure his duck hook. And he didn't keep him out of the rough. But he did keep him on the golf course—the most wild and erratic duck-hooked shots would not fly out into the street but merely onto another part of the golf course. Into a playable if not pleasant lie. (It's simply more convenient to play back from the next fairway than to try to play out of a rut in the trolley lines.) What about the right-handed slice-hitters? Theoretically, they could go off the course on the right, of course. But there weren't so many of them. And none of them could duck-slice the ball the way most of the better-trained duffers could duck-hook one. So the odds that they'd hit into the street were not nearly so great.

Once a trend like that gets set, it endures. For thirty or forty or fifty years, golf courses tended to fit into the same pattern: If there were roads around, the hole pattern was counterclockwise; if there weren't, the designer could get more creative.

So if you're a right-handed golfer who hits a draw or hook, you know that the counterclockwise course was designed to forgive your own worst faults—it's meant at least to keep you on the course when you duck-hook the ball. That may or may not give you a vast sense of security, but at least you know how the designer felt about the relative threats of the rough to the right as compared to the left. And you can examine them with a critical eye as to how they'll affect a bold philosophy of play.

(In recent years, it should be noted, golf courses have been built much farther from the city than in the past—cars can get out farther in an hour than a horse and buggy could get in a day. So the new courses do not suffer from the old disciplines.

The LaCosta Country Club in California—where the Tournament of Champions is held—is laid out completely and fluently in a clockwise direction, for example. For my part, I encourage and applaud the trend to a more creative design; I think it will lead to far more thoughtful and challenging golf courses.)

This is a trend—a useful hint—you can get as to how a particular golf course was conceived. And how it might be played.

But you can also learn, by a close look at the overview of the course, whether it otherwise favors the draw or the fade.

Augusta National, for example, is very much a course that plays to a draw. There are, doubtlessly, certain spots on which you'd rather go down the right side than the left side to a particular hole. But in general, the vast reaches and best positions on each hole come into play to the golfer who plays the draw rather than one who plays the fade.

To be sure, some of this is apparent only when you play the course. But by looking at a diagram of the course, you can see—as at Augusta—that the pronounced doglegs are to the left. Which is to say that they yield most to golfers who play a draw. There are, in fact, only one or two holes that bend to the right—and on some of them the bend is all but imperceptible. So here's a course that determines your strategy of play— a draw, not a fade—without really altering your philosophy of play.

You can also use the diagrams fruitfully to see what holes have a sharp dogleg and what the yardage is on those holes. From this, you can determine on what doglegs it's rewarding to be bold in trying to cut the dogleg. Part of the decision is in distance; part of it is in what lies beyond the blind shot if you make the shortcut over the inner angle of the dogleg.

If the total length of a dogleg hole is, say, 350 to 400 yards or so, a par-4 with a narrow fairway, it would not always be worthwhile to shoot blindly over the trees—over the corner of the dogleg—to try to shorten your second shot. You can reach the green and make the par 4 anyway, just by shooting down the fairway to the corner, and turning the corner with your second shot.

But if the dogleg hole is a par-5, let's say 500 yards or more, and if you're looking for a birdie on the hole, then it may well be worthwhile cutting the corner. Particularly if you need the birdie on the hole to win the tournament or get right up there close to doing it. Because you may cut an entire stroke off playing that dogleg.

As an example, I was playing in the finals of the Piccadilly World Match Play championship at Wentworth, England, in the autumn of 1967 when such an opportunity arose. My opponent was Peter Thomson of Australia, who'd played splendid golf in the finals. We went into the last of a thirty-six-hole match in which we'd traded the lead back and forth quite a few times. I was one-up on the thirty-sixth—leading by one with one hole to play (which meant, of course, that he had to win the hole to tie me and force a playoff).

The eighteenth hole at Wentworth is a 495-yard par-5 hole that doglegs to the right. Theoretically I could have played it safe, by hitting down the fairway on my tee shot, turning the corner on the second, reaching the green with a long third shot, and hoping to two-putt. But that wouldn't have been *me*—and that wouldn't have beaten off the challenge of Peter Thomson.

So I cut the corner. My drive was as sweet as anything I could have wanted: I went over the trees and played a little fade right into the heart of the dogleg. It set me up for an easy second shot that left me just off the edge of the green. I chipped up six feet from the cup. One putt would give me the birdie, two putts a par. In the meantime, Peter hadn't made it into the clear; he caught the rough with one of his shots and wound up 130 yards from the green with three shots to go to make par. He didn't make it. After he missed a putt that had to drop for a par 5, he conceded the hole to me: Even if he sank the next putt, I could take three putts from six feet out and still tie him. (My putting hasn't been sterling—but it's not *that* bad.)

So cutting the corner on the dogleg gave me the advantage that won the hole, and with it the tournament.

To be sure, you can't know everything about a dogleg by studying it on a diagram. There are some very important things you can learn only by going out on the course. The fifteenth hole at Pleasant Valley, where I won the Kemper Open in 1968, is a 341-yard par-4 hole with a gentle dogleg to the right. There's a lagoon off to the left, and a creek splits off from the lagoon to go through the fairway about 200 yards or so out. It would seem to be a good example of a dogleg that you don't have to risk cutting the corner on—you can play straight down the fairway, around the gentle corner, well within your skills. But what you can't tell from the diagram is this:

The tee is elevated. So is the green. So the fairway in between is really a valley—some would say "canyon"—that slopes down from each direction. And the slope is steep enough, particularly on the tee side of the water, so that—if your tee shot falls short of the creek—the ball will roll down and down until . . . Gulp! Splash! Sob! But you won't fall short unless you flub the shot. The question is what happens if you execute the shot well and clear the water with no trouble? Then you're on an uphill lie, still a lengthy way from the hole, with the green elevated above you and guarded rather formidably by traps. For most golfers, even a good many pros, that offers a rather difficult challenge. That's the time to look for another way to get to the hole, one that will eliminate at least one of the disturbing factors of the second shot: the length, the lie, or the danger of the hazards.

In such a case, it would seem that the wisest thing to do is to cut the corner—to drive over the trees in the right-hand rough to try to get the ball well beyond the water and fairly close to the green. You'll still face an uphill lie if you land short of the green, but you'll be a lot closer to it and thus more hopeful of chipping in close to the pin than if you're using a fairway wood far down the slope—trying to catch the ball on a downswing while you're working on an uphill lie. Of course, you can get into trouble cutting the corner on the dogleg. But the significant thing about a hole like this is that you're in trouble even if you play it safely. Though the hole is not extraordinarily long, the "safe" way down the fairway can lead you into more difficulty than the risky way, cutting the angle. But you cannot know that until you see the hole; a diagram alone won't tell you.

What else should you determine from the diagrammatic sketch?

Look for the holes that run parallel to each other. You can learn quite a bit by watching what's happening on a parallel hole that you're soon to play. On the first tee at Augusta, for instance, you can see the action on the ninth green—the two holes are parallel. Similarly on the second tee; you can see the eighth green. At Firestone, you can seize an even more immediate bit of intelligence: On the second tee you can see the third green, on the third tee you can observe the fourth green; you can not only check the pin placement and the wind trends, but watch a player putt to see how fast the green is.

There are, to be sure, certain engaging hazards to holes that are parallel. In the 1971 Houston Champions International, Bob Rosburg shot a 64 for the course record at the Champions Golf Club and the next day went on to hit one of the most bizarre holes-in-one ever seen in pro competition. He was teeing off on the thirteenth hole just as Lee Trevino was teeing off on the neighboring twelfth hole. Trevino swung, saw his ball arc toward the green, and heard a roar go up: He thought he'd holed his tee shot. *He* hadn't, but Rosburg had—in the wrong hole. For Rosburg, swinging at almost the same instant as Trevino, pulled his shot from the thirteenth tee. The ball hit high up in a pine tree, bounced back at an acute angle, careened across a pond onto the twelfth green, and trickled into the cup—just as Trevino's ball came down. It would have been a great split-screen shot for television—but if they'd *tried* the shot, they could never have done it.

In all of this, my point is to suggest that you learn as much about the course as you can—*before* you set a spike onto the course. It's like going on a trip: You usually buy a road map, choose your routes, know where the shortcuts are, know whether going off the expressway is going to be rewarding in some other way, and so on. You just don't start driving aimlessly on a road in order to get from New York to Chicago. Similarly with a golf course: You just don't start hitting a ball aimlessly around it. You look at its "map" and you see what it has to offer: where the birdies are, where the dangers are, how one hole is related to another, where the shortcuts are and whether they are as rewarding as some other way around the course, what you can do to make the course bend to your own philosophy. After all, the course was carefully designed—if not by a rational man, at least by a purposeful one. And you can learn something of that purpose—and how you can deal with it—by studying the overview in advance.

XI

Think the Way the Pro Thinks

WHEN I step out onto a golf course—with intent to conquer —I do so with two questions in mind:

1. What can I find out about the "trouble" on the course, and how it will affect my philosophy of play?
2. How can I make the most of each hole on the course— in effect, what is the strategy of the hole?

Those are, in fact, merged and come as one, not two efforts: I don't play a course once to find out the quality of the trouble, and then again to find out how to make the most of it. Both thoughts are always in my mind, no matter how often or how rarely I play the course. But for analyzing a think-through, we'll take the process part, the easier to examine it by.

First, let's examine the "trouble" and how it can affect the strategy of boldness.

I usually start by watching to see what kinds of trouble are emphasized and what are de-emphasized.

At Augusta, for example, the rough is not really terrifying. It is not dense or crowded, and its greatest problem is in playing the ball out of the pine needles that are scattered in so much of the rough. (The problem: Moving one set of pine needles may stimulate another cluster of pine needles and move them in a way that would cause the ball to move, attracting a penalty. That sensitivity is not customary among leaves or in grass. So you must be very careful in setting yourself up to hit out of a pine-needle-covered rough, particularly when you're placing the club down behind the ball and then moving it back into your backswing: One small miscalculation will cause the pine needles to move, and they'll cause the ball to move. Similarly, in coming back in your downswing into the ball: You can't hit the divot before you hit the ball—you should hit the ball first, to keep the pine needles from moving the ball, and then hit the ground and the pine needles second.) There are roughly thirty-two sand traps at Augusta, not an overwhelming number. What there is—and what makes Augusta so challenging a course —is water, and the way it keeps coming into play on the most decisive shots of a hole. It is not simply that the water hazard costs you a penalty if you land in it, but that it can warp the whole thrust and force of your game. (For the most part, I'd recommend that you never try to play the ball out of the water. Among the pros, the rule-of-thumb is that some of the ball must be exposed above the water. Otherwise you can't get the club down and under it in order to get it out of the water. In addition, light bends as it passes through water, and the view you get of the ball may actually be considerably in error. If you want to see just how much the water can "bend" the pic- ture of something only a few inches below the surface, try this experiment: Fill one of your wife's saucepans—the one in which she boils eggs—with water and put a long-handled spoon in it. The spoon handle will seem to bend dramatically just below the water level, though you *know* it's still straight—and you can prove it by lifting it from the water. That one experiment will cure you forever of the temptation of going after a ball that lies only an inch or two below the surface of the clearest and most beckoning water.)

The way that Augusta's water changes your game is suggested by the action at Amen Corner, that retreat embracing the eleventh, twelfth, and thirteenth holes in the southeast corner of the course, where Rae's Creek flows slow and brown under two stone bridges into a forest of pine. The series of holes is inextricably linked with the mystique and history of the Masters. Sam Snead almost blew his Masters win in 1952 in this series of holes. I've won a couple of Masters here and lost a few, and I think that Gary Player and Jack Nicklaus and Lee Trevino and scores of others would agree that the series is the hingepin of success: If you beat these holes, if you can play the eleventh and twelfth in par and then birdie the thirteenth on two of the four rounds, you're going to be very hard to beat in the Masters. But they are also holes where the bold player can wipe himself out—put himself out of business—with the ill-considered risk. He can go into this series of holes leading the tournament and come out trailing unless he's a bold player who plays them with his head—and executes every decision well. For there's almost no way you can keep the water on any of several of the holes—on one day or another—from playing an influential and even destructive part in your game.

Take the eleventh hole, a troublesome 445-yard par-4 in which water tends to come into play almost any way you approach the hole. For the green is narrow in width and guarded on the left front by a pond and on the left rear by a stream. (Both are, in fact, parts of famed Rae's Creek, which splits and curves around a spit of land to the left of the eleventh green.) If you play an approach from the left side, you'll find water between you and the green, as well as considerably behind it. If you play down the right side, you avoid the water in front, but the water at the rear can come into play for long shots if you overshoot badly. The method most commonly used is to play the tee shot down the middle or to the right of center, then to hit the approach shot to the right, hoping to bounce the ball off a hump or slope that rises on the right of the green; that ricochet will, hopefully, put the ball on the green without much danger of it going directly in the water behind the hole. But even that constitutes a rather singular way to play a shot: The fact is that there is no way you can play this hole without the water warping your approach.

Back in 1966, Gary Player published an instructional article in a magazine explaining how to play the eleventh at Augusta without going into the water. He pointed out that in thirty-five rounds at Augusta, he'd never gone into the water at the eleventh. That year—you guessed it—he played an approach shot on his first round that went over the green and into the water. He wound up with a two-over-par 6 and finished the tournament with a dismal 299. If confidence won't help, neither will boldness and the momentum of success. In the 1968 Masters, Bruce Devlin shot three rounds in the 60s, yet did not win the tournament because just once he decided to risk going boldly over the water. The result: He took a disastrous 8 on this par-4 hole. Those extra four strokes were the difference between a clear win and fourth place. Bruce wound up with a 280 for the tournament, while Bob Goalby was the winner with 277. "I think of that eight every time I play the eleventh hole," Bruce said later. "I'll never gamble with the water again."

Quite obviously, other golf courses emphasize other hazards. Those in the arid parts of the country are going to lean a little more heavily on sand than on water. Those in the Northeast and Middle West—where vegetation in the summer is lush—are likely to lean a little more on rough than on sand: People can learn to play out of sand traps, but every shot in the rough is a different and tormenting challenge, and nobody can learn to handle all the possible shots out of the rough.

Perhaps that's why I prefer to have sand traps defining the challenge to the golfer instead of trees and heavy rough, even though historically I've been stronger out of the rough than out of the sand. The reason is due more to an expectation of what a course should be for all players rather than a worry over what it is for a professional. For the fact is that sand traps are much fairer ways of penalizing golfers who stray than is a tangled rough of grass and brush. The sand traps are stable penalties—they penalize every golfer who gets into them in approximately the same way. But a rough—grass and bushes—does not offer equal harassment. Luck is an important factor in the hazard that the rough offers. Consider two different players on the same hole who drive into the rough on the left side, only a few feet from each other. With good luck, one can come up with as good a lie as he might have enjoyed if he'd stayed on the fairway. With bad luck, the other player—lying only a few feet away—might be in so bad a position that his ball is unplayable.

By the same token, a player can drive into the rough quite a few times during the course of eighteen holes and, if he gets lucky on the places that his ball drops in the rough, he could come in with a very acceptable score—while an unlucky player who hits the rough only a couple of times and comes up in unplayable lies both times might draw penalties that would send his score soaring.

Another question I ask myself is:

Where is the trouble located?

We've seen how a water hazard some 390 or 400 yards out in the fairway affected my bold play and Jack Nicklaus' safe play on the eighteenth hole at Baltusrol. We've seen also how the water in Amen Corner at Augusta—particularly as it clusters and circulates around the greens—affects the direction, power, and club choice of the approach shots. So by examining the location of the trouble, as well as its nature, you can analyze ahead of time what kind of choices will be forced upon you in planning a strategy of boldness.

The fact is that the location of the trouble—and its significance—is even more varied than its basic emphasis. The important thing is to understand how the location of the trouble relates to how the entire hole is played.

It is easiest to do this on the par-3 holes. You can stand on the tee and measure all the vexations that face you. You can see where the sand traps are, where the pin is located, which way the green slopes, and what it falls off into. You can also see what the wind is doing around and over the green; all you have to do is watch the tops of the trees that surround the green.

But this doesn't necessarily make the choice easy. For there are some par-3s that are so locked in trouble that you don't have a choice of whether or not to get into trouble; your only choice is what kind of trouble you prefer.

The fourth hole at Baltusrol is an example. It's a 183-yard par-3 over a large pond onto an undulating, even, double-tiered green that slopes down toward the water in front. The higher tier of the green, on the left, narrows sharply as it drops off to the lower tier on the right, where the collar of the green borders a stream feeding the front pond. Other than that, the green is merely guarded like the crown jewels. There is a series of three traps that guards the back, another trap that guards the left front—in the narrow gap between water and green—and a three-foot stone wall that guards the green in front. If your shot is short, it goes into the water. If it has the power but is low—i.e., on a long iron—it'll hit the stone wall in front of the green and bounce back into the water. If it has too much power, it'll run over the green into the sand at the rear. If you hit the green on anything but a perfect spot, the ball will be endangered by the front slope toward the water or by the narrow tier to the right.

Robert Trent Jones, the architect who helped redesign this hole, was challenged about its fairness. He was, like some golf course architects, not altogether happy about the challenge, and marched with a committee from the club out to the fourth tee. He put down his ball, addressed it, hit a long iron—and calmly sank a hole-in-one.

"I don't agree with you," he snapped—and walked off, having forever proven his point.

But for most golfers, the choice of clubs from the tee of this hole can be anything from a four-iron to as much as a three-wood. In general, the pros would go for too much club and risk the trouble in the back of the green. They don't want to mess with the trouble in the front: Going into the water means a bogey at best, unless you pull off a small miracle and hole the pitch shot from across the pond—while going into the sand at the back always offers the option of blasting up and out, close enough to the pin to hope for a one-putt.

On the longer holes, you have to begin thinking of how trouble and triumph are linked—though you may only see the trouble from the tee. Consider the choices forced on you by fairway traps and bunkers. They are used by some designers to force the long hitters off the tee to pull up and drop their tee shots a little shorter than usual. Otherwise, they can take the gamble of trying to hit long enough to carry over the fairway bunkers and perhaps finding themselves out of control and in the rough as they strain to reach for the longer shot. (The rough, as I've suggested, is often a less equitable hazard than are sand traps.) Fairway bunkers are also used to pinch off the golfer in a direction away from the easiest approach to the green. If the fairway traps are on the left—tempting the golfer to the right—you can usually figure that there's a reason for this, beyond the everyday satanic glee of the architect. I'd tend to look to the left as being the most inviting approach to the green. And then I'd determine whether I'd be more confident and successful going to the left—and daring the sand traps—

on my tee shot. Or whether I'd do better to challenge the hole with my irons.

From time to time, you will find bunkers on both sides of the fairway, trying to pinch you in and short of the hazard. You may take one look and decide that the architect is trying to tell you something: like, play it safe and come up the middle, short of the sand. You may also find that he's trying to tell you something else: No matter where the pin is located, you've got trouble on your hands.

The seventeenth hole at Firestone is an example. It's not a particularly exasperating hole, but it does ask that you make certain perceptions and—because of the way the hazards and target are linked—make certain judgments on the tee about how much guts you've got. It's an uphill 390-yard par-4—with four traps set in tee-shot range, two on each side of the fairway. The hill runs about three-quarters of the length of the hole, and the bunkers are set into the sides of the incline—i.e., the ball will run down into them even if you get the ball out pretty much in the middle of the fairway, even with the traps; the ball may roll down toward or into them. Most golfers consider the right-side bunkers to be more treacherous than those on the left side. But the real choice is right, left, or considerably long or short of the bunkers on either side. Whether to go long depends on your strength and distance off the tee; most people —other than pros—can't count on outdriving the bunkers all the time. Whether to go short depends on your sense of caution; going short generally means that you're relying on your middle-iron play to reach the green in less than three shots. If your iron play is stronger than your control of a tee shot, you'll go short—perhaps with a three-wood—and play to the iron. Whether to go right or left depends simply on one question: Is the pin placed to the right or left on the green? For the green is actually two putting surfaces, separated by a huge hump roughly down the middle, running from front to back. If the pin is on the right side, you'd do well to accept the risk of playing your tee shot to the right—assuming you can get your tee shot out past bunker range. If it's on the left, you must play left. Otherwise, you'll be playing blind over the lip of a bunker, trying to reach a pin that is screened from you by the hump in the green. That's only to avoid putting up and over the hump, if you have to go from one side of the green to the other (the roll is tremendous, and the speed that's developed is quite considerable). The alternative is to play from the opposite bunker, short of the green, and then chip up to the green on your third shot. That pretty much takes care of your chance for a par.

On occasion, you'll find still more trouble farther along in the fairway. Here the location and the nature of the hazard become significant. For, if the hazard is a tree or outcropping of trees, you can usually play around it—though you might have to choose between your strengths with a hook or a fade. Similarly with bunkers: If you can control the ball, you can frequently play around a bunker if you can't play over it. But if it's a stream that cuts across the fairway, there's no way you can play around it; you must be prepared to play over it. That may involve not just a decision on your fairway shot but on your tee shot—and how you set up for the combination of troubles that leads to the water.

Take the seventeenth hole at Quail Creek, near Oklahoma City. It's a 459-yard par-4. The green is well bunkered and guarded by trees for the errant shooter, but the front opens well to the fairway, and the green is comfortably large. There *is* one little thing: a creek that runs right across the fairway, some 80 yards in front of the green. If you're a little short with your first two shots—if the second one bounces along the fairway, say, 375 yards out—your ball will drop into the creek. But if you can get out there far enough on your tee shot, then you can get over the creek easily. (Alternatively, if you can get out there short enough on your first two shots—say, 360 yards—then you can get over the creek easily and into good position for getting in or near the hole. That way, also, means that you've accepted the likelihood of a bogey or more on the hole, because you won't reach the green in less than three strokes.) But the rest of the fairway is designed to frustrate the golfer who plans to go over the creek comfortably in either two shots or three. For the fairway is built in several levels, each of them cunningly placed to cause problems for golfers of various capabilities. The second, and higher level, for example, is some 230 yards out—about where you'll have to be beyond to get over the creek on your second shot. So mentally you've got to climb that slope with a long tee shot if you hope to go over the creek with your second shot. The lesser tee shot also has to climb up a slope to a higher level. So what you do to cross the creek depends very much on what you do off the tee. In 1964, I came up to this hole with a critical opportunity in the last round to win or lose the Oklahoma City Open. I attacked the hole by going for a position that would not only cross the creek but also bring the green into range for a precise second shot. It would take, I judged, brute strength on the first shot, great finesse on the second. So I rammed a drive off the tee that carried 300 or more yards on my first shot. Now I was in an easy position to clear the creek, only 80 yards away. In fact, I was in a great position to control my next shot quite precisely by using a short iron to the green. So I took out an eight-iron and lofted the ball onto the green some 14 inches from the cup. From there, it was one putt and a birdie to take the lead in the tournament, and I ultimately won the championship.

On occasion, you will encounter a hole on which you don't have to look for trouble—it's all over the place. In rich and diverse quantities.

Such a hole is the sixteenth at Firestone. It is a par-5 hole of deceit and deception, filled with fairway sand traps, a water

hazard fronting the green, and the flinty character of a
bear with a backache. My clear and totally objective perspective on this hole was shaped only slightly by the ruinous 8
that I took on it in the 1960 PGA—at a time when I might have
won the PGA and put together what then was called "the
American Grand Slam": I already had won the Masters and the
U. S. Open that year.

The fact is that I feel this is a terribly unfair hole, not only
for professionals but particularly for the everyday kind of
golfer who must endure it.

For one thing, the hole is long—604 yards, with a slight break
to the left that gives it the flavor (but not the opportunity for
short-cutting) of a dogleg.

At that length, you're going to need three very muscular
shots just to get on the green in a regulation three strokes. If
your tee shot goes "only" 280 to 300 yards, you're not even halfway there, yet. You've got to hit a fairway shot that is about as
good and then come up with an approach shot that has power
and great control, to put the ball precisely on the green and
not in the water or the sand traps around the green.

The strategy of the hole demands that you hit down the right
side of the fairway on your tee shot. (If you go to the left, the
bend of the dogleg will screen your line of sight from the
green, and you'll wind up shooting blindly on your second
shot, perhaps into any of several hazards that await you closer
to the green.) But there are a couple of sand traps down there
on the right, just about far enough out to catch most tee
shots. (By and large, the pros can outdrive them—but not by
much. And not every time.) The occasional golfer is going to
have trouble outdriving them. So he may choose to go to the
left—which is a bad position for the second shot.

On your second shot, from the fairway, you do want to position yourself to the left side of the fairway. The reason is
simple: From there you'll now be able to see the green and the

hazards—the water is to the right, while the opening to the green is on the left. But playing your fairway shot to the left offers trouble. For there is a fairway bunker about 450 yards out from the tee, and it roams from the middle of the fairway over toward the left fringe. So it's going to catch any fairway shot that is not strong enough and high enough to clear the bunker.

If you've gotten out 280 yards on your tee shot, you can figure to clear the bunker with a strong two-wood on your second shot. But if you haven't, you can't: That second fairway bunker catches an awful lot of good amateur golfers. That's what I mean about this hole: If you're a good amateur golfer, how would you like to find yourself—after two shots at the extremes of your power—lying in a sand trap, 150 yards from the green, with nothing between you but a large water hazard and more sand. The way I feel, this isn't a hole for golfers; it's a hole for psychiatrists—group therapy for every foursome that passes this way.

The fact that you're near the green hasn't reduced the potential for trouble. If you've stayed, somewhat defiantly, on the right side of the fairway, the only trouble you have is the huge pond and its tributary that curls to the right—and the slope of the green, which favors a run over the green and into a sand trap at the rear.

If you're on the left, you had better be *deep* along the left side. For the opening to the green is broader there. You can, of course, still go over the green and into the pond-feeding stream on the far side. (The green is relatively narrow and sometimes fast enough to prevent the ball from holding on it readily.) So your third shot has got to have power and have loft —it's got to reach the green, if you still are shooting for par, and yet it must go high enough and come down with enough backspin to hold on the green. That means you must hit a lofted-iron hard. For most nonprofessionals that's trouble in itself: It demands something that the club can't give them—power and, at the same time, precise control—and which therefore must emerge from the skills of the golfer himself. And that *is* trouble.

Perhaps the most meaningful trouble with this hole is that it has no compensating balances. On most golf courses, you are rewarded for dealing successfully with trouble—you can make your next shot more acceptable or you have a good chance at a birdie or eagle. That's the point of looking to what and where the hazards are and gearing your game to dealing with them. But on this hole at Firestone, you are not rewarded for overcoming difficulty. You are simply faced with yet another difficulty, and another and another. In the end, if you succeed, you rarely have a chance to pick up a stroke on par (unless you happen to one-putt). So there is no reward for your skills. They must be employed defensively instead of boldly—you are playing to avoid a bogey or double bogey, not to earn a par.

That is, perhaps, the most significant thing to learn about holes that have such constant and unremitting difficulties: They cannot fit into a strategy of bold enterprise, but only into a strategy of determined defense.

One more aspect of trouble that is worth determining as you think through a course: the individual character of the hazards you encounter.

Consider the rough: We've already seen how the density of foliage of the trees can make a difference in your play in the rough. We've seen how pine needles can exert a different kind of discipline than a leaf-covered ground. We've seen how tough, bristly grass can provide a different—and sometimes predictable —lie than do the longer, softer, more pliable grasses. And we've seen how these differences will affect your club choice and your entire strategy for playing out of the rough.

But the rough is never constant. The rim of rough grass bordering the fairway may be very narrow, with the dense underbrush and tree line crowding up to it to provide a more ominous threat. Or it may be rather broad and generous: After

all, when the fairways are narrowed for a professional tournament—and it's not unusual for them to come down to a width
of 28 yards—the narrowness has to come from *some*where. It
usually comes from the rough area bordering the normal-width
fairways: The grass is allowed to grow long, and the rough
thus encroaches on the former fairway. Nobody, after all, starts
hauling in freight-train loads of trees to plant full-grown as a
new rough edge to the fairway, just so the fairways can be
narrowed by the threat of trees instead of long grass.

So the strip of rough alongside the fairway may be somewhat broader and more in play during and just after a tournament than it is for the regular use of the club's golfers. At the
just-acclaimed sixteenth hole at Firestone, for example, that
becomes a factor on the tee shot. For the rough on the right
side is not a terrible threat to sanity or to your score. If you
play to a fade—if your tee shot moves left to right—you may
choose to bring the rough into play as a potential landing area.
It will allow you to "let out" a little more on the tee shot, so
that you can curve the ball in there beyond the right-side sand
traps. Otherwise, you might feel constrained to come up easy
to make sure you land in the middle of the fairway somewhat
short of the sand traps. The latter not only costs you length—
which is important on this hole—but also a good position to
angle the ball deep to the left on your second shot. But if you
land in the rough fringing the fairway on the right, you'll not
only be closer to the hole—presumably—but you'll have a better
shot at angling off to the left, beyond the left-side fairway trap.
And perhaps you can then get deep enough to the left on your
second shot so that you can play to the green a little more
securely on the third shot. Thus what seems to be "reckless"—
deliberately accepting the shot into the rough as a viable possibility—has a certain logic. *If* you execute the second shot as
well as the first.

The same is not true of sand traps: You never want to play
your way into them deliberately in competition (though—as

we shall see—the pros sometimes do it in practice rounds). Certainly there are some players—notably Gary Player—who've practiced playing out of sand traps so persistently that sand is, for them, a nuisance but not really a hazard. Back in 1969, I think it was, Gary was in sand traps around the green ninety-two times during the U. S. pro tour. He got out and put the ball into the hole within two strokes on eighty-four of those occasions. Which meant that being in the trap meant—eighty-four out of ninety-two times—no more to Gary than being on the green at two-putt range.

Not all of us are quite that skilled in the sand, and so we pay detailed attention to avoiding the bunkers. But we know that it can't always be done. Thus it is important to know all about the sand traps and prepare ahead of time for the difficulty of playing them. The things to think about are sand, size, and the lip of the trap.

As we've seen, the sand is not the same all over the country. You cannot test it to determine its quality. You cannot swing through it a couple of times, as you can do in the rough. In fact, you can't even touch it beforehand with a club without incurring a penalty: I once lost momentum in a tourney because I thoughtlessly let a club touch the sand—other than in my shot—as I fought my way out of a trap. But there are no rules against using your eyes—or your feet: You can learn much about the substance of the sand in a trap simply by walking through it to address your shot. That's why you see so many pros playing deliberately into trouble—into a sand trap—in the practice round before a tournament: They figure to learn a little about the sand by having to walk through it, and they learn a lot about it—before the strokes count for money—by having to play out of it.

Dry, powdery, deep, or very fine sand is usually more difficult to play out of. (And the artificial sand made out of silicon compounds is usually finer than the most powdery of real

sand.) In such sand, the ball tends to bury itself in its own depression. Such sand is so dense and—literally—heavy that the
clubhead loses much of its speed as it tries to cut through it. So
you will have to dig your feet deep in the sand to take a very
firm stance; then you will have to concentrate on hitting
smartly behind the ball—about an inch behind it—and staying
with the shot all the way through. If you quit on it, the club
will quit on you. Now here's the compensating balance: The
sand slows the clubhead, so you've got to swing hard to get
through the sand, but you've got to remember also that on a full
explosion shot—necessary in this sand—the ball tends to roll
with considerable force after it hits the green. That's because
so much of this powdery sand gets between the ball and the
clubhead that it neutralizes the effect of the club's grooving,
and it's all but impossible to get a pronounced backspin on the
ball. So you must have the speed and force of the swing under
rather precise control. And you've got to know what will
happen if the ball rolls and rolls on the green: Is the green narrow at your proposed impact point? Is there more sand or still
grass on the other side? Or, as a likely alternative, can you chip
the ball precisely on the near edge of the green and hope it
carries up to, or near, the cup?

In coarse-grained sand, or shallow sand, there's a cushion-
like phenomenon that tends to make the clubhead bound up
and into the ball. So I'd suggest using a half-explosion shot out
of this sand and hitting about an inch or so behind the ball; that
will help avoid skulling the shot. On the whole, coarse or
shallow sand allows you to get more distance on the ball. But,
because less sand gets between ball and clubhead, you'll also get
better backspin, so that the ball can bite more effectively into
the green. On wet, coarse sand, the ball tends to sit up more
highly than otherwise. But it's a good idea—in walking through
the sand and setting yourself up—to see whether the wetness
is superficial or deep. If it isn't deep—if it's dry an inch or so

down—you may find that the clubhead will cut through it as it does through dry sand. So you must play the ball in that way.

Still another consideration, in thinking your way through the sand, is how deep the base of the trap is. You can sometimes determine this in walking through the sand or taking your stance. For in very fine, powdery sand, in particular, your feet will tend to slip and slide—unless they feel a solid base only slightly below the top layer of sand. If you feel the base, you should not plan to go deep with the clubhead; it will simply hit the base and bounce back up off it. This is, quite obviously, one of the many insights that a pro will gain by playing deliberately into trouble in a pretournament practice round: If his feet can't feel the base, he can play through enough sand traps so that his swinging club can make the search for how far down the base is, each time he tries to blast out of the sand.

Two other aspects of the sand traps can be examined by eye, not by feel.

One is the severity of the "lip" at the top of the trap. Does the grassy top overhang the sand in such a way that it thrusts out broodingly over the trap? If so, a lot of shots exploded out of that trap will nick the lip and either drop back into the sand or career off in some direction that you haven't anticipated. So you're going to have to pick a club that will pop the ball up and over the lip, even if the club doesn't offer distance. If the top of the trap does not have such a lip—if it rolls over smoothly into the turf and contour of the course—then you can play the ball cleanly to the pin without worrying about the "pop" or loft you need to get on it to clear the lip vertically: You can simply play the "slant" of the ball in your preferred trajectory to the hole, using an iron, perhaps, instead of a wedge.

The other aspect is the size of the trap. For in a strategy of boldness, you look to the bunker's size not simply as a factor of going in—of being captured by the trap—but of getting out.

For if the trap is large enough, and you've landed in the reaches of it far from the lip, you may find that the angle from that lie is just enough to let you get out of it with a longer iron instead of a wedge. (Whereas you'd need the wedge to clear the same lip if you were lying under it.)

Another thing you can learn about a sand trap, and a country club—at a single glance—is whether the trap is furrowed. If the trap is furrowed—which is rare in these days—you know you've got problems and the club has money. For the reason furrows are rare is economic: It costs a great deal to hire the help to do the handwork needed to keep a trap adequately furrowed.

That fact has smoothed a lot of furrowed brows—among golfers. For furrows provide a hazard within a hazard. They allow the ball to lie deeper in the sand, though exposed, and thus make it more difficult to dig out with the clubhead. You've got to concentrate on cutting down and through the sand and exploding from under the ball, knowing you have to move all the sand piled up in the furrow between clubhead and ball (assuming the furrows run perpendicular to your line of play). The fact is that furrows take away some of the control you have over the ball, and thus contribute to rising scores—not only in blasting out of the sand traps but in the inability to place the ball precisely where you desire for the follow-up shots.

For years, one of the distinguishing marks of the Oakmont Country Club near Pittsburgh was the severity of the furrows in its sand traps. In fact, the ground crews at Oakmont had a special instrument to carve deep and difficult furrows: It was a 3-foot-wide metal bar with a series of V-shaped teeth in it, each set about the width of a golf ball apart. The traps were raked with this device for something like forty years, during which Oakmont became renowned as (a) a great course and (b) a terribly difficult one. Four U. S. Opens were held there in the past generation. In the first two—1927 and 1935—the winners' seventy-two-hole totals were the highest since World

War I: 301 for Tommy Armour and Henry Cooper in 1927 (Tommy won the playoff) and 299 for Sam Parks, Jr., in 1935. (You have to go back to 1913 and Frank Ouiment's 304 at Brookline to find a winning score higher than Armour's.) Finally, the United States Golf Association, sponsor of the U. S. Open—appreciating how the furrows in the sand were making furrows in the players' foreheads—stepped in and suggested several changes. The officials at Oakmont were gracious enough to accept them; the old furrow rake was retired, and in the two U. S. Opens that have been held there since then—1953 and 1962 —the winning scores were 283. Not a record—that's a 275 by Jack Nicklaus in 1967 at Baltusrol near Springfield, New Jersey, and by Lee Trevino in 1968 at Oak Hill near Rochester, New York—but somewhat more encouraging than what had been known in the past.

*

Even when you've analyzed all the trouble—real and potential—thoroughly, you should go on examining each hole on the course in all its enterprising detail. For any one of a score of such observations will help you to think through the course and shape your game to make the most of it.

I start in the expected place: I examine the tee first. Is it elevated or not? An elevated tee will usually mean a longer carry on your tee shot—which may be very significant on par-3 holes—while a lower tee looking up to an elevated green may mean that the tee shot will run short. How are the tees angled into the fairway? If you want to land on the right side of the fairway, should you tee up on the right side of the tee, assuming you have a straight shot or a fade? If you hit a fade from the right side of the tee, the ball will start out to the left and carry up and over the middle of the course before curving back to the right. That's fine—but if the fairway angles off slightly to the left, you may find your ball landing too *much* to the right. In that case, you'd tee up more toward the middle of the tee in order to get the angle into your chosen landing area.

How big is the tee? If it is small and relatively inflexible, you won't be able to adjust to changing weather conditions. That is to say: On small tees, the tee markers can't be moved forward enough to keep the hole's distance constant if the wind is in your face. Or backward if the wind is behind you. At some clubs, the tees are large and the tee markers are changed from day to day or even from round to round so that the yardage and character of the hole can be kept constant, regardless of wind and rain. Indeed, the analytical golfer can learn something about the grass and ground conditions out on the fairway and green by studying where the tee markers have been placed in those clubs where the care of the tee is conscientious. If the clouds are lowering and the skies are muttering and the sun has been blocked out, and the tee markers are still placed far back on the tees, then the golfer might suspect that—though rain or squalls are swirling around the club—the fairway and the green on that hole are still dry and fast.

The thoughtful golfer will also use the position of the tee markers to determine not only what club to use off the tee but how much his own best drive is favored. On the seventeenth hole at Pleasant Valley, for example, the basic decision must be made at the tee. The fairway of this 402-yard par-4 is narrow, and the green is guarded by water on the right front and on the rear. There are several tees open for use, not much separated from each other. But if the tee markers are on the right-hand tee, which is placed forward, a good player will work off the tee with a one-iron or four-wood, hoping to be in a position to go up the alley on the left of the fairway, which leads into the green. If the tee markers are set on the left and to the rear, the same player is likely to tee off with his driver, hoping he can get in the same position to go up the alley on the left. One advantage of playing off the left tee: The right-to-left driver gets a better shot at the fat part of the fairway, and the alley in front of it, than he does off the right-hand tee.

Then I'd examine the fairways: Are they wide or narrow? Are they flat or sloped side to side or undulating? Can you find a place in each fairway that is flat so that you'll have a level lie for your next shot? Can you reach that level lie with your golfing skills? If not, what does the fairway look like at the point you can reach? Is the fairway grass long or short? If it's long, you know that you will not get as long a roll on the ball that lands in the fairway; the thickness of the grass will simply slow it down.

Next, I'd go on to examine the greens: Are they large or small? Are they flat or undulating or broken and sloping? If they slope, do they tilt away from the tee? Or toward it? Or do they tilt to one side or to both sides? How thick and deep is the collar around the green? Can you come off it with a putter, or will you need some other club?

Most important: Where is the pin placed? On big greens, the placement of a pin can affect profoundly the golfer's choice of a club as he is about to hit to the green. In some places, a deep pin placement may lengthen the hole 20 yards or more. In other places, a forward pin placement will shorten the hole but also make it more difficult to reach from the fairway. Another consideration: A pin on the left side of the green is more inviting to a golfer who normally hits a "draw"—who moves the ball from right to left. That's how pin placement can inhibit you: That same pin on the right front of the green will frustrate the "draw" shooter and respond to the golfer who's got control of a "fade."

In examining the pin placement, look for the best possible "ball placement." Or—to put it another way—the best possible "putt approach." For you not only have to know where the pin is but where you want to place the ball when you get onto the green. The pros go for the pin whenever feasible. Sometimes it's impossible, of course. And sometimes they feel that it's wiser—and more conservative—just to get into a good position on the green. If it's the latter, they've not only studied the pin placement but also the contour of the green, so that they know what side of the green provides the easiest putt to the pin. As a last resort, they'll simply hit onto the "fat" part of the green—the place where the green bulges most and offers the largest target for the golfer hitting from far out in the fairway . . . or far out in the rough.

One aspect of pin placement is as common to the country club as it is to the pro tour: The location of the pins can change not only the strategy of your game but the whole mood of those playing. I've seen the entire field at the Masters change from a mood of high and exhilarating aggressiveness to a nervous defensiveness simply because the tournament committee changed the pins in a certain way. (On the pro tour, the location of the pins is changed on every green before every round. The tournament committee has usually graded pin locations from the most severe on every green to the most accessible. Obviously, eighteen holes of "most severe" locations is going to alter significantly the attitude of those playing the course. In fact, a mixture of twelve to fifteen "most severe" locations out of eighteen over-all has a depressing effect.) In the 1969 Masters tournament, some twenty-five golfers finished under par, and eleven finished in the 60s in the first round. To the folks at Augusta, that kind of scoring is sacrilegious. So when they changed the pin locations for the second round, they chose the severe locations on many holes. The whole style and strategy of the tournament changed almost immediately. No longer were the pros going, almost routinely, for birdies on the par-5 holes. Until that moment, old men, young rookies, and light hitters were approaching the hallowed thirteenth and fifteenth holes with an enterprising destructiveness. Even Deane Beman, who is a more accomplished "position player'" than a soaringly long hitter, tried to reach these greens in two shots; he used a driver and a long iron—and he fell short. But on this day, the pin positions were so severe that pros drew back, rolled their eyes heavenward, as if supplicating a kinder God, and proceeded to play it safe. The result was that only four golfers went under par that day, and two of them were amateurs who, perhaps, didn't know how frightened they should have been. Of the players who finished in the top ten, five were well over par—with 73 to 75—that day.

Certainly one of the most important aspects of "thinking" your way around the golf course is to look for—and even map out, if necessary—the opening to each green.

The opening is simply that route to the green between—or sometimes over—all the hazards that imperil the approach to it.

Every green has one. Or, I should say, *almost* every green has one (some greens I've seen have openings so narrow as to be almost imperceptible). But it is the style and structure of the opening that gives the hole, and usually the entire golf course, its character and its challenge.

Not all openings are difficult. But enough of them are to make life (a) interesting or (b) intolerable, depending upon your manic balance.

The more challenging the approach, the more stimulating is the hole. On paper, it may seem that there are few bunkers guarding the green and that the opening is pretty wide—until you get out there and see that there is an outcropping of trees just where the normal right-handed player with a "draw" will line up for his fairway shot. Or that a spit of water trickles out a few feet into the fairway and closes down the available opening to half of what it looks like on paper. It may look like the area in front of the green is fairly wide open—treacherous, of course, but not laced with bunkers—until you suddenly discover that there's a hazard set out in the fairway that shuts down access to the green to a path in the fairway only a few yards wide. The first hole at Merion, a par-4, 355-yard hole, is an example. The green itself is well trapped on the sides and the rear, to catch errant shots, but the traps do not curl around in front to close down the approach. It just happens that there's a bunker out in the fairway, about a short iron in front of the green, and which just happens to curve so that much of the front of the green is cut off as you view it from the tee or fairway. That bunker leaves an opening on the left side of the fairway (with the green set to the right in a shallow right dogleg). But over farther to the left is another trap, and farther up on the left, at the distant point of the dogleg's hinge, is yet another trap and a line of pine trees. So this hole is "guarded" at a considerable distance from the green, and the gate is out on the left corner of the dogleg. It is a small area, only a few hundred square feet, and if you hit it exactly in the middle, you'll have a clear and open approach to the green. Of course, if you don't hit it quite right, you'll wind up in any one of three traps close to the gate (there are at least four others lining the fairway short of the gate) or in the pine trees beyond it.

The sixteenth hole at Oakland Hills in Birmingham, Michigan, is another and perhaps even more extreme example. This is a 405-yard par-4 hole touched up—long after the course was built—by Robert Trent Jones. The green is irregularly shaped —not quite oblong, not quite kidney-shaped—and set in a dogleg to the right. The green is guarded well on the left and rear by traps, on the right rear by trees, and on the right and right front by a pond that curls in front of the green. The approach on the "front" of the green is narrow enough. But that isn't the "gate" to the green. The opening is back in the fairway a couple of hundred yards out into the fairway. For that water near the green is part of a large, meandering pond that winds up with a large, gnarled thumb sticking into the fairway, from right to left, just at the hinge of the dogleg. It cuts off so much of the fairway as to leave an opening to the green only a few paces wide at the extreme left of the fairway. Once you get past it, you have a nice sweep to the narrow front of the green. Of course, you *can* come up the fairway before the hinge, ignore the opening to the left, and drive down the edge of the lake to the right. They tell me that some summers they sweep two hundred balls a month from that lake.

If you study the location of the openings closely, you'll find that on the good courses they tend to have one thing in common: They take you the long way around to get to the hole. I mean, if you want to play through the opening, you'll sometimes have to go considerably out of your way to get there. For this is the compensating balance of golf: The easiest way home is usually the longest one also. It's the subtle cunning that tempts you to go the wrong way, or the long way, that provides so much delight in analyzing holes.

Take, for example, the 388-yard par-4 sixth hole at the Seminole Golf Club in Palm Beach, Florida. Let's examine the hole backward, from green to tee, to appreciate the countervailing pressures of the layout.

The green is closed off on the far side by a sweep of tall Australian pines. It is flanked on both left and right sides by fairly large sand traps. There is another set of traps both left and right on the approach to the green, but the actual "front" of the green is fairly wide and open. However, this is *not* the opening to the green. The opening is actually about 90 or 100 yards out from the hole. It is a strip of fairway about 25 yards wide, and it opens into a long alley that leads down to the green. The gate is actually formed by a series of vast sand traps—four of them altogether, including two that we've already mentioned—that are planted in the fairway on the right of the gate as you face the green. On the left, the rough—studded by palm trees—sweeps into the fairway, pinching in toward the sand traps. That leaves the narrow opening into the alley—*our* opening.

Now, as you keep backing up, you will see that there is plenty of fairway running off to the right. It's just that those four huge bunkers cut off easy access to the green from the right side. If you want to go through the opening, you've got to play to the left. But the curve and sweep of the fairway keep moving the golfer to the right. In fact, as you back up to the tee, you'll find that the "pressure" is *from* the left to move right on the fairway. That's because three more large sand traps are built on the left not too far off the tee. They keep making you "think right." And beyond them, the rough on the left makes the curve inward, which further urges you to the right. So the whole "motion"—the "dynamics"—of the hole is to get the golfer to move right, while the opening to the green is far off on the left. If you respond to these dynamics, it'll likely take you two shots to get through the opening and perhaps a third onto the green. Then you have to one-putt to get your par.

Since not everybody can count on one-putting all the time—I speak from lamentable experience—the pressure on this hole demands so devious a route that the golfer seeking the opening concedes that he's going over par by one or two strokes. If he's lucky.

Of course, there is an alternative. Nobody is forcing you to go through the opening on this hole or any other. I mean, it's not part of the moral law. You can look for another way to get into the green, if you're willing to take the risks involved. Those risks involve going through or over the hazards, not around them.

It's a little like walking up to a fenced-in pasture. You can always go down to the gate in the fence and go through it easily. But it may be the long way around, and you're tempted simply to go over the fence. The fence may offer certain hazards. It may be high. It may have barbed wire. It may have a muddy ditch in front of it. Or it may have all three: It may be a high, barbed-wire fence with a muddy ditch in front of it. But if you think you can get in that way, you're likely to try it, instead of going the long way around to find the gate.

That's what you do in golf: You look for a place through

the fence that doesn't involve going through the gate. It means tackling a hazard and perhaps tackling two or three of them —sand traps, trees, and water. If you make it, fine! If you don't, it's like catching your trousers on a barbed-wire fence or falling flat in a muddy ditch: It's going to cost you something. In golf's case: more strokes. Next time, maybe you'll go back around through the gate.

But this is the genius of golf on a well-designed course.

The easier the approach you select, the more strokes it costs a player to make that approach.

The more perilous the approach you venture to take, the fewer strokes it will cost you—if you can overcome the hazards successfully.

You can't make that choice whimsically. For if you can't overcome a particular hazard or series of hazards, it's going to cost you something—more strokes than if you'd gone the easy way, through the gate.

So the practical thing is for a golfer to tackle only those hazards that he knows he can beat. If he feels he can use his irons so skillfully that he can invariably go over a sand trap, then he'd do well to try it. And if he's so confident about blasting out of a sand trap that it constitutes no hazard, then he'd be foolish not to tackle this kind of hazard as part of his approach to the green. For even if he fails, he knows it won't cost him much. And confidence is the name of the game.

But a golfer who's intimidated by water would be wise to avoid this kind of hazard. Similarly with one who hates trees or tangled rough: If you don't have the strength to slash your way out of there, then you'd do very well to make sure you don't get in there.

Thus the "thinking" thing to do is not only to determine where the opening is to every hole but to analyze what kind of hazards are involved with the opening. Then you can pick and choose what hazards—and thus what holes—you can conquer.

If you are not in the least bit intimidated by sand traps—if you *like* them, perhaps—then you wouldn't look for the gate on the left on the sixth at Seminole. You might simply accept the flow of the fairway to the right until you could shoot over the sand traps that guard the green on that side.

Such analyses cannot help but improve the score of any golfer: The first step to success in any venture is to understand the problem in all its detail. For there are many aspects of golf that offer a tantalizing illusion, though you may not know it *is* an illusion until you've made a bad shot. Everybody is susceptible to such illusions, even a pro who's won a million dollars playing the game.

One sun-drenched day a few years ago, I was standing on the rim of a crater on the Hawaiian island of Molokai next to Frank Duane, a golf course architect with whom I am associated in my own company, called Course Design.

On this occasion, Frank was explaining the details of a course he was designing—and I would get involved in, financially speaking.

"We'll make this hole a par-3," he said, gesturing out to where lava had once blackened the slopes. To me, it looked less like a golf hole than a geological dig. You wouldn't need a caddy cart on this hole; you'd need a lunar rover. You wouldn't measure the hole in yards or feet; you'd measure it in light-years.

Yet when the hole was actually laid out, it came to 190 yards—a good par-3.

What Frank had done was exploit an illusion into a work of high art. He had perceived with his mind's eye the exact dimensions of a vision that nature would allow him. I was enraptured by the illusion—as will the golfers be who negotiate that hole.

But illusion is for the eye, not the score. To score well, the golfer simply must overcome the vastly increased gifts of golf course designers to present illusion in vaster and more alluring terms. That's why I'm for such logical developments as the charting of holes—the detailed note-taking of how far it is from various points on the course to the front of the green. And the significance of other details, such as how large the green is, where it's deep, where it's narrow, and what its over-all design and dimensions are. For by marching off and marking down the exact yardages of the key points on a golf course, you free yourself from illusion. The game—already one of inches—cannot be played by guess and by God. You have to give Divinity some decent kind of help.

Not too many years ago, I might not have bothered with the charts. When I was somewhat younger, I'd take a look at a golfing situation and *know* —viscerally, cerebrally, instinctively —exactly what I had to do. Nobody had to tell me it was 162 yards from the gnarled bole of an oak tree to the front of the green and that I'd need a five-iron to make the shot. I just reached for the five-iron and let it rip—and somehow things always worked out.

But in those days, I had plenty of time to get the feel of a golf course before the tournament opened. I'd usually get in two or three days of practice on any one course before competition opened, so I'd have a very good feel of it. I wouldn't know precise yardage points, but I'd know how far the ball would go from point to point if I applied a certain club to it.

Now I don't get that much chance to practice the course before the tournament opens. Usually I'm off somewhere else on some phase of my professional activities. To be sure, I have a certain advantage in experience; I've played some courses so often that I can remember what club is needed in a given situation. Nevertheless, I frequently use charts. They're not too sophisticated; sometimes they're only notes scribbled on a scorecard. Sometimes they're only notes gathered for me by a caddy who'll work the tournament with me.

But I've found them enormously helpful in eliminating the

illusions that surround certain holes—illusions of fact or mind. And every illusion that's eliminated from a round of golf is likely to be converted into a reality called "triumph."

For evidence, let's hark back to the approximate start of charting—to the 1961 PGA championship at Olympia Fields outside of Chicago. Among those close to the leader as the tournament entered its final phase was Jerry Barber, a determined and extraordinarily hard-working man who made the most of a rather slight frame. He helped make up his lack of great power by writing down the various details of the course and pacing them off to the green so he could make the most of his position strategy. He was, to my knowledge, the first pro to write charts as a formal method; he preceded Jack Nicklaus by several years in doing this. On this occasion, he'd gone to Olympia Fields the week before the tournament not just to practice but to pace off and write down on a little chart the exact distances from every significant feature on and around the fairway to the front of the green. (He used a stable terminal for his measurement; he couldn't measure to the pin because the placement of the pin would be changed every day.) In the closing round, the charts became pivotal. Jerry was playing as a partner with Don January, the tournament leader, and was making a belated "charge" to seize the championship. They reached the par-5 520-yard eighteenth hole with Don still in the lead. They were both playing fairway shots, with Jerry consulting his chart as he went. He saw Don take out a six-iron when—by Jerry's own charts—he was a four-iron from the hole. "I knew right then he didn't know how far it was to the green," says Jerry. It was valuable insight for Barber: He figured that he'd have a little edge in insight to match Don's edge in muscle. It paid off: aided by three long putts—20, 40, and 60 feet—on the last three holes, he tied Don in regulation play and beat him the next day in a playoff.

Today, the detailed plotting of the golf course is common.

Jack Nicklaus rarely steps onto a tournament course without a pad and pencil in his pocket. And Gary Player sometimes sits down at night to work over a rather meticulous plan of the course that he's gathered, so that he will not only know where everything is on every hole but—as best as can be done ahead of time—how he must place each shot to conquer that hole.

The systems in use range from those as simple as my own to highly developed and detailed charts. Sometimes a golfer will make a table of figures for each hole, showing the distances along with other pertinent details. At other times he will take the club diagram of the course and write in distances. At still other times, he'll prepare a distance chart first and then sketch in the hole on the chart. (It's just a matter of having a series of vertical lines on a piece of paper, with the distance between each line representing a certain distance on the golf course— say, twenty-five yards or fifty yards. Then all he does, as he makes his rounds, is sketch in the hole over this network of lines.)

There is another value to marking off the yardages. For if you do it carefully, you'll discover details about the golf course that you never noticed before. All too often, walking a golf course is, for some people, like walking through an exhibition of French Impressionists: You look but you don't see. But once you have to measure and mark down something precise about each detail, a new and larger meaning comes over you; you suddenly see something that you never before knew. And you begin to appreciate relationships that heretofore escaped you. Not only that there is a particularly inviting opening to the green, but how wide it is, how far the various hazards are set from frequent lies in the fairway and around the green, and how they're interlocked—how trees complement bunkers and how humps complement water holes. And, most of all, how the whole hole comes together—tees, fairway, and greens —in the hands of a brilliant golf architect, and how it might be taken apart by a brilliant golfer.

In all of this, there is a recognition that it is the mind as well as the muscle that offers opportunity for playing winning golf. And it is by use of the mind—in detailed and enterprising ways —that can help give the game a new dimension. And give the philosophy of boldness a strategy of reality.

XII

The Externals
—How to Avoid Their Foulup

IN ALL of this, the factors affecting your strategy have involved the cerebral man. There are other factors that are more external: The other players, for one thing, and the way the golfer—and his playing partners—treat themselves and the dignity that is golf.

An opposing player can upset both the golfer and his strategy. This is more common in casual, everyday, and allegedly friendly golf than on the pro tour: The partner who moves deliberately into a putter's line of sight on a putt, or who mentions—lugubriously—on a tee shot, "I had dinner with your boss last night" (or "your banker") is exclusively part of amateur golf, not of the professional tour. In all my years on the pro tour, I can remember only one incident in which I felt sure that my playing partner was deliberately trying to upset me.

He succeeded.

It was in my first year on the tour. In one particular tournament, I was teamed with a pro who had both a reputation for (a) hurried, impatient play and (b) for using it to harass rookies on the tour. On this occasion, he took out an iron and, while I was standing farther up the fairway, played a shot past me toward the green. There was still a group on the green, which gave me the illusion of security: It didn't occur to me that any golfer would try to play past me and into another group still putting. In fact, the first I knew of it was when his ball went flying past me as I was examining my lie in the fairway. Then—while I waited for the previous group to clear the green—he marched past me and stood in the center of the fairway. Apparently he was determined to stay there until after I made my shot. I asked him to move; he didn't. I asked again and then again; he moved a few paces, then a very grudging few paces more. I marched down the fairway to get him to move. He didn't. I then marched over to an official: "I have a right to a shot free of casual obstacles. Will you please get him to move out of the path of the ball?" At the officials' request, he moved—but he achieved his aim: In my rage, when I got up to the green I three-putted the hole. Then I went over to him and I reminded him that he'd been reported by other players for such actions and that I would make an official complaint about his behavior. But just in case he didn't get the hint, I added, "If you ever do that to me again, I'm going to wrap this club around your throat. And if you don't think I can do it, let's go over behind those trees and settle this matter right now." I mean I was *hot:* Ol' Pap once told me I couldn't throw a club, but he never said anything about bending it ever so gently around an opponent's throat.

The matter ended there. Without a fight. And I was never harassed again by this pro or by any other.

All this is not to say that there aren't personal feelings among the golfers on the professional tour. When you set 90 to 150 different personalities hurtling from one town to another for up to forty weeks a year—with all the concomitant strains of constant travel—and when you add to that the pressures of money, frustration, competition, and occasional deep loneliness, you're very likely to find surfacing the extremes of the human personality: anger, bitterness, envy, despair—as well as a profound camaraderie, caring, warmth, and generosity. But when you're on the golf course, the competition is solely a professional matter, not a personal one. Certainly there are irritations: There are some players who are annoyed by the vociferous interest of the gallery—and who come gradually to understand that a large gallery can be used by the best of golfers . . . to stop shots that are bold enough to carry over a green, to stop shots that carry through the fairway into the rough. (They also realize that it is the ardent interest of the people who watch golf, in person or on TV, that has made the professional tour so financially rewarding for all of us.) There are impatient pros who go ape over the more studied habits of the slower players: Jack Nicklaus can drive some golfers nuts, not only by playing with them but simply by showing up in the same nine holes with them; he's been the target of complaints by pros who feel that four or five or six holes back they're being held up while Jack stands over a putt for one or two eternities.

But these are matters of professional pique, not personal animosity. Every golfer wants to do his best, and he does not want the external influences of other golfers to jeopardize his own best game. He knows that those influences are not personal; they are not even aimed at him in a professional manner. They simply arise within the framework of the game—the professional tour—and must be viewed as part of the working conditions, not as a matter of personal persecution.

So there are no classic feuds in golf, as there are in so many other sports.

There are classic contests—that develop out of the professional skills, and pride, of the competitors. Jack Nicklaus and I, for instance, love to get together in a twosome. We love it when we're playing with each other as a team: Our team victory in the PGA team championship in 1971 was our third in five years in that competition, and most years we manage to collect at least $20,000 in team winnings. We also love it when we're playing against each other, perhaps because the high skills of one draw out the competitive edge of the other. Yet we've never exchanged an angry or irritable word, not only because we respect each other as golfers but because we also respect each other as human beings.

Moreover, there is a realistic limit on how much we can play against each other in the normal tournament on the pro tour. For we've had some sobering lessons on the pitfalls of playing each other instead of playing against the golf course.

Perhaps the best all-around example of what I'm talking about took place during the 1967 U. S. Open at the Baltusrol Golf Club in Springfield, New Jersey. Jack and I were first paired together in the third round of the tournament, but we began working on each other during practice before the Open. For in one of his practice rounds, Jack shot a thoroughly admirable 62.

"Were you shook when Nicklaus shot that sixty-two?" one of the newsmen asked me.

"Well, I can't imagine why anybody would get shook by that, unless it was Jack," I said, as innocently as possible. "Because he didn't get it when it counted."

Jack was equal to the riposte. "Well," he said, "I think I'd rather have my sixty-two than what Arnold shot in practice today." I'd struggled through with something humiliating—a 67 or something like that.

No way to figure it but one: Jack and I were ready for each other. He shot a 71 in the first round; I shot a 69. He shot a 67 in the second round; I shot a 68. He had a 138 after two rounds; I had a 137. When we were matched in the third round, his gallery met mine in a collision of hopes and emotions that could only be matched by the outbreak of war in the Middle East. (One kid wriggled through the crowd, looked me over critically, and said, "Palmer's not *really* in bad shape—for a man his age." It's the kind of observation that inspires a vast appreciation in you—for infanticide.)

Jack missed a chance to go one-up on me when he missed a 15-foot putt for a birdie on the second hole. Then he missed a 15-inch putt for a par. When he stood over the ball for a third —and tap-in—putt, somebody in the gallery called out, "Miss it again, Jack."

On the par-3 fourth, I was looking for a birdie 2; my tee shot hung a fraction short and dropped into the water, and I wound up with a double-bogey 5. On the sixth, Jack got back at me—with a bogey. On the seventh, we both whumped our tee shots into the rough. On the eighth, I got my tee shot to within 15 feet of the pin for a good try at a birdie 2. "Sock it to 'em, Arnie," cried out somebody in the gallery. Jack was in a sand trap at the time, but he recovered for a par, while I two-putted. Jack bogeyed ten; I missed a birdie when I missed a 15-foot putt. We both got pars on eleven, and I hit a poor putt on twelve.

Somewhere out there, a spectator called out: "How about a couple of birdies? There are forty thousand people out here rooting for you two guys."

Ultimately, the word got through to us: We weren't leading the tournament any more. Marty Fleckman, an amateur who'd led everybody on the first round with a 67, was charging through, and now he'd passed both of us and was leading again on the third round. Behind him, Billy Casper was about to pass us by, with Deane Beman and Don January right up close behind him.

We were both so deeply involved in beating each other that, unthinkingly, we'd turned the round into match play. We were so interested in winning the round from each other that we'd forgotten there was a National Open on. The result was that we were playing pretty sloppy golf. Thus, whatever we did to each other, we were certain to help everybody else. By the sixteenth hole, at least three other golfers had passed us, and a couple of others were about to join them. By that time, Nicklaus had come up to me and said, "Let's stop playing each other and go out and play the course."

Which we did—without notable results. Jack and I finished the round tied up at 210 for the tournament. Fleckman was at 209, and Casper, January, Beman, and Gardner Dickinson were all at 210 or 211. If Jack and I hadn't suddenly realized what we were doing, as opponents, we might have given the whole thing away in the third round.

As it turned out, we came back at each other in the final round, playing the course instead of each other, and had a brilliant and enjoyable time. There was only one thing wrong with it all: Jack won. The round, the tournament, and the title.

Behind all of this is a suggestion of the enduring imperative of the pro tour: We all must accept the discipline of self-survival. The almost puritanical drive toward professionalism—even when personal feelings are high—is one of the reasons the pro tour itself survives. Without it—with personal feelings running rampant—the tour would be chaos. For another part of that same self-discipline involves the rules of golf. The players must help each other to live with them and within them, instead of launching an internecine war of deceit and disillusion. For the rules are strict and stringent, and sometimes they are quite costly. On the sixteenth hole of a playoff for the 1950 U. S. Open title at Merion, Lloyd Mangrum picked up his ball to blow an insect off it. He was seeking no unfair advantage, but that pickup nevertheless cost him two penalty strokes and any hope of overtaking Ben Hogan. In the 1968 Masters, Roberto de Vicenzo did not notice that there was an erroneous score on his scorecard. His playing partner, Tommy Aaron, himself caught the fact that he'd marked down a "4" on Roberto's scorecard instead of a "3" for the seventeenth hole, and he rushed to tell Roberto about it. (The players are responsible only for marking down the score of individual holes but not for adding up the total.) But—terribly pushed and rushed by the TV crew, who wanted to get him ready to go on-camera—Roberto had not noticed the mistake when he looked over his card; he'd already signed it and turned it in at the scorekeeper's table. That error—by then immutable under the rules of golf—cost de Vicenzo a chance to tie for the Masters title. "What a stupid I am!" said Roberto—blaming himself, not Aaron. And most emphatically not involving Bob Goalby, who had the mixed fortune of winning because Roberto did not tie—and who was unfairly put down because of that victory.

The fact is that few sports are so stringently self-regulated by the competitors themselves as is professional golf. A pro considers it no contest when he's asked to stake his honor against an illegal—or even unthinkable—ethic. Lee Trevino came to the Westchester Classic, in the summer of 1971, from a brilliant streak of golf in which he'd won the U. S. Open, the British Open, and the Canadian Open. But in the Westchester, he played a ball on which he felt he deserved a penalty. He called it on himself, notified the officials, and sacrificed a stroke. That single stroke—which he called against himself—was enough to put him below the cut (the two-round score that would eliminate perhaps one-third of the field). He was out: He could do nothing else for the rest of the week but go fishing—which he did, with his usual enormous aplomb. But the important thing is that, through sheer integrity, he eliminated himself from the richest golf tournament in the world.

Something similar happened to me in the 1972 Florida Citrus tournament. It was being played in Orlando, which I now consider my second home (and where I own a fine club called Bay Hill). It was also a tournament in which I was defending champion. But I wasn't playing very good golf at the time and I knew I was very close to falling below the cut. On the par-4 third hole of the golf course—the twelfth hole of my second round—I hooked my second shot into the rough to the left of the green. I removed a loose impediment and then took a practice swing—which is permissible in the rough. In the process of taking the swing, the ball moved ever so slightly. I was the only one who saw it move. I played out to a double-bogey seven on the hole, finished the round, and then told a PGA official about the ball moving. Quite properly, the PGA assessed me a one-stroke penalty on the incident—and that dropped me one stroke below the cut. It was the first time in eighty-five tournaments that I'd failed to make the cut.

It is gratifying that my action is not singular: Many, many players "turn themselves in," so to speak, when they've violated a rule, no matter how unintentionally. I've known of only three cases—in all my years on the pro tour—where players were penalized for failing to uphold this self-discipline. Two of the cases, including one in Great Britain, remain secret. The third, which took place early in 1972 at the Greater New Orleans Open, involved a visiting pro from a Latin American country who changed a "5" on one hole to a "4." The one-stroke change enabled him to make the cut. But he was discovered; a number of persons—including other pros—testified to the fact that he'd gotten a 5 on the particular hole, and his privilege to play in the United States was withdrawn. (For regular members of the PGA tour, the penalty for cheating can run as far as suspension from competition for a year.) On the other hand, I know of many, many cases where players voluntarily accepted the sense of self-discipline, even though it could cost them a coveted championship.

Such an incident—perhaps even an ennobling one—took place in the 1960 Masters. Dow Finsterwald was in the heat of the struggle for the lead when, *after* putting out on one hole, he took a practice putt. What he didn't know is that there was a local rule against such strokes. It was printed on the back of the scorecard, but Dow had not remembered it. The penalty for such action is two strokes but, because he didn't remember the rule, Dow turned in his scorecard with a 71 instead of the

73 (with penalty included). The next day, he was about to do
it again when Billy Casper walked up to him and reminded
him of the rule. Dow studied the scorecard and—with enormous
integrity—went immediately to the officials and admitted that
he'd violated the rules the day before. They talked it over and
decided to penalize him the two strokes under the rule, instead
of disqualifying him for turning in an erroneous scorecard.
Those two strokes were just enough to keep him out of a playoff with a bloke who won the tournament—a good friend of his
. . . named Palmer.

The exchanges between players about potential rules viola-
tions are intended to help, not hinder. And sometimes there is
a higher justice in all this. In the third round of the 1968 U. S.
Open at Oak Hill Country Club near Rochester, New York,
Bert Yancey had a five-stroke lead over his nearest pursuer, Lee
Trevino—his playing partner. Trevino had bogeyed the tenth
hole, and Yancey had to begin to feel that things were moving
rather dramatically—and all his way.

On the eleventh green, Trevino was "away"—farther from
the cup than Yancey—but Yancey's ball was in Lee's putting line
to the hole. So Yancey marked his spot with a coin and then
picked up his ball and pocketed it. But he took an appropriate
further step: He carefully measured a putter head's length
away from where his ball sat, and placed the coin there. He did
it to keep the coin, as well as the ball, out of Trevino's path of
putt. Lee sank the putt for a birdie 2, while Lee's Fleas whooped
with pleasure. Perhaps Yancey was distracted for a moment by
the noise. In any case, he put his ball down where the coin
was, instead of where it had landed—a putter's head length
away. He was about to address the putt when Trevino called,
"Hey, did you move the coin back before you put the ball
down?"

Yancey stopped in midbreath. "I forgot," he said. He leaned
down and carefully corrected his mistake. It was, he knew,
a very near miss. Had Trevino kept his silence until after

Yancey putted—or even if he too had forgotten about the moved coin—Yancey would have been assessed a two-stroke penalty. That, combined with Lee's birdie, would have cut Yancey's lead to two strokes—and he still had the putt to play. Not to mention seven more holes. More than that, had Yancey not remembered the mistake until after he'd signed the card—and had it then been called to official attention—Yancey would have been disqualified. And Trevino would have immediately become the leader of the U. S. Open.

"I'm not that kind of guy," said Lee. "Who wants to win that way?"

He's right. "He's a gentleman," said Yancey. "He's a pleasure to play with."

The higher justice emerged almost immediately. Lee not only birdied the eleventh hole that day but also twelve and fourteen, and the next day he went on to shoot seven strokes better than Bert Yancey and capture the U. S. Open for himself.

One thing I've always felt in accepting the discipline of the rules: Don't do it ignorantly. Like most other pros, I make a determined effort to know the rules thoroughly and to know how to apply them. My intent is simply to know as much or more about the rules as the men who impose them. For there've been times when the decision makers were individuals who've been recruited to work on a particular tournament—people of good enough will but who haven't devoted their lifetimes to golf and its rules. Simply by knowing the rules well, and how they've been applied, I've been able to save myself a stroke here and there—and sometimes something more.

Take, for example, a hole-in-one that might never have been—and a fine that would have been—if I didn't know the rules.

It took place while I was practicing for the Carling World Open at the Oakland Hills Country Club in Birmingham, Michigan, in 1964.

It developed on my second shot off the first tee of the

seventeenth hole—you've got to admit there aren't many holes-in-one that come on the second shot. (The fact is, though I sank the ball on a single swing, I didn't have the guts—or the cheerful deceit—to classify it among my eight holes-in-one.) For what happened is that I "flew the green"—I sent my tee shot on this par-3 194-yard hole—reeling off far beyond the green on the fly. Instead of going down and playing the ball out of the distant rough beyond the hole, I stayed on the tee, set up another ball, and—since it was only a practice round, with a couple of good friends as companions—I teed off again. With a four-iron. This time I was a shade more accurate: The ball hit the green and bounced and bounced and bounced . . . right into the hole. There wasn't even time to celebrate the shot. For immediately the controversy arose: Was it legal? Hadn't I taken a "Mulligan," so to speak? If that was the case, the single-shot drop-in didn't count as a hole-in-one—except in my personal dreams—and I might even have been susceptible to a fine: Under PGA rules, a $25 fine was to be assessed players who hit a second shot to any green in practice. But I had been a member of the PGA players committee, and I knew that there was an exception to the rule: It did not apply when the green was missed on the first shot. So I was willing to concede the reality—that it was not really a hole-in-one—but not the fine. For there was a principle at stake . . . well, I managed to make my point. On the fine. And never mentioned the hole-in-one-plus again. At least until now.

Or take a more important issue: the 1958 Masters tournament.

Going into the twelfth hole, I was leading Ken Venturi by one stroke. It had been raining heavily during the week, and the "embedded ball" rule was in effect. On the par-3 155-yard twelfth hole, I hit a six-iron from the tee over the hole, and it plugged in the soft turf near a trap beyond the green. Under the "embedded ball" rule, the player is allowed a free drop if his ball becomes embedded in its own pit mark. The rule applies to the whole area of the golf course except (a) the teeing ground and the putting green of the hole being played and (b) all hazards on the golf course. The area in which my ball was embedded was clearly not on or part of the green; I'd overshot the green by a perceptible measure. It was clearly not in a sand trap; it was beyond it. So I felt that the "embedded ball" rule should apply because none of the exceptions could apply. But the official on the spot disagreed. We had quite a discussion at the time, and finally I asked that the entire rules committee be assembled and polled so that we could get a ruling on the matter. I was willing to stay right there, holding up the entire tournament if need be, until we got that ruling. But while we waited, we worked out a compromise: I'd play two balls—the one that was embedded and one that developed out of a free drop. With the embedded ball, I got a double-bogey 5. With the provisional ball I got a par 3. On the next hole, the 475-yard thirteenth hole, I was in a determined mood. I hit a long drive, used a three-wood to carry over Rae's Creek in front of the green, and then sank the putt for an eagle 3. It was not until the fifteenth hole that I learned that the rules committee had decided in my favor. I got a 3 for the twelfth hole instead of a 5—and I won the tournament by a single stroke.

On the other hand, knowing the rules won't help unless you are resolute enough to use them. One of the most embarrassing and frustrating moments of my professional life involved a lapse in resolution on my part. It took place in the 1965 PGA championship tournament at the Laurel Valley Golf Club—the club that I represent on the pro tour. (I grew up at the Latrobe Country Club—and now I own it—but for more than a decade I've represented the Laurel Valley Golf Club on the pro tour. From a time well before I even began thinking of owning Latrobe Country Club. The Laurel Valley Golf Club is located only about 15 miles from my home, and I have many cherished friends there—which is why I've been proud of my affiliation with them.) The PGA is the only major championship that has eluded me, and there was a certain feeling that I might finally take it when it was scheduled into Laurel Valley. It wasn't just that all my old friends were around; it was that the late President Eisenhower made a special trip up to Laurel Valley to be there for the PGA—and perhaps for my long-sought triumph. Everybody seemed intent on the idea that "this" was going to be "Arnie's year."

I was there to make them believe it. As far as the first hole. For on that hole I made an error of omission that ruined it all. I pulled my approach shot to the first green into thick grass at the bottom of a gully. There was no way I was going to be able to get out of there without my club striking some wooden railings that protected the sides of a temporary bridge across the gully. I was fairly sure about the rule: I could take a free drop two club-lengths away from the obstruction, which would give me plenty of room to clear it on my swing. But to make sure, I asked for an official to rule formally on the situation. The official was slow in getting to us.

Eight minutes passed, and finally two marshals—no doubt feeling they were helping the tournament by getting it moving again (and perhaps helping the "home" pro)—began tearing down the wooden supports. I should have stopped them, no matter how long it took to get an official ruling. I knew what the rule was. But I for some reason just stood there, perhaps loath to stop people who were so obviously eager to help—people who were trying to keep this tournament from being marred by an extraordinary delay on the first hole. Back in 1958, I was more patient and insistent. But this time, I lacked resolution: I let them go ahead, and then I played a delicate pitch shot out of the long rough up to about six feet from the hole. And I got my par 4. Which was not too bad a recovery.

On the second hole I got a birdie and I was really rolling, until—maybe an hour or more later—at the sixth tee I saw Jack Tuthill, the PGA tournament supervisor, come chugging up in a golf cart to advise me that I'd been assessed a two-stroke penalty for the removal of an obstruction at the first hole. He was right. There was absolutely no doubt in my mind that he was right. But I was so mad at myself—so transcendentally enraged —that I could have kicked myself halfway around the world. I went to my playing partners, Al Geiberger and Bob McCallister, and asked them to tee off on the sixth hole before me so that I could have an added minute or so to collect myself. They were gracious enough to agree. But it didn't help: I hit a poor tee shot into the rough on the right, skimmed the ball with a wood farther along in the rough to the right—and hit a spectator along the way. But now I got control of my emotions—which is a fundamental point of the game—and I got the ball on the green with my third shot. I two-putted for a par 5, and I wound up with another reason for being mad: I thought I could have gotten a birdie on the hole. The whole episode was a costly one— three strokes when you figure the penalty and the blown birdie. I never quite regained my stride: I shot a 72 that day, but the next day I soared to a 75. And after that I never even approached par: I finished thirty-third in the tournament—on a course that I know like the gentle light in my wife's eyes.

So the rules are important, and not only as a discipline. The good golfer must know how to work with them as well as within them. It is a discipline that is part of the heightened goals of golf. For you can make the rules work for you—if you know how—as much as against you.

Which is the point of the whole strategy behind the philosophy of boldness—to take advantage of every one of the tiniest openings toward victory.

An Afterthought

IT ALL started a long time ago as a dream that endured—to play the game with an unreachable perfection.

The dream goes on. And so does the pleasure.

I still experience—as does every golfer—the exaltation of the hard shot truly achieved, the bold play boldly made.

I still experience—as does every pro—the exaltation of the hard, clean, totally self-reliant requisites of the pro tour. In no other aspect of life is the competitive challenge of life so pure and uncomplicated: Success rests solely on the individual —on what you do, not who you know. That is what lures us all back to the pro tour time and time again—that above money itself.

It is what brings us all to golf—on the amateur level as much as the professional: It is a way of testing ourselves while enjoying ourselves. My test is always to go for broke—to try to win when common sense says it's all over.

That's still the way I go at the game: to hang loose and look for the shot that'll win.

It's a good way to live.

For me—and, I hope, for you.